AWAKENING

A HISTORY OF THE BÁBÍ AND BAHÁ'Í FAITHS IN NAYRÍZ

HUSSEIN AHDIEH
HILLARY CHAPMAN

AWAKENING

A HISTORY OF THE BÁBÍ AND BAHÁ'Í FAITHS IN NAYRÍZ

Bahá'í
PUBLISHING
Wilmette, Illinois

Bahá'í Publishing
415 Linden Avenue, Wilmette, Illinois 60091-2844

Printed in the United States of America on acid-free paper ∞

16 15 14 13 4 3 2 1

Library of Congress Cataloging-in-Publication Data
Ahdieh, Hussein.
Awakening : a history of the Babi and Baha'i Faiths in Nayriz / Hussein Ahdieh and Hillary Chapman.
page cm
Includes bibliographical references.
ISBN 978-1-61851-029-7
1. Bahai Faith—Iran—Nayriz. 2. Bahais—Iran—Nayriz. I. Chapman, Hillary. II. Title.
BP330.A33 2013
297.9'3095572—dc23
2012049805

Cover design by Andrew Johnson
Book design by Patrick Falso

In loving tribute to all of the Bábí and Bahá'í children of Nayríz and as a gift to their descendants, Bahiyyih Amelia, Naim Alexander, Ari Jalal, and Thomas Vahid, my grandchildren.

—Hussein Ahdieh

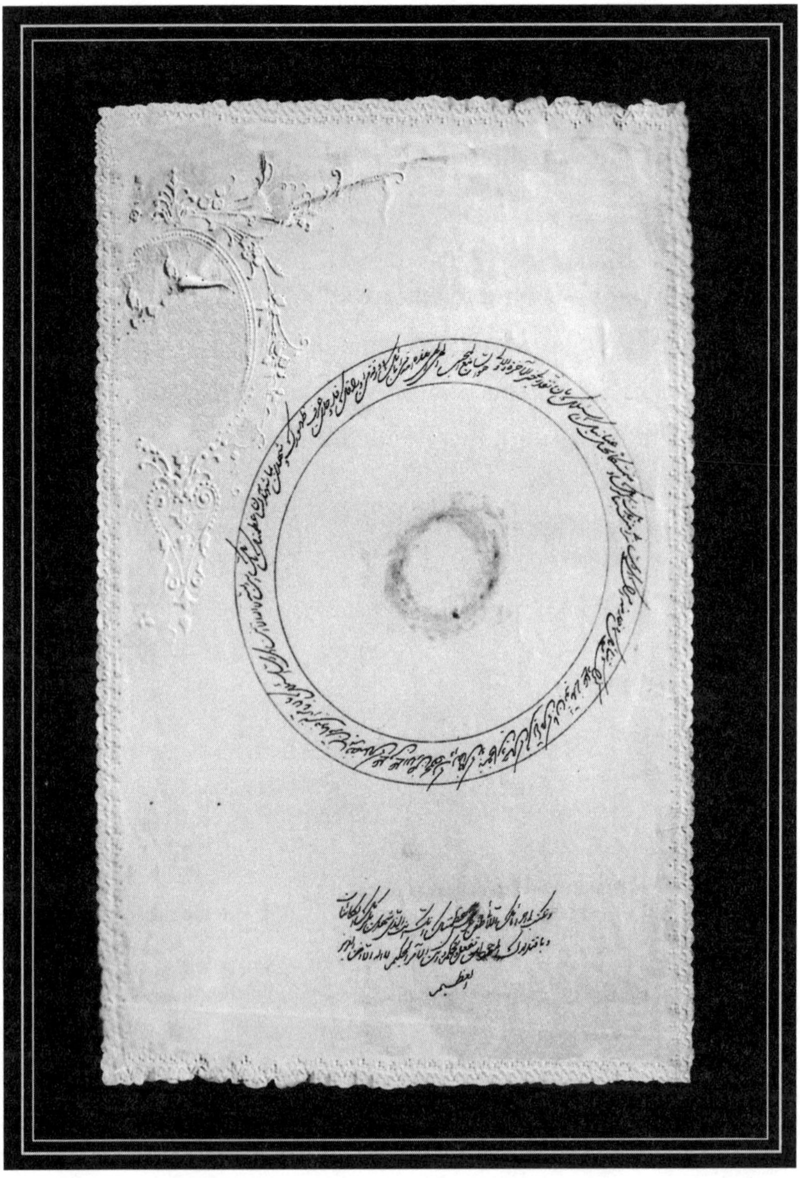

Tablet from Bahá'u'lláh to Khávar Sultán, wife of Mullá Muḥammad Shafí.

CONTENTS

Introduction 1
Background 7

THE BÁB, VAḤÍD, AND NAYRÍZ

In the beginning 19
1 / The town of Nayríz 21
2 / The Báb 35
3 / Vaḥíd 53
4 / Separate Ways 59
5 / Vaḥíd Nears Nayríz 71

NAYRÍZ, 1850

6 / The Great Announcement and the Heroic Stand at Fort Khájih 79
7 / Massacre of the Faithful 91
8 / Punishment 103
9 / Attempt on the Life of the King of Persia 115

NAYRÍZ, 1853

10 / Upheaval in Nayríz 123
11 / Battle in the Vineyard 133
12 / The Bloody Mountain: Darb-i-Shikáft and Bálá-Taram 139
13 / Death of the Commander 149

14 / Sacrifice of the Faithful 161
15 / The Long Road into Captivity 171
16 / The Transformation of the Bábís into Bahá'ís 185

NAYRÍZ, 1909

17 / The Kingdom of Persia in Chaos 207
18 / The Invasion of 1909 213
19 / Suffering of the Faithful 225
20 / The Temple Sacrifice 237
21 / The Third Day 245
22 / Flight to Sarvistán 251
23 / The Passing of 'Abdu'l-Bahá 259
24 / Exodus 267

Appendix A / List of martyrs of the Nayríz conflict of 1853
as listed in Shafí''s manuscript 283
Appendix B / About our Sources 287
Notes 291
Bibliography 323
Index 331

INTRODUCTION

By the early 1800s, centuries of power and wealth had corrupted the clergy of Persia.

A movement for spiritual renewal, the Shaykhis, came into being. They believed that, according to prophecies of the past, God was about to send the promised one, the "Qá'im," Who would arise and purify Islam.

In their teachings, they emphasized devotion to the Ímáms 'Alí and Ḥusayn, the two central figures in Shi'ite Islám after Muḥammad; by these names, the Shaykhis also referred to two figures who would be the "Twin Manifestations of God." The Qá'im would arise first, followed immediately by a second Manifestation of God.

The Shaykhis pored over the Qur'án and the hadiths, the oral traditions of Islam, but, unlike other religious scholars, they interpreted these traditions allegorically—not literally—and concluded that all the signs were now visible and that a new Age of Divine Revelation was upon them.

And it came to pass that at this very time, a young merchant from Shiraz, Siyyid 'Alí-Muḥammad, who would be titled "the Báb," meaning "the gate," arose to claim to be the fulfillment of Islamic prophecy, the bringer of a new Revelation, and the forerunner of an even mightier one.

The claim and teachings of the Báb spread like wildfire throughout the cities and villages of Persia. Many of the Muslim faithful were attracted to the message, but many of their mullás violently resisted it. Among those places touched by it was the quiet, agricultural town of Nayríz, in Fárs province.

This book tells the story of how the Báb's Revelation came to Nayríz and convulsed its social order, resulting in three major episodes of persecution in 1850, 1853, and 1909.

The Revelation of the Báb came to Nayríz through Vaḥíd, one of the most influential clerics in Persia. He had given up everything to serve as the Báb's disciple. He proclaimed the new Divine Message in 1850 to large, enthusiastic crowds gathered in the Great Mosque of Nayríz. The clerics became alarmed, and he and a group of followers were forced to defend themselves in an old abandoned fort outside the town. The confrontation ended in a massacre. The conflict renewed itself three years later, but this time with 'Alí Sardár, a local hero, as the leader of the Bábís. He, along with hundreds of other Bábís, their wives and children, put up a brave defense in the surrounding mountains. But they were eventually overcome, and the men were slaughtered, and the women and children were taken prisoner. Within less than ten years, normal life returned to Nayríz, and a new and vigorous Bábí community prospered and became a Bahá'í community when Mírzá Ḥusayn-'Alí declared Himself to be Bahá'u'lláh, the Promised One prophesied by the Báb. The Bábís of Nayríz accepted this claim. They were subjected to frightening persecution in 1909, when eighteen were killed and hundreds driven from their homes, their properties destroyed.

We begin our account with a description of the daily life of this nineteenth-century agricultural Persian town, its people, and their beliefs. This is followed by a brief history of the Báb's extraordinary life, to help the reader understand why so many people would give their lives for their belief in Him. The story of the persecutions in Nayríz are also placed in the larger context of the unfolding of the Bábí and Bahá'í Faiths and the political changes in the kingdom of Persia.

Vahíd, and the events of 1850, have been covered in other important sources, such as Nabíl-í-A'ẓam's *The Dawn-Breakers*, an early account of the birth of the Bábí and Bahá'í Faith, and *God Passes By*, by Shoghi Effendi, a history given special authority by Bahá'ís due to the high station of its author. We have included additional information from other sources, such as an account of Vaḥíd's arrival written by hand on the wall of a local mosque. The mountain battles of 1853 are told using details from the unpublished memoirs of Muḥammad Shafí', an eyewitness, as well as established sources currently available only in Persian—Faizi, Rouhani, and Mázandarání, and the recent scholarship of Dr. Ahang Rabbani. The persecution of 1909 is recounted using Faizi, Rouhani, and a new source—the unpublished memoirs of Shaykh Bahá'í Ahdieh, among others.

We had two goals in preparing this narrative.

The first was to render it in a storytelling style that would make this history accessible to a broader audience for whom the Persian names, background regarding Islam and Persian society of the nineteenth century, and the Bahá'í Faith may not be familiar, while maintaining the highest standard of accuracy. We have provided a brief overview of Islam following this introduction, and to preserve the flow of the narrative, we have addressed discrepancies that were found in the sources by providing explanations in the endnotes rather than in the main text. In cases where sources did not agree—and there were many—we made a best guess based on available knowledge about the times, other existing sources, the quality of the sources, and comparison with similar situations, and we have placed alternate interpretations in the endnotes in order for the reader and researcher to evaluate our conclusions for themselves. We have also provided a more detailed explanation of the main sources in Appendix B. Although we have included stories from the personal memories of individuals that are impossible to verify with historical certainty, there is a factual basis and a purpose behind every story we included.

The second goal was to memorialize the individuals who suffered so much during these conflicts. This is why the book contains so many names. In many cases, the single mention of an individual will be the only trace of his or her suffering. We have limited the number of Persian names in the text to those of the individuals who are central to the thrust of the story and of the martyrs and their direct family members. We have provided the names of other martyrs and family members in the appendix and endnotes.

The amount of information about specific people in this history varies. For many persons, we could find only a little information regarding their lives, and so the references to them are brief. The amount of space given to individuals is in no way an evaluation of their merits or the degree of their suffering. In covering the education of the Nayríz Bábís—and later Bahá'ís—we have written much about the service of Mullá Muḥammad Shafí' because we have his written accounts of those days but not those of others.

Women are largely invisible in the historical record and were given secondary status in nineteenth-century Persian society. To give the reader a more complete picture, we have included as much as we could find about the contribution and suffering of women and children during these events; this includes a perspective from the unpublished memoirs of a local Bahá'í woman. We have attempted to humanize the people in this story by giving background information and anecdotes about them.

We also have provided descriptions of locations to help the reader more closely experience the world of the early Bábís and Bahá'ís and to guide future researchers who may revisit these events and make additions and corrections to this history. These descriptions were made largely from personal memories and photographs given to us by former residents of Nayríz.

This story takes place over the course of the life of the Báb, Bahá'u'lláh, and 'Abdu'l-Bahá. In the 1850 and 1853 conflicts, the protagonists are all Bábís; by 1909, they are all Bahá'ís. This was a period of great spiritual ferment. The Báb not only challenged all the old traditions but also generated powerful spiritual feelings among His followers, who felt they had been born again into a new spiritual age. His new teachings spread rapidly around Persia. This tumult and spiritual fervor prepared the way for Bahá'u'lláh, Whose majesty could be seen as the culmination of the Báb's Mission. Bahá'u'lláh's son, 'Abdu'l-Bahá, would be the one to hold the Bahá'í community together after being appointed his Father's successor and given sole authority to interpret the Bahá'í holy writings. He also took his Father's teachings out of the Near East when he traveled to Europe and North America.

This story has been recounted from a faith perspective when relating to the Báb and Bahá'u'lláh Who, the authors believe, were invested with divine knowledge and authority. The authors believe that anything having to do with the Báb and Bahá'u'lláh is sacred history, while everyone else in this narrative—other than the Central Figures of the Faith—is subject to human fallibility because they are products, in part, of their environment, culture, and education. If you are unfamiliar with the figures of the Báb and Bahá'u'lláh, please read the brief overview that follows this introduction.

Finally, this project would not have been possible without the great generosity of friends who volunteered many hours with editing, translating, researching, and recalling the names of people and their memories of Nayríz. These include Ṭáhirih Ahdieh, Íráj Ayman, Soheil Bushrui, Anita Ioas Chapman, Shahrokh Faní, Brett Gamboa, Robert Hanevold, Nabíl Hanna, Faruq Izadinia, Nura (Shahídpúr) Jamer, Tatiana Jordan, Frank Lewis, Iraj Mítháqí, 'Álí Nakhjavaní, Michael Penn, Rosann Velnich, Martha Schweitz, Christopher White, and Ehsan Yarshater.

We would also like to thank our editor, Christopher Martin.

A complete list of the names of all the volunteers who gave us such valuable service can be found at http://www.nayriz.org. We are profoundly grateful to each and every one of them.

DR. HUSSEIN AHDIEH AND HILLARY CHAPMAN
FEBRUARY, 2013 CE / 170 BE

BACKGROUND

The Báb and Bahá'u'lláh

The Báb and Bahá'u'lláh are often referred to by Bahá'ís as the "Twin Manifestations" of God. This means that each was chosen by God to be His Manifestation—One who perfectly reflects all the divine attributes of God such as mercy, power, bountifulness—to be the Revealers of His Word, to reinfuse humanity with spiritual life, and to move human civilization forward.

The Báb lived in an Islamic world and claimed to fulfill Islamic prophecy. He also announced that He was preparing the way for a second Manifestation of God, "Him Who Will Be Made Manifest."[1] In 1863, Bahá'u'lláh declared that He was this Manifestation.

In the following decades, Bahá'u'lláh revealed numerous writings which came to form the Bahá'í holy writings. All religions, Bahá'u'lláh taught, originated from the same transcendent God; all Manifestations of God had revealed the same religion, and as humanity's capacity grew from age to age, more of God's truth could be revealed to it. Bahá'u'lláh explained that He was ushering in an age of maturity for the human race in which the world's population would come together in one common faith and become interdependent and peaceful. This would be the Kingdom of God. The purpose of the Bahá'í Faith is to unify humankind by infusing it with a new spiritual life and to guide it toward the golden age of peace promised by Bahá'u'lláh.

Islám

Muḥammad was born in 570 CE, in Mecca, an important commercial center on the trade routes between Yemen and Syria. Mecca was also a center for worship so that, at certain times of the year, festivals with trade and cultural exchange took place, and all armed conflict ceased. Worship centered on the Kaaba, a square building around which the statues of the Arabian tribal gods stood, awaiting the prayers of devotees.

The tribe to which Muḥammad belonged maintained the Kaaba shrine and provided hospitality for the pilgrims. Muḥammad was orphaned early in life and then raised in the home of his uncle Abú Talíb, the head of their clan and father of a boy named 'Alí. In this world, social status, friendship, and marriage were all determined by one's tribal and clan affiliations. Belonging to a clan was also essential for one's protection because feuds between clans could last for generations. A constant state of conflict over access to resources such as water and control of trade routes existed among the tribes.

Muḥammad became known for His honesty and His deeply spiritual nature. At age twenty-five, He married Khadíjih, a widow whose trading business he managed. They had several children. Their household included 'Alí, the boy with whom He grew up and His future son-in-law. Muḥammad received His first divine revelation while meditating on Mount Hira, near Mecca, in 610 CE. The angel Gabriel appeared to Him and told Him to read certain revealed words. Khadíjih was the first to believe in Muḥammad as a Manifestation of God, followed by 'Alí, and then Zayd, a freed slave who served them.

His close friend, Abú Bakr, became the first to believe in Him outside of his immediate household.

Four years after this Revelation, Muḥammad proclaimed to His clan and others in Mecca that He was a Manifestation of God. His message of the Oneness of God and the need to submit to His authority aroused furious opposition from Meccans because these beliefs challenged their long-held traditional beliefs in tribal gods. Then Khadíjih and Abú Talíb died, leaving Muḥammad without any clan protection. His life was in danger.

But Muḥammad's message had found believers in the nearby town of Yathrib. A delegation from there arrived in Mecca in 622 CE to pledge allegiance to Him and offer Him protection. Accepting their offer, He and some of His Meccan followers moved to Yathrib, which would now be known as Medina, the "City of the Prophet.'" Muḥammad's move from Mecca to Medina in 622 CE marks the beginning of the Islámic calendar.

In Medina, Muḥammad served as a peacemaker between feuding tribes. He set about building a community that would worship God and obey His newly revealed laws, such as those on prayer and fasting. There in Medina, the first mosque was built, and the first call to prayer sung out. The Meccans, and those hostile to the new Faith in Medina, attacked Muḥammad and his followers in a series of armed conflicts until, in 630 CE, Muḥammad entered Mecca, destroyed the idols of their tribal gods, and ended the resistance of the Meccans.

The following year, Muḥammad received representatives from tribes all over Arabia who came to submit themselves to His will, which was submission to the divine will, or "Islam."

Muḥammad taught the unity of God, set out new laws of prayer, fasting, almsgiving, and pilgrimage, and established a higher form of justice—including greater rights and protections for women. He became known as *al-Amin, the Trusted One,* for His fairness, gentleness, spirituality, and simplicity of life that grew out of His nearness to God. Most importantly, His spiritual teachings were enshrined in a book, *the Holy Qur'án,* which would become the source of spirituality and moral guidance for His followers.

Divisions gradually developed among Muslims after the death of Muḥammad in 632 CE. Two major branches of Muslims grew apart, the Sunnis and the Shi'ites. This split, which would only emerge after several decades of internal conflict, had its roots in the period immediately following the death of the Prophet.

Shi'ites believed it was Muḥammad's intention that 'Alí be His successor. 'Alí had grown up with Muḥammad and was the first person after Khadíjih to acknowledge Him as the Messenger of God. He had been referred by Him as His succesor, had acted as His secretary, been chosen as His brother, carried the standard in two important battles, and been left in charge of the faithful when Muḥammad was away. According to a hadith considered reliable, Muḥammad, on His way back from His final pilgrimage, said to His followers: "Of whomsoever I am lord, then 'Alí is also his lord." In a more controversial episode, Muḥammad called for pen and paper on His deathbed to prevent Muslims from being led into error. Some who were with Him said that the Book of God was enough and that illness was overwhelming Him, at which point Muḥammad dismissed them from His presence so as not to hear their arguing. Shi'ites believed that He intended to write 'Alí's name down as His successor.[3]

But it was Abú Bakr, Muḥammad's father-in-law and the first convert outside of His own family, who became the leader of the Muslims. 'Alí accepted Abú Bakr's leadership to preserve unity among the Muslims especially since, with Muḥammad gone, many recanted and turned against the Muslims. 'Umar, a prominent believer, succeeded Abú

Bakr, and 'Alí did not advance a rival claim. 'Umar continued the Arab conquests, this time of Persia and her empire.

Shi'ite Islám

'Uthman was chosen as the Muslim leader after 'Umar's passing. Under 'Uthman's rule, there was considerable unrest in the vastly expanded Muslim territories. Rebel delegations came to 'Alí asking him to take over, but he refused, though he tried to mediate between them and 'Uthman. The rebels eventually killed 'Uthman and again came to 'Alí, who accepted the request for his leadership and, in 656 CE, became the head of the Islamic world.[4]

Over time, Sunnis and Shi'ites developed different systems of authority. Sunnis elected one individual to be the political ruler, while clerics would be responsible for all religious questions. The Shi'ites believed that God chose one man at a time to be the spiritual leader of the Muslims, the Ímám. As the successor to the authority of Muḥammad, the Ímám received divine guidance, interpreted the Qur'án, and applied the sacred law. Divine guidance flowed through him to the believers.[5]

One branch of Shi'ism claimed that there were twelve such Ímáms and considered 'Alí to be the first. The most well-known Ímám was the third Ímám, Ḥusayn, the grandson of the Manifestation of God and the son of 'Alí. He was massacred along with his family and followers at Karbilá by the army of the caliph, a violent event that continues to be commemorated annually up to the present-day with great emotion by the Shi'a faithful. In all the towns of Persia, there were men who reenacted the massacre of Ḥusayn and his family. Ḥusayn became the model for what it meant to be a true follower of Islam, and to give one's life for one's faith became a religious ideal of Shi'a Islam.

According to the Shi'a tradition, the twelfth Ímám is believed to have gone into occultation, a mystical form of concealment. Four in-

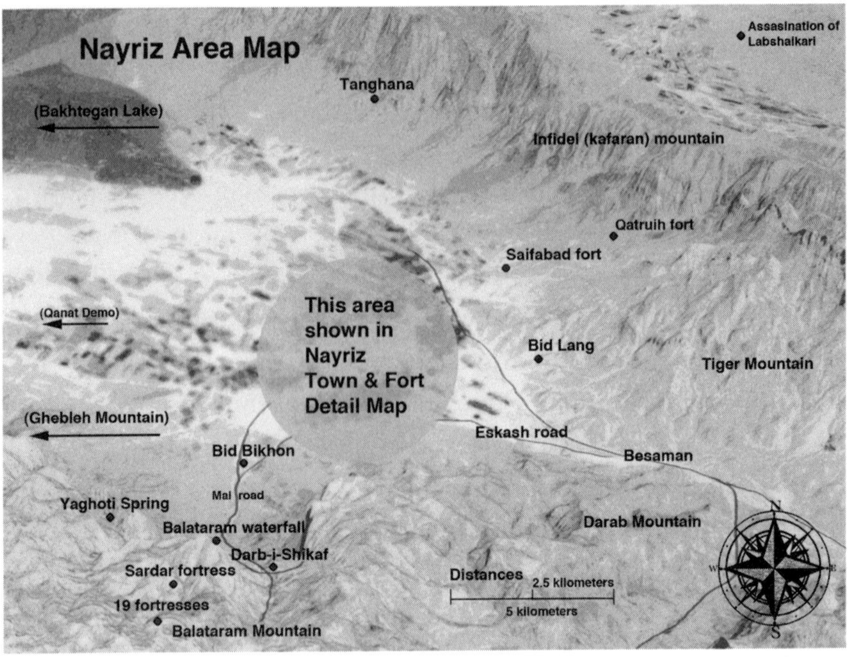

dividuals, or "Gates," successively became the intermediaries between the Hidden Ímám and the believers. When this period lasted longer than the normal lifespan of a human being, Shiʿites came to believe that the Ímám was being hidden by God from the believers for some future time, when he would come again.

When the twelfth Ímám returned, he would be the Qá'im, the "One who arises," and the Mahdi, the one who "guides the people" of Islam.[6] He would return with his chosen ones—his enemies would return as well—and he would lead the forces of righteousness against the forces of evil. He would then rule, after which Christ and all the Ímáms, prophets and saints would return.

Until then, society would be guided by the educated clergy and legal scholars who interpreted the Qur'án and the hadiths. These educated

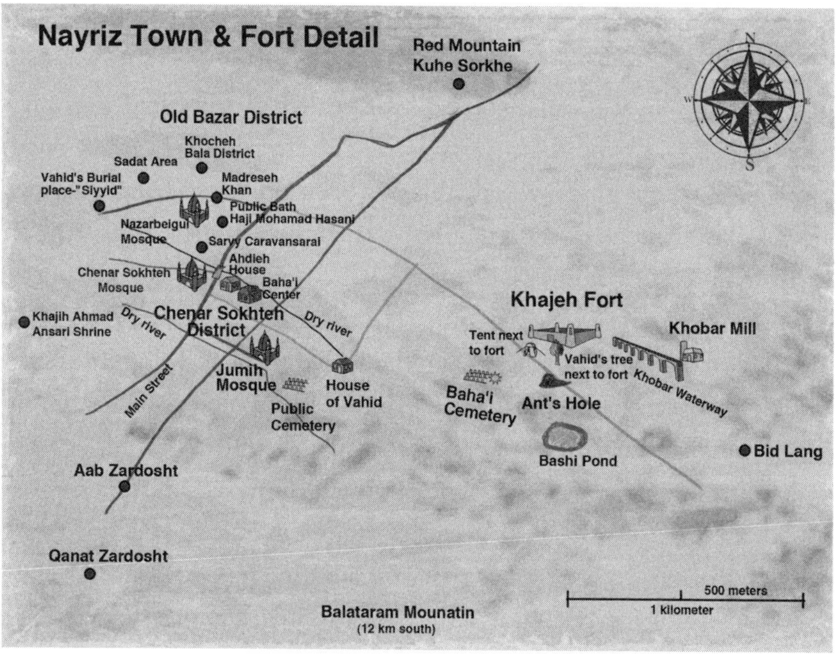

clerics became the representatives of the Hidden Ímám and fulfilled the functions of the Ímám, such as receiving the religious tax, leading Friday prayer, and putting judicial decisions into effect, among others.[7]

For centuries, Shi'ites were a minority in Sunni kingdoms. In 1501 CE, Shi'ism found a homeland in Persia when a new dynasty declared Shi'ism the official form of Islam in its kingdom.

The use of violence

It is often believed, in the Judeo-Christian world, that Islam spread primarily through the use of violence, while Christianity spread through the teaching of the Word of God. This mischaracterization of history does not do justice to the true teachings of Muḥammad and the history of Islám.

Muḥammad was born into an Arab tribal and nomadic world; Jesus was born into a settled agrarian kingdom ruled by Romans through local kings. The economic and political reality of the tribal world necessitated that a tribe fight for resources and territory. In every tribal society anywhere in the world, this has been the case. Tribal societies always existed in a constant state of low-grade warfare. After the end of Roman rule in Western Europe, for example, the large Germanic tribes fought each other constantly for centuries. They then developed into the structure of medieval agrarian kingdoms, so the fighting diminished. Even so, the European Middle Ages were characterized by annual small-scale warfare over territory and disputes.

Arab tribes, like tribes everywhere, fought one another over essential resources such as water, trade routes etc. Muḥammad did not cause this state of constant conflict; it originated in the tribal structure of Arab society. What Muḥammad did was to help temper this violence much like the Catholic Church tempered the violence of the Germanic tribes. In the societies in which they lived, both Muḥammad and Jesus were seen as peacemakers.

Once the Arabs had taken over the near East, the traditional heartland of Christianity, the local people gradually became Muslims for many reasons, such as their preference for Arab rule over their former rulers, the depth and suppleness of the Islamic scripture, the theological and philosophical culture that was built on it, the rapid progress of the Muslim societies, and personal belief, among others. It was not characteristic of Arab rule in the early Muslim centuries for people to be forced to convert under the threat of violence, though occasionally this did happen. In the early Middle Ages in Europe, Charlemagne, a tribal king of the Franks and the dominant political figure of the early European Middle Ages, coerced rival tribes to convert or die as he consolidated his power over most of Europe.

From a Bahá'í perspective, God's religion spreads through divine power and human agency. Over time, human ego mixes its own ideas and behaviors into religion. So it was with Islam. After it spread dramatically and transformed societies, its followers slowly drifted away from the holy scriptures and incorporated their own ideas, their own local customs and prejudices, their own political ambitions, and their own theological concepts and distorted Islam to fit all of these. As the light of truth was dimmed, manmade beliefs manifested themselves. For example, the concept of *jihad*, which in its purest meaning referred to the struggle against one's own lower self, became a rallying cry for violent attacks against opponents. The concept of *nusrat*—rendering assistance to God—accepted the use of coercion and violence.[8]

This was the unfortunate state of religion in Nayríz, whose people had become victims of their religious leaders—many of whom pursued their own self-interest and distorted the true faith of Islam. The use of violence in religion was a feature of this distortion, as well as economic profiteering on the part of the higher ranking clerics.

The Báb, as a Manifestation of God, appeared for the purpose of renewing God's religion by purifying it. Part of this purification was the teaching that all forms of offensive warfare would have to be renounced. He was also preparing the way for a second Revelation. After His martyrdom, Bahá'u'lláh proclaimed that He was the One Whom the Báb had foretold. As a part of the new Revelation, Bahá'u'lláh forebade any form of violence in matters of religion:

> *"Beware lest ye shed the blood of any one. Unsheathe the sword of your tongue from the scabbard of utterance, for therewith ye can conquer the citadels of men's hearts. We have abolished the law to wage holy war against each other. God's mercy hath, verily, encompassed all created things, if ye do but understand."*[9]

THE BÁB, VAḤÍD, AND NAYRÍZ

IN THE BEGINNING

The old Zoroastrian priest made his way through the narrow streets of Nayríz to the fire temple. He worried about the rumors that the army of the King of Persia, the King of Kings, had been defeated at Nahávand by those Arab barbarians who had invaded the Western provinces and crossed the great mountains. It was unimaginable to him that these invaders were inside the Persian Empire and spreading like an unstoppable plague. He prayed silently to Ahura Mazda for protection of the Kingdom of Persia and his city, Nayríz.

Nayríz had prospered with its mild climate and the plentiful orchards and vineyards covering the mountain slopes. The King of Persia made the city a center for the manufacturing of weapons and employed its craftsmen for the building of the magnificent capitol, Persepolis. Persian engineers had designed a system of underground canals to bring water down from the mountains into town. There was much to be grateful for.

The old priest stepped into the sanctuary of the temple. He tried to clear his mind of his worries about war. Surely these foreigners would not be allowed to triumph. He rang the bell to mark the beginning of the watch and picked up the tools used to maintain the fire. The Arabs, it was said, brought with them a new God, Allah, and a new Holy Book. He shuddered at this thought and prepared himself to read the liturgy . . .

1

THE TOWN OF NAYRÍZ

The old Zoroastrian priest of Nayríz died before he saw his temple's fire go out.

Three centuries passed. Minarets rose above his fire temple. It became the Great Friday mosque of Nayríz. Gradually, the educated townspeople became Muslim, followed by the common people.

The call to prayer went out from this Great Friday mosque and could be heard through the jumble of mud-brick, stone, and wood, one- and two-story houses that made up the neighborhoods of Nayríz. In the unpaved spaces and dark alleys between the homes, people walked along with donkeys, cows, or horses. This commotion kicked up a lot of dust during the dry season. During the rainy winter, the mud made walking quite difficult. Through all seasons, a traveling salesman made his way with his wares—clothes, soap, hats, pottery, makeup, string—in baskets swaying from side to side in the rhythm of the steps of his donkey, and beggars waited for the chance to carry a man's load and kiss his hand in hope of some reward. Men walked past them dressed in a cloak or a heavy coat but always with a hat on, and women went about completely covered by a black chador under which they wore bright colors and a white veil over much of their faces.[1]

The call to prayer could be heard in the bazaar—or market—district, the northern part of town. Here were found the government buildings, a major bathhouse, the caravanserai where travelers and traders could stop with their animals and stay overnight, and the Sádát neighborhood where the clerics lived. It could be heard in the Chinár-Súkhtih district in the southern part of town where one main street ran north-south and was lined with stores so the residents could shop in their own area. The northern and southern parts of Nayríz were divided by a canal that was dry most of the time. When it rained—and it could rain quite hard, especially in the cold winters—the canal would overflow, causing flooding, especially in Chinár Sháhi, the neighborhood that bordered it.

The call to prayer could be heard in private walled gardens around the edge of town where apricots, grapes, quince, walnuts, and almonds grew. Walled villages and the old abandoned fort Khájih, an echo of a past conflict, lay about beyond the town.

The call to prayer called forth the water from under the ground of the southern mountains blessing this otherwise hard brown land with vineyards and orchards. This water then flowed through underground canals to several distribution points from which it was channeled into smaller canals above ground to irrigate individual properties.* At

* These underground water tunnel systems, quanats, built in ancient Persia, brought underground water from the mountains to town. The water ran above ground and powered mills that were used to grind corn and wheat. The water was distributed to town through another series of canals from large distribution points surrounded by a high wall. The Zardosht (south of Nayríz) and Khobar (southeast of Nayríz near Ft. Khájih) quanats had such distribution points.

dawn, Nayrízís would release the water. At the larger wells, a person would have to walk down slippery stone steps carrying a bucket to get to the water, which often had small worms or bacteria in it.[2] If a person fetched water at the springs, which were further away, they would take large containers made of pottery and strap them to their donkeys. The low-lying northern mountain, known as the "mountain of the Infidels," was all dirt and rock except for the occasional scraggly bush.

The call to prayer echoed in the foothills of the mountains south of town where orchards of figs, almonds, walnuts, and pomegranate trees grew up alongside fields of cantaloupe, watermelon, white flowers, and pink roses for making rose water. The scent of blossoms and the freshness of the air could revive any weary soul. Fields of wheat and cotton fed and clothed people. Poppies grew and were smoked as opium and traded in small quantities.

The call to prayer could be heard by shepherds and their dogs going through town as they gathered the goats and other animals of their neighbors to take them out to pasture. Up in the mountains, hunters preyed on the wild pigeons, quail, and deer. Donkeys crisscrossed the slopes, carrying their owners out to orchards and vineyards or loads back into town. Stars filled the night skies with light that shone down on the makeshift stone huts covered by branches sheltering tired farmers and hunters and on the wolves and tigers stalking silently around the rocks. It lit the way for the shepherds bringing the animals back to their owners, the sheep bleating to be let in when they had reached their pen.

The call to prayer could be heard by a woman going through labor in her home as she struggled through birth pangs, hoping a boy would emerge. The midwife and other women assisted her. These early days were the most dangerous moments for newborns. Families feared the evil spirits that took the life of a newborn, so small rituals were performed for protection.

The call to prayer could be heard in the homes where the children of the wealthier citizens were being taught. There were no formal kindergartens here.[3] Outside such a wealthy home, school was taught by a mullá or a teacher to whom students paid cash fees. Boys and girls learned together until they were ten years old. The girls' formal education almost always ended at that point. Students would have learned the alphabet, pronunciation, and basic math by rote; short passages from Qur'án were used to introduce the reading of scripture. Students of all ages worked in the same room—there were no grade levels—and came up to the instructor to show her what they could read or write. They sat on cushions or mats, and they got out by noon to go help their families. Only the more able or wealthier students would continue their education, which would consist of the same subjects but with more advanced literary texts. Any misbehavior by students was punished by caning or beating of the soles of their feet.[4] Most boys in Nayríz would soon be learning their fathers' work, and the girls would be by the side of their mothers acquiring the skills to maintain a household and weaving carpets.

The call to prayer could be heard by the child who was ill lying near her mother. Eye and ear infections were very common. All children had lice, and the only way to get rid of them was to shave the child's head. There were no doctors with medical training. Herbs, made from local bushes and trees, and poultices were used. For poor people, these home remedies were all the medicine that was available to them; in the richer, bazaar district, there were a few more options. The only dental care was to rub charcoal on one's teeth; an infected tooth was pulled out manually by a person in town who had some experience at this. This same individual would bleed people by using leeches or pricking small holes in the patient's shoulder and sucking out the blood to remove infections, or so they believed. A flu infection would spread through town very quickly.

The call to prayer could be heard by healthy children playing outside. But they had to be careful. A scorpion might jump out at them from behind a stone or a snake slither suddenly forward from a hole in the ground. Wolves were always about and were known to feed on small children, even coming inside a home to do so.

The call to prayer could be heard by families negotiating a marriage for their children, who were often second or third cousins. The marriage partners may have been chosen by the families when they were still very young. The needs of the families and the economic and social advantages of the marriage played the major role in choosing a marriage partner. The marriage feast was an event lasting several days with religious ceremony, music, feasts of lamb kebab, sweet lemon juice and halva, and parties for the families to get to know one another.[5] It lasted three days, and the abundant food and meat were shared with the poor.

The call to prayer could be heard by the nervous bride on the day of her marriage when she was being prepared for her appearance—she would have to be accepted by the groom and his family. She was made up with beautiful designs in henna—a dark orange dye—drawn on her hands. After dinner, the groom and family members, carrying torches and accompanied by music, came to get the bride who was now fully made-up but had her face covered. She was led to the groom's house, a Qur'án was displayed, and, sometimes, an animal slaughtered in her honor. A room had been prepared for her and the groom in his family home. In a town like Nayríz, a handerkchief might be used to determine the girl's virginity the night of the wedding.[6]

The call to prayer could be heard by the newly married young woman settling into her husband's family home. She would have to find her place in the extended family home and carry out the chores of the household. Her family had provided her new husband with a dowry, and he controlled its use. She would be expected to obey him; she must not speak back to him. In the course of an argument, her new husband might hit her; since this was common, she would have to accept it. When her husband came home drunk, she would have to be especially careful. She could wield greater influence over the decisions that were made in the family once she got to know the other women in the household and the personality of her new husband with whom she could learn to interact and negotiate.[7]

The call to prayer could be heard by the new husband watching his new wife enter his family home. He hoped she would get along well with the other women in the family, that she would provide him with sons, that she would be a good mother, that she would be pleased with him and eager to serve him. He hoped that she would try to maintain her appearance for him by using black eyeliner, make-up and perfume, if they could afford it. He knew that, in time, he could marry a second, younger, wife; he could also take a temporary wife for a few weeks or months if he could pay the fee to the mullá.

The call to prayer echoed in the courtyard of the new couple's home. Their home faced inward, with rooms around the courtyard and often a small barn or pen for animals. Rooms were used for multiple purposes.[8] Some, though, were for the women and children who were expected to stay in them if male company came over. There were no private bathrooms; the public Turkish-style bath had to be used to wash. A family would bring clean clothes, towels, brushes, soap, everything they would need for the public bath; rich families had servants bring all of this. Nor were there any toilets in the home. In the back of the house outside, there was a hole in the ground. At night, light could only be created by small oil burning lamps which filled the closed rooms in winter with smoke but did not give off much light. Richer families imported large lamps from Shíráz.

The call to prayer could be heard by a man receiving other male guests in the public rooms of the house. He poured water over his guests' hands and then served them black tea and offered them a water pipe with which to smoke tobacco or hashish; opium was smoked through a regular pipe with a long stem and small bowl at the end of it.

The call to prayer could be heard by the dervish who came into town to perform. In the streets, he hung up large canvases with paintings of famous battles. Then he reenacted well-known stories to the delight of onlookers. He also recited poetry in praise of the Ímám usayn and chanted prayers. The townspeople rewarded him with food, money, or shelter.[9]

The call to prayer could be heard by the men farming their land, tending their orchards and vineyards, and husbanding their animals. Some men worked as craftsmen and belonged to guilds. Bakers, butchers, grocers, foragesellers, coalsellers, and small shopkeepers and traders who worked in the bazaar also had their own guilds.

A very industrious man would have gotten up well before sunrise, made his way through the dark lanes and stopped at the houses of his field hands to wake them up. They would have arrived at his property on the mountainside by sunrise. Out there they could still hear the call to prayer. After some hours of work, the industrious man would have gone to another field he owned and, on the way, stopped by a garden of his nearer to town to collect fruits. He might have finished the day by going to his small store in town where he sold fabric and shoes. After such a day, he might have sat by the fire in his home and sewn the shoes together with a piece of material on top and rubber on the bottom.[10]

The call to prayer could be heard by educated men reading over a Qur'án or a legal document. They were local clerics or government and military men who worked for the central government in Shíráz.[11] The city had a governor who was appointed from Shíráz, usually due to his family's influence and the wealth that paid for the position. There was also a military commander in charge of soldiers stationed there and an overall religious leader, the Shaykhu'l-Islám.

The call to prayer could by heard by a woman lost in thought as she sat in the women and children's section of the house. A man who was not a family member had entered the home, and she had to stay in that area of the house. Her whole social and emotional life was lived within the home and the extended family, while men could express their emotions publicly, make friends, and socialize in a variety of ways. They gathered with other men and drank alcohol, smoked opium, or had young boys dance for them before selecting one. They enjoyed gambling with cards and backgammon, though they often got into fights as a result.[12]

The call to prayer could be heard by the poorer women who were baking bread together in a large open oven. They had brought the wheat and corn to the mill where waterpower turned two large circular rocks that ground the grain into powder, which the women then mixed into flour. The wealthy women had others do this for them. On festive occasions, sweet bread would be made. Much of a woman's time was spent preparing meals—stew with rice and chicken, if the family had money, cucumbers, watermelon, and homemade cookies. A samovar kept water hot all day for the black tea that was always offered to guests. They also wove cotton for clothes, using natural dyes for color. To wash the clothes—a difficult task—the poorer women and servants would go down to the stream or the springs and wash together; away from the men, their tongues would loosen, and they would laugh and share news. When the day's work was done or they could take a break, the women sat around together and ate watermelon seeds and raisins.[13]

The call to prayer could be heard as neighbors visited one another. A person had to be very aware of another's social status and observe specific social rules. In a conversation, the person of lower social status should speak less and listen more; when giving a gift, the person would have to make sure that it was valuable enough for someone of higher status. All gifts had to be reciprocated.[14]

The call to prayer could be heard on the greatest gift-giving day of the year, New Year's Day. Preparations for it began one month prior when people would clean their homes, gardens, and clothes, and make cookies and sweets. Then came the great day of celebration. This pre-Islamic festival included Zoroastrian aspects such as the use of fire. Bonfires would be lit and jumped over, feasts were prepared and eaten, eggs were painted, the elderly were paid respects by the young and gifts were given out—often coins. If the family had means, an entertainer could be hired, such as a man with a performing monkey. The visiting and gift-giving and celebrating went on for thirteen days. All of this display of friendship often eased tensions between neighbors and family. On the thirteenth day, it was considered a curse to stay in town, so people would head out to open fields.[15]

The call to prayer could be heard by the elderly man who increasingly had to stay in the family home to be taken care of by those who were younger. The day of his death eventually came. It was announced from a rooftop accompanied by the beating of a drum. Visitors began walking to the house and entered already crying and wailing. The gravedigger came to wash the body, which was then placed in a casket, transported to the cemetery, and buried. Two sticks were sometimes put into the ground so the deceased man could lean on them to rise up and answer the questions put to him by angels. The mourners then returned to the family home, ate sweets, drank tea, and listened to verses read from the Qur'án. Food was shared with the poor. Forty days went by, and the bereaved family held a memorial. They went to the cemetery and asked a mullá to come with them. They offered prayers. Then the next day came. The call to prayer sounded. Life continued.[16]

The call to prayer went out, and all Nayrízís responded to it. Many made their way faithfully to the mosques, washed their faces, entered, knelt, and followed the prayer leader with a series of movements—standing with palms uplifted, bending over with hands resting on the legs, kneeling and prostrating themselves, and touching their foreheads to the floor.

Few people, though, understood much about the Islam taught by the Prophet Muḥammad. In their daily lives, they trusted in magic and spirits.

They believed in ancient forms of foretelling the future. They threw pebbles on the ground to see which shapes were made. They counted rosary beads—usually used for prayer—in special ways to determine the outcome of an undertaking. A Qur'án might be opened at a specific time to a random page and the verses read to make a decision. They saw signs in nature—such as the howling of dogs, the movement of smoke in the air, an involuntary sneeze—as harbingers of things to come.[17]

The sky held great meaning: an eclipse caused terror, comets were seen as omens of ill fortune, the phases of the moon could influence people. The zodiac was consulted before planting or deciding on a marriage. Throughout the calendar year, special days commemorated major events in the lives of the Ímáms of Islámic history, and people believed that certain days were better than others for taking trips, marrying, building a house, or hunting.[8]

Healing could be obtained by sleeping near the tombs of holy men. A person might leave a strand of hair there to share in his sacred power. Trees could also have this power if associated with someone holy, and Nayrízís would tie a piece of cloth to it, each piece representing a wish.[19]

Evil spirits were believed to be behind misfortunes such as mental illnesses and crazed animals. Some spirits were thought to dwell in particular locations, such as waterfalls, because they had been barred from heaven. There were specific verses from the Qur'án and acts of abstinence that could help a person gain control of such a spirit. There were good spirits as well that could be summoned for assistance.[20]

And everyone dreaded the evil eye. People with the evil eye might bring about terrible events even if they didn't want to. Stories were common of the evil eye—given through a passing gaze—injuring or killing a person. Parents protected their children against this by having them wear talismans or overcoming it by repeating specific Qur'ánic verses. A ceremony took place in which a woman who worked magic against the evil eye came to an afflicted person's home. She put a tray in front of the accursed, covered it with a white kerchief, dipped her finger in a bottle of oil, and let a drop of the oil fall on the kerchief. With each drop, a curse would be removed. The names of those who had given the evil eye were said aloud. The kerchief was then picked up and thrown into water. The names were repeated, and the kerchief taken out of the water. The curses were gone.[21]

People most often used the Qur'án in this way—as a book of charms and as a talisman. Few could actually read it. They owned miniature versions of the Qur'án worn around the neck in little pouches for protection against evil spirits.[22]

Many of these magical beliefs were claimed to be found in the volumes of hadiths, the accepted traditions from the Prophet Muḥammad and the Ímáms. Some hadiths were verifiable, but many were not, and all were interpreted and reinterpreted by local religious scholars, mullás, diviners, and elderly men. The beliefs of the people were really locally held folk beliefs that had been cast into a Muslim mold but that had no connection to Muḥammad's Revelation.

Whatever a Nayrízí knew about Islám came from the mullá. The mullá was someone who could read and write and had studied the Qur'án. To the average believer, he was the authority on all spiritual and many legal matters. Many Nayrízís worked the land and felt themselves inferior to these robed men who could read the holy text, and if a prominent cleric came to Nayríz and spoke to them, his word was absolute.

Nayrízís also learned stories about the history of Shí'a Islam from yearly public reenactments of famous events, especially the story of the martyrdom of the Ímám Ḥusayn. The constant use of this story reinforced the idea that martyrdom was the highest act of religious devotion. The belief in giving one's life for God and of defending true religion even with violence were deeply held in the hearts of the faithful masses.

The most powerful release of their spiritual emotions came during Muḥarram, the month when the Third Ímám had been martyred.* From the pulpits, the mullás recounted stories about the Ímám Ḥusayn. The men crowding into mosques and women standing behind curtains and on the roofs were moved to begin their mourning. The faithful would come out of mosques with their emotions lit. Men then marched down the streets holding up signs and symbols honoring Ḥusayn and began

* This month would become especially dangerous for Bahá'ís because the religious fervor of the faithful was then directed against them by the clerics, and many acts of violence were carried out as a result.

to beat themselves with their hand, with chains, and even with swords, making small cuts in their foreheads. As the march continued, the men would bleed more and more profusely. Red rivulets ran down their bare torsos, spattering their young sons who walked alongside them dressed in white, the color of martyrdom. On the sides, the women wailed and ululated. The whole community participated in this powerful and violent display meant to honor Ḥusayn and share in his suffering.

These beliefs were reinforced by the mullás in the mosques built in the different neighborhoods of Nayríz. Several mullás served in each of these mosques. The most important mullá was the one who led the prayers on Friday; the principal, or "Great" Mosque of Nayríz was located in the Chinár-Súkhtih district. A leading mullá had real authority over people and access to wealth from the land owned by the mosque and monetary contributions from the faithful. The people of a town like Nayríz trusted their clerics completely and obeyed their decisions. But their clerics had little true understanding of Islám. So, when the faithful bent their knees at prayer, their minds were full of little understood teachings, unquestioned traditions, and ancient magical beliefs.

Over the centuries, the mullás—the spiritual leaders of the people—had become more concerned with maintaining their position in society and enriching themselves through the ownership of a mosque's land than with living a life of submission to God's teachings.

This was true everywhere in Persia.

By the early 1800s, many Shí'a Muslims believed that Islam needed to be cleansed. The hope that the Qá'im, the "One who will arise," would appear to sanctify Islam became widespread. A new movement, Shaykhísm, dedicated to seeking and finding the Qá'im, came into being. The Shaykhís were told by their master that the time had come and that they must go and seek this Promised One.

To find Him, one would have to journey to S͟híráz, the capital of the province of Fárs.

To go on a long journey, one had to join a caravan. The organizers of a caravan announced its departure long in advance, and those who wanted to go with it prepared clothes, food, and money. Women rode in howdahs, large wooden compartments fixed to a donkey or camel. People said good-bye to their families. The departure was a big event. After all, the countryside was full of highwaymen and bandits, and if someone became ill, there was little that could be done. The journey from Nayríz to S͟híráz could take five days.

Leaving Nayríz for S͟híráz, one would have to take the road that wound away from town southwest toward Iṣṭahbánát, the fig-growing heartland of Persia.[23] Rows of fig and almond trees planted by the Nayrízís on the mountain slope to the left stretched all the way to Iṣṭahbánát. The road continued uphill, a view of the valley opened on the right, and then the road went down towards the town of Iṣṭahbánát and forked. The southern fork led to Fasá, while the northern one led to S͟híráz. To the north, the land leveled out into low hills. The right horizon became jagged brown mountains, and the road led through the small town of Sarvistán. Mountains appeared on the left and grew closer to the road as those on the right receded far into the distance. On either side, small groups of nomads, covered against the cold and sun, slowly crossed the dry landscape on their donkeys. Soon the road passed near the edge of a salt lake. This lowland turned marshy, with reeds breaking the water and standing along the road.

Finally, the road rose uphill to S͟híráz, the poetical heartland of Persia.[24]

2

THE BÁB

In the courtyard of the house in Shíráz, the little girl, Khadíjih, chased the other children around. Their laughter echoed throughout the house and into the street. One boy, 'Alí-Muḥammad, who had lived there in the home of his maternal uncle since His father had died, watched them. He was more serious than other children—His own mother had worried about how calm He had been as an infant. He was never anxious or restless, and His mother wondered, "Why is this child not like other children?" Still, Khadíjih and the other children liked Him because He was so kind to them. 'Alí-Muḥammad and Khadíjih lived next door to each other and spent much time together.[1]

Around age six, the boy was brought to the Qur'ánic school located in the convent for mystics in the poultry quarter near his house.* The

* The schoolmaster, Mullá Fatḥu'lláh Maktab-Dár, who worked for Shaykh 'Abid, became a follower of the Báb after His Declaration in the mosque in Shíráz. The school was located in the Tayr marketplace (Afnán, *The Báb in Shíráz*, 12). According to Mírzá Abú'l Faḍl, cited in Nabíl-i-A'ẓam, *The Dawn-Breakers* (51), the Báb was age six or seven; according to Afnán, *The Báb in Shíráz* (12), he was five.

morning of the interview, He arrived with a small tray of sweets and a student's Qur'án. He was met by the school's owner and schoolmaster, Shaykh 'Abid, and some older students who were all eager to meet this extraordinary child.* He was asked to read the opening words of the Holy Qur'án. The boy asked for an explanation of this famous passage, and the teacher pretended not to know, instead asking the boy what He thought they meant. To everyone's astonishment, the boy gave a deep, original explanation of the spiritual ideas in this passage. Later, the teacher brought him back to his uncle: the boy's abilities were so extraordinary that he felt unworthy to teach Him. The uncle scolded the boy and told Him to be silent in school and follow the example of the other students. Back in school, though, the boy's intuitive knowledge could not be suppressed. One day, the learned Shaykh 'Abid was discussing a difficult scientific topic with his seminary students. He told them that he would research the answer that evening and tell them what he had found the next day. Suddenly the boy—Who had been listening nearby—spoke up and gave a thorough answer to their question. The seminary students told the Shaykh that they had never discussed this with the boy, and all were amazed at his knowledge.[2]

School could offer little to Khadíjih's friend. At age fifteen, He joined His uncle's trading business and left Shíráz for Búshihr, a port city on the coast to the west, to work in trade. Though young, he ended up managing His uncle's trading business and developed a reputation for extreme honesty and fairness as well as thoroughness. One evening after he had left, Khadíjih went to sleep and had a vivid dream. In it, she saw 'Alí-Muḥammad standing in a green meadow filled with flowers.

* The interview was on a Thursday morning, according to Mullá Fatḥu'lláh Maktab-Dár.

He was praying toward Mecca and wearing a coat. This was not the ordinary outer coat that people wore—it was embroidered in threads of gold with verses from the Holy Qur'án. His face radiated a powerful light. Once she had awoken, she remembered this powerful dream and went to ask the mother and grandmother of 'Alí-Muḥammad what it meant. They explained that 'Alí-Muḥammad—even though still a teenager—always prayed with His whole heart and soul, and this was being shown to her in this dream. In Búshihr, He could be seen offering prayers with great devotion on the roof of His house under the blazing midday sun.[3]

After five years in Búshihr, 'Alí-Muḥammad left to visit the holy cities of 'Iráq.* While in Karbilá, He attended the class of the disciples of Siyyid Káẓim, the leader of the Shaykhís. When Siyyid Káẓim saw Him come in and sit down, he stopped speaking. A student asked him to continue his discussion, and Siyyid Káẓim responded that there was nothing more to say as the Truth was as obvious as a ray of light, at which point a ray of sunshine shone upon 'Alí-Muḥammad.[4]

At the request of His mother and uncles, 'Alí-Muḥammad returned to Shíráz. Again, after falling asleep one night, Khadíjih had another, even more astonishing, dream. This time, Fáṭimih, the daughter of the Prophet Muḥammad, asked Khadíjih for her hand in marriage to the Ímám Ḥusayn, the Third Ímám, whom all Shí'ah Muslims revered. When her mother heard about this dream, she became excited, telling her daughter that it meant something very great was going to happen to her.[5]

---

* The holy cities in Iraq are Najaf, burial place of 'Alí, the First Ímám; Karbilá, burial place of the Third Ímám, Ḥusayn; Kazimayn, burial place of the Seventh and Ninth Ímáms, and Samara, burial place of the Tenth and Eleventh Ímáms (Balyuzi, *The Báb*, f. p. 41).

Later that day, the mother and grandmother of 'Alí-Muḥammad came to the house to see K͟hadíjih's mother. The children and young people greeted them warmly and showed their affection by kissing the grandmother on her shoulder; out of respect, they waited outside the sitting room for permission to come in and sit down because only the mothers would sit in the presence of the grandmother. They were silent waiting for the grandmother to speak first. K͟hadíjih went to get some refreshing fruit juice for the older women and served them. She then left the room so the women could talk in private, though her older sisters went in to participate. After awhile, the guests got up to leave. As she stood there to bid them good-bye, K͟hadíjih was very surprised when the mother of 'Alí-Muḥammad kissed her on the forehead on her way out of the house. K͟hadíjih didn't know what this meant. Her mother, seeing that she was puzzled, explained to her the meaning of her dream: 'Alí-Muḥammad's mother had asked for K͟hadíjih's hand in marriage for her son, 'Alí-Muḥammad.

K͟hadíjih felt great joy when she heard this. She had known 'Alí-Muḥammad all her life—He was her neighbor, her relative, and her playmate when they had been children. She had experienced His kindness. She knew how much her elders admired and respected Him, and so He must be a great man. Her heart stirred with emotion as she looked forward to her union with 'Alí-Muḥammad. God certainly had blessed her.

The households prepared the marriage feasts. Two months later, on Friday, August, 25th, 1842, the marriage day came, and the families held feasts in each home. By custom, the wedding consisted of two separate celebrations, one for the men and the other for the women. The men gathered in the house of the groom's uncle, Ḥájí Mírzá Siyyid 'Alí, while the women celebrated in the home of the bride's father. The leading Mullá of S͟híráz, S͟hayk͟h Abú-Turáb, read a marriage oration in the home of the bride. The uncle of 'Alí-Muḥammad accepted the marriage offer, as was the custom. Then the wedding moved to the uncle's home where the two young people were joined in wedlock.[6]

So began their life together.

The household consisted of the young couple, the mother of 'Alí-Muḥammad, and two Ethiopian servants, Mubárak and Fiddih. They took up residence in a home on Shamshirgatha Street.[7] This unpaved street was typical for its time—on either side of the street were brick and mud walls with no windows, as all homes faced inward. One arrived at a dark wooden door with a round brass knocker on the right half. After being out on the dusty streets of town, one stepped into a small courtyard and immediately felt refreshed by the presence of a square pool of water and an orange tree. Large ground floor windows opened into the courtyard. Walking between the pool of water and the right side of the courtyard, one arrived at a set of stairs that led up to a second floor sitting room where the young siyyid* received His guests. The walls of the home were made of stone and brick. Windows with small colored panes on their edges and framed by woodwork gave the home decorative highlights.

'Alí-Muḥammad treated His young wife with great care and kindness, and her relationship with His mother was very affectionate. Khadíjih could not believe her good fortune.[8]

❋ ❋ ❋

One night early in their marriage, she awoke with her heart pounding in fear. She told her husband that she had seen a great lion in the courtyard of their home. She had her arms around its neck. The beast circled the courtyard two and a half times. He explained that it

* The term *siyyid* is a title used to indicate that the bearer of the title is a descendant of the Prophet Muḥammad.

meant their life together would not last more than two and a half years. Hearing this, she became anguished. His soothing words and affection calmed her, but He was also preparing her for her future tribulations.

Soon Khadíjih was pregnant. Her delivery was very painful and dangerous. 'Alí-Muḥammad named their son Aḥmad. But little Aḥmad died not long after. 'Alí-Muḥammad's mother was furious at Him for not preventing the death of their little one. He responded calmly that He was not destined to leave children.

The little baby, son of 'Alí-Muḥammad and Khadíjih, was buried under a cypress tree.[9]

Later, his father would write:

> O my God, my only Desire! Grant that the sacrifice of My son, My only son, may be acceptable unto Thee. Grant that it be a prelude to the sacrifice of My own, My entire self, in the path of Thy good pleasure. Endue with Thy grace My life-blood which I yearn to shed in Thy path. Cause it to water and nourish the seed of Thy Faith. Endow it with Thy celestial potency, that this infant seed of God may soon germinate in the hearts of men, that it may thrive and prosper, that it may become a mighty tree, beneath the shadow of which all peoples and kindreds of the earth may gather. Answer Thou My prayer, O God, and fulfill My most cherished desire. Thou art, verily, the Almighty, the All-Bountiful.[10]

❁ ❁ ❁

Life continued in the household. In the mornings, 'Alí-Muḥammad would sometimes go to work at His uncle's trading house in the customs area of town. In the afternoons, He would go walking in the fields outside of Shíráz. In the early evening, He performed the evening prayer and then wrote letters and meditations. Days when He did not go to the trading house were spent in prayer in the upper room overlooking the courtyard.[11]

One day, He came home earlier in the afternoon and asked that they eat dinner sooner than usual, as there was something He had to do. Fiddih cooked a meal, which they ate in His mother's room, for the family. Then 'Alí-Muḥammad went to His room for the evening.

Later that night, after everyone had gone to bed and the house was quiet, Khadíjih heard 'Alí-Muḥammad get up and leave their room. She didn't think anything of it, but when He didn't return, she grew concerned. Finally, she got out of bed and walked out into the dark house to see where He was. She did not find Him anywhere. Had He gone out? She went downstairs and crossed the courtyard to check the wooden door that led out into the street. It was locked from the inside. As she crossed to the other side, she looked up. A light shone in the upper room. He used this room for guests, but there had been none that evening. So she walked over to that side of the courtyard and nervously climbed the stairs to the upper room. Reaching the top, she saw her husband with his hands raised up in supplication, chanting a prayer in his beautiful voice. Tears rolled down his face. A powerful, unknown light emanated from him. She began to shake with fear at this sight. She couldn't move; His majesty overwhelming her. At that moment, He turned to her and made a gesture that told her to go back. This gave her the courage to go back down the stairs, cross the courtyard, and get back into bed. For the rest of the night, she could not sleep, as she kept reliving that powerful scene. What did it mean? Had something terrible happened that He was in such tears? Her restless state of mind kept her up all night. The call to prayer announced the dawn from a nearby mosque.*

---

* Afnán, "The Bab in Shiraz," v. 16, *Witnesses to Babi and Baha'i history* (f. 65, p. 34), explains that, according to the Báb in the Kitáb Fihrist, the "First descent" of

Fiddih brought the samovar for the family morning tea, which they had in 'Alí-Muḥammad's mother's room. When Khadíjih saw her husband seated in the room, she became pale because He had the same majesty she had seen the night before. After her mother-in-law had left the room, He motioned for Khadíjih to sit near Him and passed her His cup of tea. Drinking from it calmed her down. He asked her what was bothering her, and she told Him that she had seen a great change in Him. He was no longer the man to whom she had been married for two years, nor the same young person she had known all her life. He had been transformed. She didn't understand what was happening, and this made her nervous.

He answered her, "It was the will of God that you should have seen Me in the way you did last night, so that no shadow of doubt should ever cross your mind, and you should come to know with absolute certitude that I am the Manifestation of God Whose advent has been excpected for a thousand years . . ."[12]

Hearing this, she fell prostrate before Him, believing what she heard. She would serve Him the rest of her life.

He would later reveal the following about her:

> O well-beloved! Value highly the grace of the Great Remembrance, for it cometh from God, the Loved One. Thou shalt not be a woman, like other women, if thou obeyest God in the Cause of Truth, the Greatest Truth. Know thou the great bounty conferred upon thee by the Ancient of Days, and take pride in being the consort of the Well-Beloved, Who is loved by God, the

---

God's Spirit on the Báb was on the fifteenth of the third month of 1260 AH, or April 3rd, 1844. So this may be the date of the incident remembered by Khadíjih Bagum.

Greatest. Sufficient unto thee is this glory which cometh unto thee from God, the All-Wise, the All-Praised. Be patient in all that God hath ordained concerning the Báb and His Family. Verily, thy son is with Fáṭimih (Muḥammad's daughter), in the sanctified Paradise.[13]

❋ ❋ ❋

In the late afternoon of May 22nd, 1844, a young cleric named Mullá Ḥusayn, from the northern town of Bus͟hrú'í in the province of K͟hurásán, walked through the streets of S͟híráz with Siyyid 'Alí-Muḥammad.[14] A little earlier, Mullá Ḥusayn had been standing outside the west-facing Kázirún gate of the city* when 'Alí-Muḥammad came to him and showed him great warmth. Mullá Ḥusayn thought this young man must be one of the S͟hayk͟hís of S͟híráz who had been sent out to welcome him.

The leader of the S͟hayk͟hís, Siyyid Káẓim, had died roughly five months earlier in Karbilá. Mullá Ḥusayn was one of his most devoted followers.** Siyyid Káẓim had told his disciples that the Qá'im, the Promised One, had come, that they must purify themselves completely and then, guided by prayer and with complete dedication, go out and seek Him. It was the year '60—1260 AH—a year prophecied in many of the Shi'ah traditions as the year in which the Qá'im would make Himself manifest. After Siyyid Káẓim's death, most of his disciples,

---

* It was not the Shíráz gate, as is often thought (Abu'l Qásim Afnán, 'Ahd-i A'lá Zindigáníy-Hadrat-Báb, *The Bábí Dispensation, The life of the Báb* [Oxford, UK: One World, 2000] n. 9, 70).

** According to the Gregorian calendar, Siyyid Káẓim passed away around December 31st, 1843, the "Day of 'Arafah" in the Muslim calendar—the ninth day of the last month of that calendar's year.

though, stayed in Karbilá, each with his own excuse for not following these instructions.

Mullá Ḥusayn gave up on them and began his search by praying and fasting for forty days. He was joined there by Mullá 'Alí, a learned Shaykhí, and twelve others. Mullá Ḥusayn made his way, as if guided, to Shíráz.

Mullá Ḥusayn followed Siyyid 'Alí-Muḥammad to the wooden door of His house. His Ethiopian servant, Mubárak, opened the door and welcomed them. A feeling of joy came over Mullá Ḥusayn as he followed his host to the upper room. The young man poured water over Mullá Ḥusayn's hands and served him tea. Mullá Ḥusayn was touched by the humility of this siyyid. The time came for evening prayers, and the two men stood side-by-side to worship. Mullá Ḥusayn asked silently for guidance with his search.

As the sun set, the two began to speak about Siyyid Káẓim and his teachings.[15] Siyyid 'Alí-Muḥammad began:

"Whom, after Siyyid Káẓim, do you regard as his successor and your leader?"

"At the hour of his death, our departed teacher insistently exhorted us to forsake our homes, to scatter far and wide, in quest of the promised Beloved. I have, accordingly, journeyed to Persia, have arisen to accomplish his will, and am still engaged in my quest."

"Has your teacher given you any detailed indications as to the distinguishing features of the promised One?"

"Yes. He is of pure lineage, of illustrious descent, and of the seed of Fáṭimih. As to his age, He is more than twenty and less than thirty. He is endowed with innate knowledge. He is of medium height, abstains from smoking, and is free from bodily deficiency."

There was silence for a moment and then Siyyid 'Alí-Muḥammad exclaimed, "Behold, all these signs are manifest in Me!" He went over the description just given and showed how each of these qualities was present in Him.

Mullá Ḥusayn was greatly surprised and tried to dampen the announcement: "He whose advent we await is a man of unsurpassed holiness, and the Cause He is to reveal, a Cause of tremendous power. Many and diverse are the requirements which He who claims to be its visible embodiment must needs fulfill. How often has Siyyid Káẓim referred to the vastness of the knowledge of the Promised One! How often did he say: 'My own knowledge is but a drop compared with that with which He has been endowed. All my attainments are but a speck of dust in the face of the immensity of His knowledge. Nay, immeasurable is the difference!'"

His host then repeated His claim: "Observe attentively. Might not the Person intended by Siyyid Káẓim be none other than I?"

Mullá Ḥusayn then handed his host a copy of the treatise he had written on Shaykhí teachings. This was the first of Mullá Ḥusayn's tests for Siyyid 'Alí-Muḥammad. As soon as he gave Him the treatise, Mullá Ḥusayn felt a fear come into him which he couldn't explain. His next test was for Siyyid 'Alí-Muḥammad to reveal a commentary of the Súrih of Joseph from the Holy Qur'án.

The young siyyid answered all these tests in a language of great power and with wholly original ideas. Mullá Ḥusayn listened in rapture to the chanting of his host. The power in His voice and words seemed to weave around Mullá Ḥusayn and transform him. Mullá Ḥusayn's astonishment increased with every moment. The veils fell away. He believed.

Then, looking at Mullá Ḥusayn, Siyyid 'Alí-Muḥammad spoke:

> O thou who art the first to believe in Me! Verily I say, I am the Báb, the Gate of God, and though art the Bábu'l-Báb, the gate of

> that Gate. Eighteen souls must, in the beginning, spontaneously and of their own accord, accept Me, and recognize the truth of My Revelation. Unwarned and uninvited, each of these must seek independently to find Me. And when their number is complete, one of them must needs be chosen to accompany Me on My pilgrimage to Mecca and Medina. There I shall deliver the Message of God to the Sharif of Mecca. I then shall return to Karbilá, where again, in the Masjid of that holy city, I shall manifest His Cause. It is incumbent upon you not to divulge, either to your companions or to any other soul, that which you have seen and heard. Be engaged in the Masjid-i-Ilkhání in prayer and in teaching. I, too, will there join you in congregational prayer. Beware lest your attitude towards me betray the secret of your faith . . .

After making this powerful announcement, the Báb accompanied His guest downstairs to the wooden door. Mullá Ḥusayn walked out of His Holy Presence back into everyday life, but found the whole world reduced to dust. He could see how weak he had been but, now, he was filled with courage, joy, and gratitude. Experiencing Divine Revelation had set his soul on fire. He was awake. Now, he would arise. His voice was that of Gabriel crying out: "The morning Light has broken . . . the portal of His grace is open wide; enter therein, O peoples of the world! For He who is your promised One is come!"

Mullá Ḥusayn was the first Letter of the Living—the title given by the Báb to these first "eighteen souls" who would recognize His Station and become the first apostles in the new day of God.*

* There would be eighteen "Letters of the Living." This term was used for the first followers of the Báb. A "letter" symbolizes a believer, and letters make up words which reveal meaning. The Báb was the Revealer, the One who generated these "let-

Mullá Ḥusayn rejoined his brother and nephew who noticed the great change in him. They too would become Letters of the Living. One by one, in dreams and personal revelations, the other apostles awoke. This included an extraordinary woman, Ṭáhirih, who lived in Qazvín and became a believer without ever having met the Báb over the objections of her father, a prominent cleric, and the rest of her well-known family. The eighteenth Letter was Quddús, a young man descended from the Prophet Muḥammad's grandson, the second Ímám, and with whom the Báb had been communing in the world of the spirit. He would become the most distinguished of the Báb's followers.

The Letters of the Living were now complete. The Báb prepared to go to the cities where Islam began, Mecca and Medina, to declare His Mission.

The Báb addressed the Letters of the Living:

> O My beloved friends! You are the bearers of the name of God in this Day. You have been chosen as the repositories of His mystery . . . Ponder the words of Jesus addressed to His disciples, as He sent them forth to propagate the Cause of God. In words such as these, He bade them arise and fulfill their mission: "Ye are even as the fire which in the darkness of the night has been kindled upon the mountain-top. Let your light shine before the eyes of men. Such must be the purity of your character and the degree of your renunciation, that the people of the earth may through you recognize and be drawn closer to the heavenly Father who is the Source of purity and grace . . . O my Letters!

---

ters." The eighteen Letters of the Living plus the Báb equal nineteen. The numerical value in Persian of the word *Vaḥíd*—which means "unity"—is nineteen.

Verily I say, immensely exalted is this Day above the days of the Apostles of old . . . You are the witnesses of the Dawn of the promised Day of God . . . I am preparing you for the advent of a mighty Day . . . The secret of the Day that is to come is now concealed . . . Scatter throughout the length and breadth of this land, and, with steadfast feet and sanctified hearts, prepare the way for His coming . . . Arise in His name, put your trust wholly in Him, and be assured of ultimate victory."

❋ ❋ ❋

The Báb, accompanied by Quddús, the eighteenth Letter of the Living, and Mubárak, His servant, sailed from Persia to Arabia. He wrote to Khadíjih from the port, expressing His love: "My sweet love, may God preserve Thee." The stormy seas rocked the boat. Many passengers fell ill. With little water to drink, they had to survive on sweet lemons. Throughout the tumult, the Báb revealed sacred verses, and Quddús wrote them down.[16]

One of the passengers on board was the brother of Shaykh Abú-Turáb, the leading Mullá of Shíráz who would become a great defender of the Báb. The brother envied the great respect the other passengers had for the Báb and began to speak disrespectfully to Him. The captain of the ship got so angry that he had the shipmates prepare to throw him overboard, when the Báb threw Himself on the Shaykh's brother, telling the captain that the brother was only harming himself with his actions, and they must forgive him.

They landed in Arabia in December, 1844, and proceeded to Mecca. Quddús, out of respect for the Báb, walked alongside the camel upon which the Báb rode. Once in Mecca, they performed the rites of pilgrimage. Among the pilgrims was a man named Siyyid Ja'far-i-

Kashfí, the father of Siyyid Yaḥyáy-i-Dárábí, known later by the title Vaḥíd, who would be the first to take the Báb's Revelation to Nayríz.

The Báb walked up to the door of the Kaaba, the building around which the pilgrims circled, took hold of its great rung and exclaimed three times to the large crowd of worshippers: "I am that Qá'im whose advent you have been awaiting."

The pilgrims heard these words and were astonished, but they did not understand their meaning. Over the next days, news of this strange announcement spread.[17]

The Báb gave Quddús a book of His holy writings to be presented to the Sharíf of Mecca, the man who was responsible for overseeing the cities of Mecca and Medina and who had special responsibilities for the pilgrimage of the Muslims. The Sharíf, though, did not read it, as he was busy with the pilgrimage season. When he finally did pick it up, he realized the significance of what he had been given, but by then, the Báb had left.

The Báb, Quddús, and Mubárak, made their way to Medina where Muḥammad had founded the first Muslim community. The Báb prayed intensely at the Prophet's grave and then at the grave of Shaykh Aḥmad, the founder of the Shaykhís, who had predicted the Báb's appearance.[18] Here the Báb had a vision of the early heroes of Islam, who expressed fear at what would happen to Him when He returned to Persia.

❀ ❀ ❀

The Báb, Quddús, and Mubárak landed in Persia a little more than half a year after they had left. The Báb sent Quddús on to Shíráz: "The days of your companionship with Me are drawing to a close. The hour of separation has struck, a separation which no reunion will follow except in the Kingdom of God, in the presence of the King of Glory."[19]

Once in Shíráz, Quddús was received by the Báb's maternal uncle and gave him the Báb's message. This uncle, who had raised the Báb from childhood, immediately became a Bábí. Soon the clergy were in a great uproar that a new Revelation was being proclaimed. The governor of Fárs arrested Quddús and sent soldiers to Búshihr to arrest the Báb. The soldiers found the Báb coming out of Búshihr to meet them. They were so moved by His humility and gentleness that by the time they arrived in Shíráz, the soldiers were walking behind the Báb as a sign of respect.

The governor had the Báb brought before him. In the course of the interrogation, he became so angry at the Báb's use of Qur'ánic passages against him that he had his servants slap the Báb. His green turban—the symbol of His lineage from Muḥammad—fell to the ground. Shaykh Abú-Turáb, the cleric who had married the Báb and His wife, felt ashamed at how the Báb was being treated, picked up the turban and placed it back on His head.[20] The Shaykh asked the Báb if His claim was to be the intermediary between the world and the Hidden Ímám, and the Báb denied this. Satisfied, Shaykh Abú-Turáb said the Báb would be asked to announce this publicly at the Vakíl mosque. The Báb was released into his maternal uncle's custody.

The Báb arrived at the mosque some days later to fulfill His pledge. Shaykh Abú-Turáb welcomed Him to the front of the mosque. Standing in front of the worshipers, the Báb spoke about the oneness of God and asserted the holy stations of Muḥammad and 'Alí. People thought, in listening to Him, that He claimed to be the "medium of grace from his Highness the Lord of the Age." He finished by repeating the Islamic tradition that, "The day of appearance of the Qá'im is the Day of Resurrection." Then He descended and joined the worshippers for Friday prayer, but the Shaykh encouraged Him to return home because he was worried the Báb might be harmed.[21]

But as some later realized, the Báb did not claim to be the gate to the Hidden Ímám but rather the Qá'im, the Lord of the Age. He was also the gate to "another city," to a future Manifestation of God.[22] He was preparing the ground for a mightier day, and He was revealing Himself gradually to protect His young followers who would soon face extreme persecution.

The leading mullás, enraged at the implication of what they had heard in the mosque, signed a death warrant to execute the Báb but could not issue it when Shaykh Abú-Turáb, the senior mullá in the city, refused to sign it.[23]

The Báb's mother, His wife Khadíjih, and others in His household heard the town crier announcing the Báb's appearance at the mosque. Khadíjih worried about Him. Afterwards, she heard that many had been angered by His words. To her unbounded joy, He returned to their home.[24] For a period of time now, the Báb would live in peace in their home, revealing the Word of God and communicating with His rapidly growing numbers of followers.

The Letters of the Living journeyed throughout the kingdom of Persia, witnessing to the new Revelation. A great spiritual upheaval followed in their wake. Mullás, mujtahids, and governors grew very disturbed as people listened to the accounts of the Báb's signs and wonders and were amazed.

This amazement soon reached the highest levels of the kingdom.

SSE AIRTRICITY LEAGUE

PREMIER DIVISION

Limerick FC v Dundalk FC

Marketsfield Stadium

Firday 31/08/2018 Kick Off: 19:45

Entry: T3

North Stand - Adult

marketsfield

Sporting Limerick

641241602362

Price: 15.00 euro

Gates Open 1hr before Kick Off

North Stand - Adult

15.00 euro

Order: 2211119052

Programme for the Celebration of the First Day of Riḍván

The Ḥaram-i-Aqdas, Bahjí
Sunday, 21 April 2019

CHAIRMAN: MR. PAUL LAMPLE

Excerpt from a Tablet of Bahá'u'lláh Revealed for the Occasion — ARABIC
Ayyám-i-Tis'ih, pp. 248–250

Excerpt from a Tablet of Bahá'u'lláh Revealed for the Occasion — ENGLISH
Days of Remembrance, no. 6, pars. 17–20

Excerpt from a Tablet of the Báb Addressed to "Him Who will be made manifest" — ENGLISH
Selections from the Writings of the Báb, no. 1:1, pars. 5–9

Poem of Mírzá 'Alí-Muḥammad Varqá, the Martyr — PERSIAN
Naghmiháy-i-Varqá, p. 309

Concerning the Declaration of Bahá'u'lláh's Mission — ENGLISH
God Passes By, pp. 237–240

Excerpt from a Tablet of 'Abdu'l-Bahá — ENGLISH
Selections from the Writings of 'Abdu'l-Bahá, no. 17, pars. 1–4

Tablet of 'Abdu'l-Bahá — PERSIAN
Payám-i-Bahá'í, no. 137

Excerpt from a Tablet of Bahá'u'lláh Revealed for the Occasion — ENGLISH
Days of Remembrance, no. 9

Prayer of Bahá'u'lláh — ENGLISH
Prayers and Meditations, no. 43

The Tablet of Visitation will be recited in the Ḥaram-i-Aqdas followed by circumambulation of the Shrine of Bahá'u'lláh

Tablet of Visitation — ARABIC

Children aged 3 to 10 may be excused after the fourth selection to participate in their own programme

3

VAḤÍD

In his magnificent palace, the King of Persia, Muḥammad Sháh, wondered about the conflicting reports concerning the young man who claimed to receive Divine Revelation. Who was this young man and what, exactly, were His claims? Was He insane? If so, why were the king's subjects flocking to Him—including more and more from the royal court? The king practiced Sufism, a mystical form of Islam, and was very attracted to spiritual questions and possibilities, including this one.[1] The most important question to him was, "Were these claims true?"

The king's spiritual teacher was Ḥájí Mírzá Áqásí, his prime minister—they belonged to the same mystical order. Both had read the reports from the governor of the province of Fárs complaining of the increasing disruptions caused by the spiritual teachings of this young siyyid. There was great excitement, and acceptance of the teachings was spreading quickly. The king was eager to know more. The prime minister, fearing for his own position, wanted to limit the king's access to the young siyyid, knowing He might influence the king as He had so many others.[2]

But the king wanted someone to go to Shíráz, question the young siyyid, and then report the findings back to him directly. Such a person would have to be very learned, highly respected by others so that his findings would be believed, unquestionably loyal, and trustworthy enough to tell him the truth, whatever the truth turned out to be. One man fit this description perfectly: Siyyid Yaḥyáy-i-Dárábí.

Siyyid Yaḥyáy-i-Dárábí was descended from the Prophet Muḥammad through the Seventh Ímám. His family included prominent theologians and scholars. Foremost among them was his father, Siyyid Ja'far-i-Kashfí Dárábí, who had mastered areas of Islamic law, theology, and the interpretation of scripture. His father had been on pilgrimage in Mecca at the same time as the Báb. His father was also known to pray and meditate for long hours and, as he grew older, became more attracted to mystical teachings. Most importantly for the king, Siyyid Yaḥyáy-i-Dárábí's father had written books on political theory to support the rule of the Qájárs. This helped make the dynasty more legitimate because the Qájárs were originally Turkish, not Persian. So the king knew this family to be completely loyal. Siyyid Yaḥyáy-i-Dárábí, had, in his own right, become a well-known scholar and a religious figure with a reputation for fairness and honesty, something increasingly rare in Persia. He was now among the most highly respected clerics in the kingdom.[3]

The king sent a message to Siyyid Yaḥyáy, asking him to go on a mission to investigate these claims. The king provided a special horse for the journey and a sword with which Siyyid Yaḥyáy could kill the impostor if he found the claims to be false.[4] Siyyid Yaḥyáy left in the spring of 1846.

Along the way, Siyyid Yaḥyáy stopped in the city of Yazd to see his first wife and their children.* Once in Shíráz, Siyyid Yaḥyáy went to the home of his host, the governor of Fárs, who opposed the Báb. Siyyid Yaḥyáy learned that the mullás of the city had become very hostile to the Báb and His teachings, so much so that the Bábís had to be very discreet.

Siyyid Yaḥyáy found an old friend of his who had interviewed the Báb already, and asked him for his opinion. The friend warned Siyyid Yaḥyáy not to say anything to the Báb that he might later regret as discourteous.**

The interview took place in the home of the Báb's maternal uncle. Due to the hostility toward the Báb, people who wanted to meet with Him had to come to the uncle's house. The Báb would arrive through a door connected to the neighboring house, which was owned by the Báb's family.[5]

Siyyid Yaḥyáy came to the first interview as one of the most learned clerics in Persia with a deep understanding of the interpretation of the holy scriptures, thousands of oral traditions memorized, a vast knowledge of Islamic theology and law, of language, and astrology. He was face-to-face with a pious young man who seemed to have no scholarship whatsoever. For two hours, Siyyid Yaḥyáy proceeded to ask questions on obscure aspects of a variety subjects. The Báb listened,

---

* According to Nabíl-i-A'ẓam, *The Dawn-Breakers* (350), Vaḥíd had a wife and four sons in Yazd. Rabbani (*The Bábís of Nayríz*, "The family of Siyyid Dárábí," 17) states that "it is known that the first marriage took place in Yazd, which resulted in a daughter and three sons and the second marriage was in Nayríz and brought forth a son."

** The friend's name was Mullá Shaykh 'Alí, surnamed 'Azím (Nabíl-i-A'ẓam, *The Dawn-Breakers*, 123).

wrote the questions down, and gave brief, convincing answers to each. The originality of these answers startled the great cleric. He felt a ripple of shame move through him, and he stood up to leave and told the Báb he would come back to ask the rest of his questions. Later, Siyyid Yaḥyáy's old friend reminded him of the warning not to act towards the Báb in any way he could later regret.[6]

Siyyid Yaḥyáy arrived for the second interview. He sat down with the Báb, drank tea, and ate some grapes. But when he looked at this young man, he completely forgot all of his questions. So he fumbled around and asked some irrelevant ones. The Báb answered these and then—to his guest's amazement—gave answers to the questions Siyyid Yaḥyáy had forgotten. In a confused and agitated state, Siyyid Yaḥyáy left the interview. He later met his old friend again, who reprimanded him and bemoaned the fact that they had ever set foot in the prestigious religious schools which had made them so prideful and so spiritually blind.[7]

For the third interview, Siyyid Yaḥyáy had planned a test. He would expect the Báb to write an original commentary on the Súrih of Abundance from the Holy Qur'án without telling the Báb to do so. Only then would Siyyid Yaḥyáy be convinced. As he entered the room and saw the Báb, his limbs began to quiver. Siyyid Yaḥyáy had met often with the king of Persia—the king of kings—but he had never felt this strange and powerful fear. He had to sit down. The Báb came over to him, gently took his hands and invited him to ask anything he wished. Siyyid Yaḥyáy, with his vast encyclopedic learning obtained over many years of study, had become like a child and could not form any thoughts or words. The Báb asked him if he would like a commentary on the Súrih of Abundance and if he would then accept Him as the Manifestation of God. Siyyid Yaḥyáy answered in tears with the Qur'ánic verse: "O our Lord, with ourselves have we dealt unjustly: if Thou forgive us not and have not pity on us, we shall surely be of those who perish."[8]

The Báb's uncle brought His pen case and paper. The Báb poured out verses on the Súrih without hesitating or pausing, chanting as he did so. When He finished, they drank tea as He read the commentary aloud. To Siyyid Yaḥyáy's astonishment, he heard in the commentary some of the very explanations which had come to him during his private meditations. The Báb then anointed His overwhelmed guest with rose water.[9]

He further explained to Siyyid Yaḥyáy that He was preparing the way for a divine Messenger Who would fulfill all prophecies of the past and begin a new cycle of Divine Revelation: "By the righteousness of Him Whose power causeth the seed to germinate and Who breatheth the spirit of life into all things, were I to be assured that in the day of His manifestation thou wilt deny Him, I would unhesitatingly disown thee and repudiate thy faith . . . If, on the other hand, I be told that a Christian, who beareth no allegiance to My Faith, will believe in Him, the same will I regard as the apple of Mine Eye."[10]

At the Báb's instructions, Siyyid Yaḥyáy stayed for several days and worked with His scribe to copy the commentary and verify every reference in it. Everything was completely accurate. Siyyid Yaḥyáy became certain of the divine nature of the Báb. He was now changed forever, and the Báb gave this great scholar of Islam and witness to the new day a new name—Vaḥíd, the "peerless one.'"

4

SEPARATE WAYS

The King of Persia put the letter from the governor of Fárs back on the table. This was amazing, he thought. In his letter, the governor complained that Siyyid Yaḥyáy had spent all his time with the Báb, largely ignoring him and the leading mullás of S͟híráz. There was no doubt in his mind that the siyyid had come under the spell of the Báb. The king thought to himself that if so great a scholar as Siyyid Yaḥyáy had become a believer, maybe there was something true in all of this. He sent a message to the governor that Siyyid Yaḥyáy must not be harmed in any way.

In S͟híráz, Vaḥíd wrote a letter about his belief in the Báb and sent it to a friend who would then deliver it to the king.* Ḥájí Mírzá Áqásí, the prime minister, found out about this and prevented any such direct communication between Vaḥíd and the king, fearing that the imperial

* The friend was Mírzá Luṭf-'Alí ('Abdu'l-Bahá, *A Traveller's Narrative,* 8).

court would turn towards the Báb. The prime minister communicated privately to the governor of Fárs that he wanted the young siyyid to be eliminated, but in secret.[1]

Vaḥíd had family in Nayríz and the surrounding region, so he wrote to the clergy there explaining the Báb's claim and included some of His writings. Given Vaḥíd's stature, this message alone caused many in Nayríz to become followers.[2]*

In July, the Báb sent Vaḥíd forth from Shíráz to proclaim His Message. He asked him to return first to his hometown of Burújird to see his father who was one of the most distinguished Islamic scholars in the Kingdom and about whom the Báb had written in His first book, exhorting Vaḥíd's father to embrace the new Revelation. Vaḥíd's father had heard of the extraordinary claims of the Báb as far back as 1844 and happened to be on pilgrimage in Mecca at the same time as the Báb. Though he knew of all the references to the coming of the Qá'im in the religious books, he did not become a believer. In Burújird, Vaḥíd gave his father a complete explanation of the Báb's fulfillment of the prophecies and signs in the Shí'ah tradition. Again, though the father did not reject these claims, he decided to continue on his own way. Later, a cleric—after hearing that Vaḥíd had become a follower of the Báb—asked Vaḥíd's father if his son had lost his mind. His father replied that his son had not in the sense of becoming crazy but rather in the same way that the Prophet Muḥammad had become intoxicated with the love of God.[3]

Back in Shíráz, the Báb sent other followers to Iṣfáhán. He would meet them there. He wrote a will in which all His property—His house,

* Vaḥíd's second wife, Ṣughrá, and their son, Ismá'íl, lived in Nayríz, according to Rabbani (*The Bábís of Nayríz: History and Documents*, appendix 2, 22).

furniture, and anything else in His estate—would go exclusively to His mother and wife. Upon the death of His mother, everything would belong to His wife, Khadíjih, who had been the first to recognize His station, and whom He knew would always be faithful.

As her husband's influence on the people of Shíráz grew, Khadíjih knew that He and their family were in greater danger. The local clergy and the governor were attacking the Bábís more frequently. One summer night, as Khadíjih and her mother-in-law slept on the roof, heavy footsteps coming across the neighbor's roof woke them.* The Báb appeared on the roof and told the women to go downstairs. From there, Khadíjih heard the soldiers go into the upper room, take the Báb's papers with His writings, and demand money. Then, they took the Báb, His maternal uncle Ḥájí Mírzá Siyyid 'Alí, and a visiting friend away, and Khadíjih spent the rest of the night worrying, powerless to do anything.

Later, she found that He had been taken to the police chief's house. She feared that He would be harmed there. In fact, the governor was planning to have Him killed when an epidemic of cholera broke out. When the police chief's son was discovered on the verge of death, the chief begged the Báb for help. The Báb gave him some of the water

* In Khadíjih Bagum's memoirs (16), she states that she and her mother-in-law were asleep on the roof of "our house"—it is unclear whether this means their marriage house or that of her father, the Báb's uncle, Ḥájí Mírzá Siyyid 'Alí. Shoghi Effendi, *God Passes By* (13) and 'Abdu'l-Bahá, *A Traveller's Narrative* (10–11) place this arrest in the home of Ḥájí Mírzá Siyyid 'Alí, and Nabíl-i-A'ẓam, *The Dawn-Breakers* (141) states, "'Abdu'l-Hamid Khán retired to execute his task. He, together with his assistants, broke into the house of Ḥájí Mírzá Siyyid 'Alí and found the Báb in the company of His maternal uncle and a certain Siyyid Káẓim-i-Zanjání. . . ." Afnán ("The Bab in Shiraz," 56) has this arrest occurring in the Báb's marriage house.

from His ablutions and told him to give it to his son to drink. The police chief brought the water to his son, who drank it and was cured. He reported this to the governor, begging him to let such a holy person go. The governor freed the Báb on the condition that He leave Shíráz.[4]*

Khadíjih had received no news of her husband, and none of the men in the extended family would visit her out of fear of the authorities. Instead, her sister would go to a nearby mosque, change into rags, and visit her in the guise of a beggar so she could give her any new information.[5]

The Báb was now going to leave for Iṣfáhán.** Khadíjih felt content knowing He would be safer there. She held on to the prayer He had revealed for her to ease her suffering: "Is there any Remover of

* In Nabíl-i-A'ẓam, *The Dawn-Breakers* (143), the governor, Ḥusayn Khán, set the Báb free to go where He pleased. According to Khadíjih Bagum's memories, the Báb told her it was "no longer advisable" that He stay in Shíráz and that He had been freed by the police chief without the governor's knowledge.

** According to Nabíl-i-A'ẓam, *The Dawn-Breakers* (143), the Báb sent for His uncle, Ḥájí Siyyid Mírzá 'Alí, before leaving for Iṣfáhán to give him last instructions. The Báb then left for Iṣfáhán from the home of 'Abdu'l-Hamíd Khán, the chief constable of Shíráz. 'Abdu'l-Bahá, *A Traveller's Narrative* (10–11) and Shoghi Effendi, *God Passes By* (12) do not specify whether the Báb left for Iṣfáhán from His house or that of 'Abdu'l-Hamíd Khán. Afnán (*The Báb in Shíráz*, 91) and the memoirs of Khadíjih Bagum in Balyuzi (*Khadíjih Bagum*, 20), state that He came home, went to visit Ḥájí Mírzá Siyyid 'Alí and Siyyid Káẓim, returned home and left alone, two hours after sunset, from His house to Iṣfáhán. In the first two sources and *God Passes By*, the Báb leaves for Iṣfáhán with Siyyid Káẓim-i-Zanjání; in the Afnán source, He leaves with Áqá Muḥammad-Ḥusayn Ardistání.

difficulties save God? Say: Praised be God! He is God! All are His servants, and all abide by His bidding!"[6]

Khadíjih would never see Him again in this life.[7]

❋ ❋ ❋

The Báb was in Iṣfáhán from September, 1846 CE, until March, 1847 CE. The people there considered Him so holy that when He had finished His visit to the public bath, they rushed to get the drops of water which had touched His body.[8]

Many of the clergy became jealous and plotted to stop the genuine love and respect for the Báb spreading among the people. The governor, Manúchihr Khán, who opposed the prime minister, secretly took the Báb into his custody to protect Him. The Báb would spend the next four months there without disturbance. The governor, in private, confessed his belief in the Báb, and expressed his desire to give the Báb all of his earthly possessions and properties and to go to Ṭihrán to tell the king the truth about this Revelation. The Báb accepted his declaration but declined the offer, telling him that the Cause of God would not triumph in that way but rather through the poor and lowly and through persecution. He added that the governor would not live much longer and would be joyously received in the hereafter.[9]

After Manúchihr Khán's death, the king realized that the governor's intention had been to bring the Báb and His Message to him. So the king sent soldiers to get the Báb in March, 1847, and bring Him to Ṭihrán.[10]

Ḥájí Mírzá Áqásí, the prime minister, feared that if the king met the Báb, he would be won over, and Ḥájí Mírzá Áqásí would lose influence at court. He persuaded the king to delay meeting the Báb and even to leave Ṭihrán by convincing him that there were other, more important state matters outside the capital that needed the monarch's attention. The king ordered the Báb confined to the castle of Máh-kú in the northern province of Á<u>dh</u>arbáyján to await the king's return to Ṭihrán.[11]

Máh-kú was on the border with Russia, in the most northern part of the kingdom. The Báb arrived there around July 10th, 1847.[12] His spirit touched the local people, who led rough and hard lives in the countryside of this remote region. They began to revere Him. On their way to work in the fields, they would look up in the direction of the castle and ask for His blessing.

One day, there was a banging on the gate of the castle. It was the warden in charge of the castle, who had been out riding when he saw the Báb praying near the river. He had been seized with a great fear and rode back to the castle, only to find it locked. He was now trying to get in, and he ran to the Báb's chamber and found Him there. He did not understand how this could be, after what he had just experienced. The Báb assured him that everything he had seen was real.* The warden fell

---

* 'Abdu'l-Bahá explained that seekers must investigate "reality" and not use stories of miracles as a basis for their faith because such stories can be denied and rejected by those who hear them. The deeper miracles are those that show the depth of the sacrifice of the Manifestation of God. These accounts serve as an example to transform the lives of human beings. The words and deeds of the Manifestation of God also have a profound effect on the hearts of the seekers. With the above thoughts in mind, we have included only a few of the miracles recorded from the Báb's life, remembering that the most astonishing miracles were His transcendent holiness and the irresistible power of His message and presence. We have included a few of the miracles from Nabíl-i-A'ẓam, *The Dawn-Breakers*, due to the high regard in which this history book is held. For many people still today, especially in the Judeo-Christian world, stories of miracles are a sign of the presence of God. We hope to convey some of the miraculous nature of the Báb to a broad audience for whom such stories resonate initially.

at His feet. After this incident, the warden gave permission for pilgrims and local villagers to now come freely to meet the Báb.

As temperatures plummeted and snow fell that winter, one lone believer was making his way on foot hundreds of kilometers from Qazvín to Máh-kú: Vaḥíd. After having tried to convince his father of the Báb's station, he had gone out to proclaim the Báb's Message in other cities of Luristán and from there to numerous other cities in Iṣfáhán, Ardistán, Yazd, Ká<u>sh</u>án, Ardakán, and, finally, Ṭihrán, on January 19th, 1847. In all places and to all people he met, he spoke of the Báb, including his own sister and brothers.

In early 1847, the Báb called on many of His followers to go teach His Faith in the province of <u>Kh</u>urásán, so Vaḥíd went throughout the western part of that province as well as Luristán. When he heard that the Báb was incarcerated in the mountain fortress of Máh-kú, he longed to go there. He went to the city of Qazvín and, from there, began his pilgrimage on foot to the Báb. It was winter in the mountains of Á<u>dh</u>arbáyján: the wind swirled, snow and sleet fell, and the sun came in and out of view. With the heart of a true lover, Vaḥíd trudged through the winter landscape—through dark valleys and under craggy peaks covered by snow and ice. His days with the Báb in the stone fortress helped fill his soul with strength.[13]*

❋ ❋ ❋

The prime minister heard of the conversion of Máh-kú's warden and of the many visitors streaming there to meet the Báb. Again the

* There are no sources for what took place between the Báb and Vaḥíd during this visit.

young siyyid had worked some kind of magic over the people who encountered Him. To put a stop to this situation, Ḥájí Mírzá Áqásí had the Báb moved on April 10th, 1848, from Máh-kú to Chihríq, an even more remote fortress a few days south of Máh-kú, near the border with the Turkish Empire.[14]

At the beginning of summer, the leading followers of the Báb were brought together in the town of Badasht by Mírzá Ḥusayn-'Alí, the most prominent Bábí Who had left a life of privilege to follow the new Revelation. Mírzá Ḥusayn-'Alí conferred a new name on each Bábí—*Bahá* for Himself; *Ṭáhirih*, meaning *the pure one*, for Fáṭimih Baraghání; *Quddús*, meaning *most holy*, for Mullá Muḥammad 'Alí-i-Bárfurúshi—as well as other names for the other Bábís. Later, the Báb would address them with these new names. In Badasht, over the course of a few days, many of the laws and customs of the Islamic tradition in which the Bábís had been raised were repealed, and the Báb's new laws were rolled out. Some Bábís were upset at losing the customs that had guided their lives. The break with tradition was symbolized most powerfully by the shocking act of Ṭáhirih appearing in front of the male Bábís without a veil, as a way of showing that they were all living in a new day. The old ways were being torn off and discarded so that a new vision could be beheld; the old traditions and the new faith separated. Not all Bábís would be able to behold the coming glory, however, and some immediately left the new Faith of the Báb.

* * *

Far from Badasht, the Báb's presence began to affect those in the area of the castle of Chihríq. Several prominent clerics from a nearby town, as well as many ordinary people, became Bábís. The authorities also heard that a holy man had come all the way from India to be in the Báb's presence after having seen Him in a vision.*

As a result of the growing devotion being shown toward the Báb, Ḥájí Mírzá Áqásí decided it was time to bring the Báb to trial. The trial was to take place in the presence of the Crown Prince, Nasiri'd-Dín Mírzá, and the leading clerics of Tabríz, the capital of Á<u>dh</u>arbáyján, the province in which the Báb was being held captive.[15]

In one of the towns along the way to Tabríz, the local governor decided to put the Báb to a test and offered Him one of his horses to ride to the local bathhouse. The horse was the wildest the governor owned, and the people of the town knew it. They gathered in the local square to see what would happen. The Báb approached, took hold of the bridle and gently caressed the wild animal. It calmed down and barely moved when the Báb put His foot in the stirrup. All the people in the square saw this. They followed the Báb to the bathhouse and, when He was through bathing, they hurried in to get some of the water He had used.

As the Báb approached His destination, the clerics of Tabríz whipped the people into a frenzy of emotion against Him. The trial was held in the governor's mansion. The crown prince, the leading clerics, and judges of Tabríz—the largest city in the kingdom—were gathered inside to hear this young man. Crowds pushed into the entryway and listened from over the wall surrounding the mansion. The Báb was brought in through the crush of the people crowding the gate. His

---

* The Báb named this darvish *Qahru'lláh* (Nabíl-i-A'ẓam, *The Dawn-Breakers*, 221).

personal majesty and spiritual power caused a hush to come over the distinguished audience.

The chief cleric began by asking the Báb to state His claim. The Báb answered, "'I am, I am, I am the promised One! I am the One whose name you have for a thousand years invoked, at whose mention you have risen, whose advent you have longed to witness, and the hour of whose Revelation you have prayed God to hasten. Verily I say, it is incumbent upon the peoples of both the East and the West to obey My word and to pledge allegiance to My person.'"[16]

Silence followed this declaration as those present tried to comprehend the immensity of the claim. A leading Shaykhí, the sect whose very purpose had been to find the Promised One of Islam, scolded the Báb, telling Him that such a claim had to be proved. The Báb answered that His revealed word was His proof. The Shaykhí then told the Báb, to describe the proceedings in Qur'ánic language to show them His power of Revelation. The Báb began speaking and was immediately interrupted by the Shaykhí, who wanted to correct His use of grammar. The trial descended into a series of obscure questions on Arabic grammar and anatomical science. With the proceedings degenerating completely, the Báb got up and spoke this verse from the Qur'án, "Far be the glory of thy Lord, the Lord of all greatness, from what they impune to Him . . ." and walked out. The gathering collapsed into chaos as the clerics, and judges argued about what to do. It was decided that the Báb should be given corporal punishment. He was brought to the home of the chief judge of Tabríz. The judge beat Him with rods on the soles of His feet.[17]

With this trial, the Báb's declaration reached its fullness—He was not merely the Gate to the Hidden Ímám, nor was He simply the Hidden Ímám—the Qá'im, the one who would arise to guide the people of Islam. He was the Manifestation of God Himself, the lawgiver who could change the laws of the past. Now, in this day of judgement, the high clerics had rejected Him and proven themselves, as a result, unfaithful to God.

The Báb was taken back to the prison fortress of Chihríq in early August, 1848.[18] In Tabríz, at the request of the authorities who wanted to determine if the Báb were sane and if He could be executed, He was examined by an English doctor, Dr. Cormick, the only European ever to meet Him:

> "To all enquiries he merely regarded us with a mild look, chanting in a low voice some hymns, I suppose . . . He only once deigned to answer me, on my saying that I was not a Musulman and was willing to know something about his religion, as I might perhaps be inclined to adopt it. He regarded me very intently on my saying this, and replied that he had no doubt of all Europeans coming over to his religion . . . He was a very mild and delicate-looking man, rather small in stature and very fair for a Persian, with a melodious soft voice, which struck me much . . . In fact his whole look and deportment went far to dispose one in his favour . . ."[19]

The Báb wrote a letter of condemnation to the prime minister, Ḥájí Mírzá Áqásí. A few weeks later, the king, his protector, became fatally ill. Ḥájí Mírzá Áqásí began to lose power, and the minister's enemies at court closed in. He looked for a friendly or helping hand and found none. The King of Persia, Muḥammad Sháh, died on September 4th, 1848. Ḥájí Mírzá Áqásí had fled the capital, and when he tried to return, was turned away by soldiers. He took the road to Ádharbáyján, his home province, but he was blocked from going there as well. He fled to a shrine for refuge and then was exiled from the kingdom forever. Later that year, the chief judge of Tabríz who had raised his hand to beat the Manifestation of God was stricken with paralysis, and he died slowly and painfully.[20]

That fall, Vaḥíd, back in Ṭihrán, heard that many of the leading Bábís, Mullá Ḥusayn, Quddús, and six other of the Letters of the Living, were engaged in a violent conflict with government troops in the northern province of Mázindarán, as a result of having been attacked by the troops. The Báb summoned all Bábís to help them. Vaḥíd immediately prepared to go to the fort at the shrine of Shaykh Tabarsí, but he was told all roads there were blocked because of the siege.

The battle escalated. For months, the government troops tried to overcome the vastly outnumbered Bábís. Mullá Ḥusayn was shot and killed, dying at Quddús's feet. Quddús wrapped Mullá Ḥusayn's body in his own shirt and placed him in the ground with his own hands. Still the Bábís held on. Only through deception were they finally defeated, and all the Bábís were massacred. Quddús suffered appalling torture before his death.[21]

In the darkness of His stone cell in the remote fortress prison, the Báb wept for all those who had believed in Him, who had not let public humiliation and loss of their worldly positions stop them, and who had loved Him so much that they had submitted themselves to painful deaths in His name. In the valley below, the villagers lit their home fires.

Night and day Vaḥíd, formerly the most prestigious cleric in Persia whom the Báb had called one of the "'two witnesses'" of His Cause, rode on the horse the King of Persia had given him and taught from Khurásán to Luristán, from Iṣfáhán to Ardistán, from Ardakán to Yazd, about the appearance of the Promised One. He finally traveled to Nayríz, where he would offer a last sacrifice to the Báb—his life.[22]

5

VAḤÍD NEARS NAYRÍZ

Violence erupted in Yazd after Vaḥíd's proclamation of the new Revelation. He greatly disapproved of this violence and had tried to stop it; according to the Báb's teachings, any form of violence other than self-defense was forbidden. Now, Vaḥíd removed himself, hoping to end the violence that way. He rode away from Yazd in late 1849 with two of his sons, leaving his other children in the care of his wife, and two local Bábís, one of whom was Ghulám-Riḍá-i-Yazdi.[1]

His house and property were immediately ransacked, and soldiers rode off to capture him. He made it to the mountains on foot and was taken in by his brother. His pursuers gave up and turned around.* Vaḥíd came to the district of Bávanát, where he was well-known and

* Nicolas states that the authorities in Yazd decided it would be more profitable to torture the wealthy local Bábís and appropriate their belongings, as this would fill their coffers and not be as dangerous as giving chase to Vaḥíd (Nicolas, *Seyyed Ali Mohammed dit le Bab*, 391).

admired.* From the Great Mosque, he proclaimed the appearance of the Qá'im, and many accepted his message, including the chief judge of Bávanát. Inspired by his presence, a large group of people accompanied Vaḥíd to his next stop, the town of Fasá.[2]

The governor of Fasá greeted him warmly. Once Vaḥíd began teaching about the Báb, though, the governor warned him that the people of his town were very conservative Muslims and that when they understood the nature of Vaḥíd's teaching on the appearance of the Qá'im, they would try to kill him. Sure enough, the local clergy appealed to the authorities in S͟hiráz, who wrote Vaḥíd, complaining of the disruption caused by his teaching. Vaḥíd's teaching fell on deaf ears in Fasá, so he continued on his way: "Through whichever village I pass," he remarked, "and fail to inhale from its inhabitants the fragrance of belief, its food and its drink are both distasteful to me."[3]

In the village of Runíz, his next stop, he found many people attracted to the new message. When his father-in-law, Ḥájí S͟hayk͟h 'Abdu'l-'Alí, a distinguished judge known throughout the district, received a letter from Vaḥíd that he was in Runíz, the judge came out with more than one hundred students to welcome him.

Other prominent Nayrízís walked there as well, such as Mullá 'Abdu'l-Ḥusayn, an eighty-year old scholar and religious judge in Nayríz known all over the province. After hearing that Vaḥíd had seen the Qá'im, he made his way out to meet Vaḥíd with his son Mullá 'Alí-Naqí and his grandson, Mullá Muḥammad Shafí'.[4] He became a believer right then and there.**

---

* Some sources (Afnán, *The genesis of the Bábí and Bahá'í Faiths in S͟hiráz and Fárs,* 49; Siyyid Ḥusayn Hamadámí, quoted in Rabbani, *The Bábís of Nayríz: History and Documents,* c. 6, 6) state that Vaḥíd went first to S͟hiráz.

** He is the great-great-great grandfather of Dr. Hussein Ahdieh.

Mírzá Ḥusayn Quṭbá,* and Ḥájí Muḥammad Taqí, a wealthy merchant of the bazaar, journeyed out to greet Vaḥíd as well.**

Mullá Ḥasan Lab-Shikarí, wearing a ring he had received from the Báb, brought his family out with him. He managed lands around the city of Bávanát for the great uncle of the Báb, as well as those of his own family around Shíráz. Once, when he was in Shíráz inspecting them, he saw a young siyyid with a radiant expression walking in the beautiful area known as the "Haftan," located near the gardens and tombs of the poets Háfez and Sa'dí and the city gate where Mullá Ḥusayn had met the Báb. Mullá Ḥasan had no idea of the true station of the Báb, as their chance meeting was prior to 1844. He offered the Báb, Who was journeying to Búshihr, a ride on his horse. They rode as far as the town of Marvdasht.[5] The Báb asked him if he needed anything, and he replied that he did not. Still, the Báb gave him a valuable ring. Though he had not been aware of the Báb's station, Mullá Ḥasan remembered feeling overwhelmed by the Báb's spiritual

---

* In Nabíl-i-A'ẓam, *The Dawn-Breakers*, 352, Quṭbá is described as the Kad-Khudá of the Bazar quarter, whereas 354 lists Siyyid Abú-Ṭalíb as the Kad-Khudá of the Bázár quarter. The authors believe that Siyyid Abú-Ṭalíb was most likely the Kad-Khudá of the Bázár quarter (from a private conversation with Prof. Nuṣratu'lláh Muḥammad Hosseini, December, 2010).

** Other prominent citizens listed in Nabíl-i-A'ẓam, *The Dawn-Breakers*, included Mírzá Abú'l-Qasím, a relative of the governor's from the bázár quarter, and Mírzá Nawrá and Mírzá 'Alí-Riḍá, both from the Sádát quarter (Nabíl-i-A'ẓam, *The Dawn-Breakers*, 352). Shafí' adds a few more names: Mullá 'Alí "the scribe," and another Mullá 'Alí and his four brothers. From the bázár quarter there was also Mírzá Abú'l-Qasím, a relative of the governor's, Taqí's son-in-law, Mírzá Ḥusayn. From the Sádát neighborhood near the bázár quarter came the son of Mírzá Nawrá, and Mírzá 'Alí Riḍá, a son of Mírzá Ḥusayn, and Áqá, a son of Ḥájí 'Alí (Shafí', *Narrative of Mullá Muḥammad Shafí' Nayrízí*, 3–4).

power. Now, he was coming to meet the Báb's representative with his brother, Mullá Báqir, who was head of the Great Mosque in Nayríz.*

Virtually all the residents of the Chinár-Súkhtih quarter walked from Nayríz to show their respect for Vaḥíd. Many common people followed the example of a venerable cleric such as Mullá 'Abdu'l-Ḥusayn because they looked to their clerics to tell them what to believe, and, as a result, Chinár-Súkhtih would become a mostly Bábí district. A number of individuals had accepted the Báb's claims when He had revealed a Tablet for them, but they were still unfamiliar with most of His teachings. Vaḥíd would educate them further.[6]

Once Zaynu'l-'Ábidín Khán, the governor of Nayríz, became aware of the many individuals going out to greet Vaḥíd, he issued a warning that anyone who did so would be in danger of losing his property, his wives and, possibly, his life.** This edict had no effect on those wishing to honor Vaḥíd. When Zaynu'l-'Ábidín Khán saw this, he became fearful that the population would turn against him, so he went to his home village of Qaṭrúyih, forty kilometers away, to raise troops. In that village, there were many skilled marksmen on whom he could call

* His father, Mullá 'Abdu'l Samí, had been the educator of the children of the Qájár rulers and had been driven out of Shíráz by the jealousy of the other clerics. Mullá Ḥasan's brother was Mullá Báqir (Rouhani, 138, and from a conversation with Mrs. Nura (Shahídpúr) Jamer March, 2010 CE/166 BE. The details of this story come from her grandmother, Párján, who was married to Mullá Ḥasan's grandson).

** Nicolas (*Seyyed Ali Mohammed dit le Bab*, 392) states that during this time, the authorities in Shíráz sent multiple letters to Vaḥíd listing grievances of people against him. Vaḥíd responded by asserting that these complaints were exaggerations meant to calumny him and that he would come to Shíráz at some point to clear this up. Nicolas writes that the authorities in Shíráz feared civil war as many people were gathering around Vaḥíd. These points are also found in the Qájár history Násikhu't-Taváríkh, 4–5, in the Rabbani translation. The Qájár histories portray Vaḥíd and his motives very unfavorably—as a man devoid of the talent and learning of his father, who sought rebellion and sedition.

to defend him, and there was a big fortress nearby where his men could take up position if necessary.[7]

Zaynu'l-'Ábidín Khán had good reason to fear the anger of the population: he had come to power by murdering his own brother, and many in Nayríz knew it.

After his wealthy father's death, Zaynu'l-'Ábidín Khán had plotted against his older brother who was next in line for the governorship. To gain and then secure that position, Zaynu'l-'Ábidín Khán had his brother assassinated. Then he turned on his brother's children to prevent them from laying claim to the governorship or organizing any opposition. Zaynu'l-'Ábidín Khán had them entombed in a sealed room of his residence. They could not escape. Eventually, they would starve. One of the gardeners, though, who was loyal to the brother's family, was encouraged to make a small hole in the wall and pass water and provisions to them. One of the organizers of this relief effort was Mírzá 'Alí Sardár, who later would be the leader of the Bábís in the second Nayríz conflict, along with Mullá Ḥasan Lab-Shikarí.[8]

When Zaynu'l-'Ábidín Khán was sure the children of his brother had died, he had the room unsealed but, to his amazement, found them alive! He interpreted this as a sign that they should live and released them on condition that they move to the Chinár-Súkhtih quarter.[9]

The people under Zaynu'l-'Ábidín Khán's rule had also experienced his humiliating and cruel demand that a new bride give him sexual favors, should he desire her.[10] As if this weren't enough, he had angered the local people by adding considerably to their taxation.

He feared the angry residents might rally around the illustrious religious figure, so he was not eager to have Vaḥíd come to Nayríz.*

---

* Nicolas (*Seyyed Ali Mohammed dit le Bab*, 393) implies that Vaḥíd came to Nayríz because of the popular discontent with the governor, which might create an

Two of the sons of the murdered brother did, in fact, proclaim themselves followers of Vaḥíd. Those who opposed Ẓaynu'l-'Ábidín Khán, though, had already been using the bereaved family of his brother as a rallying point against him.[11]

Before going into Nayríz, Vaḥíd visited the village of Iṣṭahbánát, his father's birthplace. He stayed in the guest rooms at the Shrine of Pír-Murád on the outskirts of the village. The clerics in Iṣṭahbánát warned villagers not to go out to meet him.* Ignoring the warning, at least twenty people came out to accompany him to Nayríz.[12]

These were all the ripples of a rising tide.

---

opening for him to be heard. The Qájár histories—Raudatu's-Safá Násírí, Táríkh Burújird, and Fársnámih Násírí—state that Vaḥíd came to take advantage of a rebellion against the governor that was already under way. We have no reason to believe that Vaḥíd, judging from his words and actions, had any interest in causing rebellion for its own sake or in overthrowing the governor. The obvious reasons to come to Nayríz of visiting his family—he had a wife, child, a home, and relatives there and in Iṣṭahbánát—and believing that he would find people receptive to the Message of the Báb seem to be reasons enough. He was on a mission to spread the Báb's teachings and had no interest in political affairs.

* Nicolas (*Seyyed Ali Mohammed dit le Bab*, 392) states that it was the villagers who opposed Vaḥíd's coming into the village.

NAYRÍZ,
1850

6

THE GREAT ANNOUNCEMENT AND THE HEROIC STAND AT FORT KHÁJIH

Vaḥíd climbed the steps to the pulpit of the Great Mosque of Nayríz, on May 27, 1850. He had lit a fire in cities and towns all across Persia by raising the call of the appearance of the Qá'im.

Now he was about to upset this ancient town's centuries-old equilibrium.

Zaynu'l-'Ábidín Khán sent Vaḥíd a message, warning him that his presence in the area was the cause of trouble and that he should leave. Zaynu'l-'Ábidín Khán had honored Vaḥíd on previous visits as a man of great learning, but not this time.

Vaḥíd reprimanded the governor for his lack of hospitality and wrote that his intention was to visit his family and friends; his wife, Ṣughra, and their son, Siyyid Ismá'íl, lived in his home in the Chinár-Súkhtih quarter.[1]*

* She was the daughter of the scholar Ḥájí Shaykh 'Abdu'l Nayrízí (Rabbani appendix 2, 22). In the coming conflict, they would accompany Vaḥíd into Fort

Arriving midmorning in Nayríz, Vaḥíd entered the Great Mosque still dressed in the dusty clothes of his journey. He ascended the pulpit, faced the large crowd, and proclaimed the appearance of a new Manifestation of God.[2]

He invoked his descent from Muḥammad, and the respect in which they had always held him as he exhorted them to accept the new message. The crowd in the mosque was amazed by the message he delivered. Many who heard believed in the Báb's teachings without hesitation.* Vaḥíd warned them that they might lose their lives, those of their family, and all their belongings for following this call. The audience, both men and women, surrounded him, shouting their willingness to lay down their lives. They triumphantly accompanied him through the streets to his house.[3]

Vaḥíd had let loose a powerful spiritual force in Nayríz. Each day the crowds at the mosque grew bigger and more enthusiastic.[4]

Seeing people fervently rallying around Vaḥíd, Zaynu'l-'Ábidín Khán feared he would lose his hold on power; other Nayrízís resented Vaḥíd as well. A strong force against him was developing.

Zaynu'l-'Ábidín Khán tried to inflame the feelings of the people in the bazaar quarter against Vaḥíd, and he mustered over a thousand

---

Khájih but survive. After the conflict, they relocated to Iṣṭahbánát, where Vaḥíd's sister, Jahán Bagum, cared for Ismá'íl as she did her own son. The two boys went to Yazd for higher education in the Islamic sciences. Siyyid Ismá'íl did not become a Bábí or a Bahá'í. He became a well-known authority on Islamic thought (Rabbani appendix 2, 16).

* Shafí', *Narrative of Mullá Muḥammad Shafí'* (2) states that one thousand people from Chinár-Súkhtih and "two-thirds" from other areas became Bábís. Mázandarání, *Zuhúr al-Haqq*, (v. 2, 409) states that four hundred people had become Bábís by the end of the first week.

well-armed soldiers from different tribes.[5]*

The Great Mosque of Nayríz

After hearing that Zaynu'l-'Ábidín Khán was bringing soldiers into the Chinár-Súkhtih quarter to attack the new Bábís, Vahíd told the twenty men who had accompanied him from Iṣṭahbánát to go and occupy Fort Khájih just outside of town.[6]**

This abandoned fort lay to the southeast outside the Chinár-Súkhtih quarter of the city. Its mud walls, mixed with straw and stone, covered several acres. Roughly in the shape of a square, the fort had towers at each of its four corners, which rose fifteen feet above the ground.[7] It had fallen into disuse, so the Bábís strengthened its walls, towers, and gate.

The nearby tower of the khobar mill, north of the fort, was used as a lookout. These mills were dotted around the outskirts of Nayríz. They each had a stone tower, twenty feet high, made of light brown bricks

* Nicolas, *Seyyed Ali Mohammed dit le Bab* (395), and Hamadání, quoted in Rabbani, *The Bábís of Nayríz: History and Documents*, c. 9, 5, state that there were two thousand soldiers.

** Afnán, *The genesis of the Babi and Baha'i Faiths in Shíráz and Fars,* 52, and Hamadání, quoted in Rabbani, *The Bábís of Nayríz: History and Documents*, c. 9, 13, have this number as "no more than seventeen."

that tapered off at the top. Here townspeople could grind their corn and wheat between two large circular stones and gather their water.

In the dead of night, Zaynu'l-'Ábidín K͟hán moved his troops to the high towers of his house in the bazaar from which the whole town could be surveyed.* He reinforced the towers and expropriated another large home nearby that was owned by the chief of the quarter who had recently become a Bábí.** On the roofs and towers of these houses, he stationed riflemen.

At dawn, the riflemen, on orders from Zaynu'l-'Ábidín K͟hán, shot at any Bábí within view. An elderly Bábí, Mullá 'Abdu'l-Ḥusayn, was hit in the right foot while offering prayers on the roof of his home.† He was able to make his way back inside his house. Later, he received a note from Vaḥíd, who offered sympathy for his injury and cheered him by telling him he was the first to have shed blood there for the Cause of the Báb.[8]

Zaynu'l-'Ábidín K͟hán ordered his men to continue firing on the homes of Bábís. He also circulated false news that many Bábís were being killed, warning any new converts that they and their families could be in mortal danger. This frightened some Bábís, who broke away from Vaḥíd and joined the governor. At sunrise, Vaḥíd went with a group of his companions to the fort for defense. That day, Zaynu'l-'Ábidín K͟hán sent a thousand men‡ under the leadership of

---

* Rouhani, *Lam'átul-Anvár* (v. 1 p. 60), places this event on May 30, 1850.

** Siyyid Abú Ṭalíb (Nabíl-i-A'ẓam, *The Dawn-Breakers*, 354).

† Nicolas, *Seyyed Ali Mohammed dit le Bab* (396), and Faizi, *Nayríz Mus͟hkbiz* (57), place Mullá 'Abdu'l-Ḥusayn on the roof of Fort K͟hájih. We have chosen the version of the story in which he is on the roof of his home because Fort K͟hájih is a little bit outside of town and the action was taking place in town.

‡ Faizi, *Nayríz Mus͟hkbiz* (58), gives the number of troops as one thousand.

Ruins of Fort Khájih

his brother, to surround the fort and cut off the supply of water. By the end of the day, there were seventy-two Bábís in the fort.[9]*

As first light appeared over the mountain, the fort's gates swung open on Vaḥíd's orders, and several Bábís came charging out, swinging their swords at the groggy soldiers.** Terrified, many of the soldiers ran.† Only three Bábís lost their lives in this battle.‡

---

* Shafí', *Narrative of Mullá Muḥammad Shafí'* (3) has this number as seventy. Seventy-two is an important number in Shí'ite history, as it is the number of companions who perished in the famous slaughter of the Third Imán, Imán Ḥusayn, at Karbilá, an event that is reenacted each year by devout Shi'ites. Siyyid Ibráhim, quoted in Rabbani, *The Bábís of Nayríz: History and Documents*, c. 7, 4, states that the number of Vaḥíd's companions going to the fort was from 180–200.

** Afnán, *The genesis of the Babi and Baha'i Faiths in Shíráz and Fars* (52), states that there were seven men.

† Nabíl-i-A'ẓam, *The Dawn-Breakers* (355); Nicolas, *Seyyed Ali Mohammed dit le Bab* (396); and Shafí' Nayrízí, *Narrative of Mullá Muḥammad Shafí'* (6) place this battle on the same day as the day the troops come up to the fort.

Prince Fírúz Mírzá, the governor of Fárs, had already counseled Zaynu'l-'Ábidín Khán to move wisely and calmly against the Bábís. Now Zaynu'l-'Ábidín Khán had suffered a complete and sudden rout at the hands of just a mere handful of these Bábís. He relayed a message from the prince to Vaḥíd that further bloodshed could be spared if Vaḥíd would just leave Nayríz. Vaḥíd replied that he was willing to leave if this would prevent more violence, but he also warned the governor to allow the Bábís access to water, or there would be another attack.* His demand was not met.[10]

As darkness fell, Vaḥíd organized two groups of seven men and boys—some not even fifteen years of age. They came up quietly on both sides of the soldiers' camp. The Bábís sprang out of the black night so ferociously that the much more experienced soldiers fled. The governor's brother and several others were killed, and his two sons

‡ Táju'd-Dín, Zayníl, the son of Iskandar, and Mírzá Abú'l-Qasím (Nabíl-i-A'ẓam, *The Dawn-Breakers*, 355). Afnán, Ḥájí Mírzá Jání and Hamadání each tell the story of a youth from Yazd who asks Vaḥíd for permission to go out on this attack and be the first to achieve martyrdom. Vaḥíd allows him and prays over him; he is subsequently martyred. According to Mázandarání (v. 2, 411) two of these three men were carrying a message from Vaḥíd to the governor conveying that the Bábís wished no overthrow of the government. According to Afnán (53), only one Bábí—the youth from Yazd—was killed.

* Shafí', *Narrative of Mullá Muḥammad Shafí' Nayrízí* (4), states that Zaynu'l-'Ábidín Khán replied by saying, "If you are the Prince of the Martyrs then I am not ashamed to call myself Shimr." Again, this is drawing a parallel between the events at Fort Khájih and the ones at Karbilá in the time of the Ímám Ḥusayn. Shimr was the one who opposed Ḥusayn and denied him water. Nicolas, *Seyyed Ali Mohammed dit le Bab* (397), states that Vaḥíd sent a trick answer back to the governor saying that he was being held by the Bábís and wanted to be rescued as a way of getting the soldiers to let down their guard. The Qájár historians give the same answer from Vaḥíd, though without adding that it was a trick (Faizi, *Nayríz Mushkbiz,* 60). The Khobar waterway ran near the fort and may have been the one that was blocked.

were taken prisoner.* Vaḥíd released the two sons with a Bábí carrying another message for Zaynu'l-'Ábidín Khán,** but when the gates of the fort were opened and the sons walked out, the soldiers mistook them for Bábís and fired, killing them.[11]

These victories increased the devotion of the Bábís to Vaḥíd and their willingness to lay down their lives for him.[12]

A stunned and frightened Zaynu'l-'Ábidín Khán fled with his remaining soldiers to Qaṭrúyih, his home village some thirty-two kilometers away. He was almost caught several times. From there, he sent a message to Prince Fírúz Mírzá, informing him of the Bábí attacks and pleading for infantry, cavalry, and heavy artillery.[13]

Now that the soldiers had retreated, the Bábís had some breathing space. Vaḥíd used this time to strengthen the fort's walls and turrets and had a water cistern built inside the fort. He organized the companions by assigning them specific roles. Áqá Ghulám-Riḍá Yazdí, who had accompanied Vaḥíd from Yazd, would command the fighting force, such as it was. Karbalá'í Mírzá Muḥammad kept watch at the gate, Shaykh Yúsuf managed the funds, Karbalá'í Muḥammad, son of Shamsu'ḍ-Dín, supervised the grounds near the fort where the Bábís grew fruits and vegetables. Mírzá Aḥmad, the uncle of 'Alí Sardár, took charge of the Chinár mill near the fort, and Shaykha would carry out executions, if necessary. Mírzá Muḥammad-Ja'far, cousin of the governor of Nayríz, chronicled the events at Fort Khájih by composing an epic poem. Mírzá Faḍlu'lláh, who kept the ongoing record of the

* The governor's brother was 'Alí Aṣghar Khán. Nicolas, *Seyyed Ali Mohammed dit le Bab* (397), states that there were three sons taken prisoner and that the Bábís pursued the soldiers all the way into town.

** Muḥammad-Ibráhím-i-Amír, the ancestor of 'Alí Nakhjavání, a member of the first elected body of the Universal House of Justice, was the Bábí.

conflict, also wrote an epic-style poem and read incoming letters. Mashhadí-Taqí guarded the jail.[14]

Ḥájí Muḥammad Taqí, a wealthy Bábí from the bazaar, helped finance the defense of Fort Khájih. He also registered each person wanting to join the Bábís in the fort. Each volunteer had to write a testimonial of his willingness to give up everything for this holy battle. Jináb-i-Bahá—the title by which Mírzá Ḥusayn-'Alí now went—praised Ḥájí Muḥammad Taqí's steadfastness in the Tablet of Job, which Jináb-i-Bahá revealed on April 9th, 1863.[15]

Another companion was Mullá Muḥammad, a talented calligrapher from a wealthy Nayríz family.* He became a passionate believer in the Báb and joined the struggle at Fort Khájih. When the conflict began, he was already the father of two very young boys. His wife walked out to the walls of the fort with their two little boys and pleaded with him to quit the struggle and come back to their home. He answered that he could not turn his back on his Beloved—meaning the Báb and His cause. Though his wife sobbed and pleaded, he was immovable in his desire to sacrifice his life. Heartbroken, the family returned to Nayríz, and Mullá Muḥammad fought on at Fort Khájih. One day, as he was patrolling outside of the walls of the fort, he was shot in the face. He survived, but the soldiers captured him. Fortunately, he was recognized by the governor's brother, who had been his childhood friend, and he was released. He went to Iṣṭahbánát with his two young sons and his father to receive medical treatment and stayed there for six months.[16]**

---

* He was the great-grandfather of Adib Taherzadeh because his son Ḥájí Mohammad Rahim was the father of Laqá Khánum, Adib Taherzadeh's mother.

** This governor's brother's name was 'Alí 'Askar. There is a complete biography of Mullá Muḥammad at http://www.Nayríz.org.

In the Chinár-Súkhtih quarter, the Bábí fervor had grown so intense that many wanted to join the fight in Fort Khájih.* The Bábís were living in a new day; they had been changed by the message Vaḥíd had brought to them. They could never go back. They would follow him into the future, even if that meant giving their lives, because this was the new life. Martyrdom was the most important way they could bear witness to the truth. It was not a death wish that motivated them but a life wish—that God was alive in the Báb, that they were now a part of Him, and that their physical lives were like death compared to this reality. Vaḥíd did not want volunteers whose belief and commitment wavered, so he was reluctant to allow them all in. Through the entreaties of his respected father-in-law, Shaykh Abd-'Alí, and the distinguished cleric Siyyid Ja'far, who had stayed in the city to educate the Bábís of Nayríz in the teachings of the Báb, the volunteers were admitted, adding greatly to the original number of defenders.

Vaḥíd sent some of these volunteers back into town to take up defensive positions. Several Bábís occupied the roof of the Great Mosque in the Chinár-Súkhtih quarter; this would give them a view of the whole area.[17]

The figure of Vaḥíd now commanded enormous respect among all the people of the district.

Bábís brought before him for judgment those men who had attacked them previously; as the de facto "chief" of the Bábís and a highly regarded cleric, Vaḥíd assumed the role of acting as a judge who

* Mázandarání, *Zuhúr al-Haqq* (v. 2, 414), notes that four hundred Bábís fought with Vaḥíd in the fort and the Chinár-Súkhtih quarter. Rouhani, *Lam'átul-Anvár* (v. 1, 63), puts that number at six hundred.

could pass sentence on individuals accused of committing crimes and transgressions.*

From his hiding place in his home village of Qaṭrúyih, Zaynu'l-'Ábidín Khán renewed his plea to the governor of Fárs, Prince Fírúz Mírzá, for reinforcements. This time he enclosed a gift of five-thousand tumans, a very substantial sum. He gave this message and gift along with his horse to his trusted associate with instructions to present this request personally to the Prince.**

After a day's ride, the messenger arrived at an old fort where nomadic tribes pitched their tents. Taking a break, he dismounted and was eating lunch in one of the tents when a Bábí, Ḥájí Siyyid Ismaí'íl, who led Friday prayers in Bávanát, arrived. He was on his way back to Nayríz from urgent business in his native village. Noticing the richly decorated horse, he asked about its owner. When told it belonged to a messenger going to Shíráz on behalf of the governor of Nayríz, he drew his sword, mounted the horse and opened the tent in which the messenger was sitting. He demanded that the messenger be tied up and given to him as he was fleeing the "face of the Lord of the Age." The owners of the tent were so terrified by his fervor that they immediately complied.

The messenger was brought back to Nayríz to stand before Vaḥíd, who asked him about his mission. The messenger explained it frankly and unapologetically. Vaḥíd let him go, but some of the other Bábís, angered by his mission and by his attitude in front of Vaḥíd, killed him.[18]

---

* Shafí', *Narrative of Mullá Muḥammad Shafí'* (5), states that some of these individuals were executed. The Laws of Bahá'u'lláh forbidding any form of violence in matters of religion had not yet been revealed.

** Mullá Báqir (Shafí', *Narrative of Mullá Muḥammad Shafí'*, 6; Nicolas, *Seyyed Ali Mohammed dit le Bab*, 400).

Zaynu'l-'Ábidín Khán sent another appeal to the governor, this time consisting of several men bearing substantial gifts. He also sent messages to the leading clerics of Shíráz in which he distorted the teachings and actions of Vaḥíd in an attempt to have them urge greater action against the Bábís in Nayríz. This clergy in Shíráz would become a driving force in the persecutions of the Bábís.[19]

Prince Fírúz Mírzá, upon hearing about the continuing conflict, ordered two regiments with cavalry and heavy artillery to go to Nayríz under the leadership of Mihr 'Alí Khán and Musṭafá-Qulí Khán.[20]* He also issued an order to his representatives in Nayríz that men from the villages in the area be gathered to fight the Bábís, as well as men from a local desert tribe.**

The British agent in Shíráz noted the beginning of these troop movements in his report covering the days between May 24th and June 5th, 1850:

> Syed Yahyáyh, a disciple of Báb, who was some time ago in Istahbánát, has it is said, assembled 1,500 men, and has proceeded to Nereez where Zeynol Abedeen Khán wishes to seize him. Outside the Town he has erected a Fort, and is engaged in

---

* Nabíl-i-A'ẓam, *The Dawn-Breakers,* states that it was 'Abdu'lláh Khán, the governor's second in command, who led the force to Nayríz, but all other sources indicate these two other commanders. It may be that 'Abdu'lláh Khán organized the forces but didn't actually go with them. A grandson of Mihr 'Alí Khán, Faraju'lláh Khán, later became a Bahá'í and told E. G. Browne about the acts committed by his ancestors in the Nayríz conflict. (Balyuzi, *Eminent Bahá'ís in the time of Bahá'u'lláh,* 28).

** Iṣṭahbánát, Íraj, Panj-Ma'ádin, Qaṭrúyih, Bashnih, Dih-Cháh, Mushkán, and Rastáq (Nabíl-i-A'ẓam, *The Dawn-Breakers*, 58).

> skirmishes. According to what is reported, the Khán has had 80 men killed. When this news reached Shíráz, the Nuseer-ool Mulk ordered a Regiment of Sirbaz (soldiers) with two guns to proceed to Nereez for the purpose of seizing Syed Yahyáy . . . On the 3rd June Mehr Ally Khán by order of the Nuseer-ool Mulk, with one Regiment and two Guns proceeded to Nereez to seize Syed Yahyáyh.[21]

Mihr 'Alí Khán arrived first with his army, followed by Musṭafá-Qulí Khán and then the army of local men.[22]

One day in the middle of June, 1850, the Bábís in Fort Khájih woke to the sight of thousands of soldiers, cavalry, villagers, tribesmen, and several cannons aiming at them.*

---

* Mázandaráni, *Zuhúr al-Haqq* (v. 2, 416), states that there were five thousand soldiers. Rouhani, *Lam'átul-Anvár* (v. 1, 72), states that there were one thousand men in the fort with Vaḥíd.

7

MASSACRE OF THE FAITHFUL

Thousands of soldiers and fighting men from the local villages surrounded Fort Kh͟ájih. Inside, the band of Bábís waited, transformed by Vaḥíd's spirit into a potent fighting force and into witnesses to the truth of the Báb's Message.

The soldiers were poorly paid conscripts without much motivation to make a direct assault on these Bábís. Instead, they built a camp with trenches on a wide open rise of red earth* just north of the fort.[1]

Once the camp was set up, soldiers fired on the fort. They hit the horse of one of Vaḥíd's attendants while he was out on his watch. Other bullets went through the turret above the gate. In response, a Bábí took aim at the officer in charge of a cannon and shot him. The guns went silent. That night, neither side left their respective camps.[2]

The next day passed without incident. When darkness fell, Vaḥíd sent the Bábís into action.** He told Gh͟ulám Riḍá-Yazdi, the commander

* The red dirt area was called *Kouhesorkheh.*

** Nicolas, *Seyyed Ali Mohammed dit le Bab,* 401, states that it was the sixth night.

who had been with him since Yazd, to lead fourteen men on a surprise attack.* This group included a ninety-year-old shoemaker filled with excitement and several very young men who had never fought. Though wholly unsuited to battle real soldiers, they followed Ghulám Riḍá-Yazdi out of the gate at midnight. They then divided into two groups and quietly approached the army camp on both sides. All of a sudden, they bolted forward crying out, "God is Great," and ran into the fray, swinging their unsheathed swords.[3]

From the Chinár-Súkhtih quarter, other Bábís could see from the flash of the guns that a battle was underway. Hundreds of them rushed out to aid their fellow Bábís. The Bábí women climbed onto the roofs of their houses—which were near the battlefield—and cheered loudly to encourage their men. The passionate cries blending with their men's calls of "God is Great" frightened the soldiers. The Bábís fought on through the night.[4]

The sun's first rays fell upon a desolate army camp and an exhausted but victorious band of Bábís trudging back to the fort, carrying their wounded and dead.[5] More than sixty Bábís and many more soldiers had perished in the nighttime battle. Some Bábís, frightened by the fierce fighting, left the fort. The army, though, had been dealt such a blow that its commanders now knew they faced a powerful opponent.**

* The Qájár official historian, Sipihr, quoted in Rabbani, *The Bábís of Nayríz: History and Documents*, c. 8, 7, asserts that Vaḥíd assured the Bábís that the cannons and bullets could not hurt them and that they would simply return to the shooters. Given what we know about Vaḥíd and his exhortations, the authors don't believe this story to be true.

** Nicolas, *Seyyed Ali Mohammed dit le Bab*, 403. Nicolas states that another attack took place the following night in which one hundred soldiers and fifty Bábís were killed. Siyyid Ibráhim, quoted in Rabbani, *The Bábís of Nayríz: History and Documents*, c. 7, 6, also notes a second outing the next day.

In the coming days, Vaḥíd thought of the future of his family, knowing that he would most likely not survive. He arranged a marriage for his daughter Ṭubá Kh͟ánum and wrote out a marriage certificate according to the laws of the Báb's holy book, the Bayán. This was the first time this had ever been done. The seals of Vaḥíd and the groom and the signatures of two witnesses appear on the certificate, with the following text written in Vaḥíd's own hand:

> "God has decreed marriage between Ṭubá, the daughter of his servant, Yahyáy, having dedicated herself to service of God, the Lord of the heavens and the earth, and the Lord of all the worlds, and His servant, Muhammad-Ja'far, the son of the late, wrongly-murdered Muhammad-Báqir, who hath consecrated himself to the service of God, the Lord of the heavens and the earth, and the Lord of all the worlds.
>
> He [i.e. the groom] consented to this marriage for the sake of God, Who is the Lord, of the heavens and the earth and the Lord of all the worlds.
>
> God hath decreed for her dowry to be nineteen mithqals of pure gold and it is incumbent upon his servant to offer this amount which is a bounty from paradise, and a heavenly instrument in establishing their union. This marriage will take place by the leave of God and His Chosen Ones and in accordance with the laws delineated by the Guardian and the Proof [i.e. the Báb], Who is the Lord of the Age, upon Him, His Father and followers be peace. Blessings rest upon the absent leaf, who by God's grace, will consent to whatever is predestined for her.
>
> Say: God is the Truth, all others beside Him are His creation and pray unto Him. Say: God is our Lord, all others beside Him are His servants and prostrate before Him.

> [Written] in the month of Sha'ban* of the sixth year of the Manifestation of the Truth."[6]

With each day, the siege of the fort became more expensive for Zaynu'l-'Ábidín Khán, who had to pay the soldiers, and his inability to finish them off would become increasingly apparent to his superiors in Shíráz. He began to panic. Sitting in his tent with his advisors, he decided to use trickery. They would cease hostilities and make a written offer of peace with their seals pressed into a Qur'án.** They hoped this would lure Vaḥíd out and separate him from his companions.

The offer read:

> "Hitherto, as we were ignorant of the true character of your Faith, we have allowed the mischief-makers to induce us to believe that every one of you has violated the sacred precepts of Islám. Therefore did we arise against you, and have endeavoured to extirpate your Faith. During the last few days, we have been made aware of the fact that your activities are untinged by any political motive . . . All that you seem to uphold is the claim that a man has appeared whose words are inspired and whose testimony is certain, and whom all the followers of Islám must recognize and support. We can in no wise be convinced of the validity of this claim unless you consent to repose the utmost confidence in our sincerity, and accept our request to allow certain of your representatives to emerge from the fort and meet us in this camp . . . This Qur'án, to which we affix our seals, is the

---

* June–July, 1850.

** This detail is not in the narrative of Siyyid Ibráhim nor in the Qájár histories, both non-Bábí sources.

> witness to the integrity of our purpose . . . We pledge our word that as soon as we are convinced of the truth of your Message, we shall strive to display the same zeal and devotion you already have so strikingly manifested . . . On the other hand, if we fail to be convinced of the truth of your claim, we solemnly promise that we shall in no wise interfere with your safe return to the fort . . ."[7]

Vaḥíd reacted to hearing the governor's messenger. He reminded them of his position as a descendant of the Prophet Muḥammad and that he had brought the word of truth. If they turn against him, they would be turning away from the religion of God. He warned them that their armies and power would pass away and that God would judge them.[8]

Then Vaḥíd received the Qur'án, leaned over, kissed it, and said, "Our appointed hour has struck."

He told his companions that they should suspend hostilities and honor this request even though this was no doubt a trick. He would go to their camp to demonstrate the truth of the Báb's Claim.[9]

Some of the companions began to sob. All of them were acutely distressed at the thought of losing the one who had come to them from the risen Qá'im. Who would be their guide?

They walked beside him as he strode out of the fort. He stopped at the big mulberry tree, turned and spoke to his companions for what would be the last time.[10] They gathered close to him while others stood on the walls of the fort straining to hear his words. He tried to ease the pain of this parting by uplifting their spirits and encouraging them in their defense of the fort:

> ". . . Our mission is to raise the call of the appearance of the Qá'im and spread the Teachings of the Báb. It is not necessary

to figure out the intentions of other people—only to declare His Mission. We have to show these people that they have responded to our teaching with violence. Now that they are offering peace, it's our obligation to meet with them and listen to their request even if it is a trick . . . Whatever the Almighty Hand wants will happen . . .We want to make sure that they cannot call this army of God an army for war but, rather an army for truth."[11]

Vaḥíd then said good-bye to each of the followers gathered by the tree. He quoted a verse from the Qur'án which he often used: "And soon will the unjust assailants know what vicissitudes their affairs will take!"[12]

Then he turned and walked with several companions, including Ḥájí Siyyid 'Ábid, toward the soldiers' camp.

Zaynu'l-'Ábidín Khán and his staff saw Vaḥíd and a few Bábís in the distance. To make a show of their respect, they came out of the camp to greet him. With great ceremony and a flourish of manners, they invited Vaḥíd into a luxurious tent specially set up for his comfort and introduced him to the other officers. Vaḥíd was given a seat along with the governor and two senior officers, while others stood. Vaḥíd's great dignity impressed them, and his powerful words confounded them: "I am come to you armed with the testimony which my Lord has entrusted me. Am I not a descendant of the Prophet of God? Wherefore should you have risen to slay me? For what reason have you pronounced my death-sentence and refused to recognize the undoubted rights with which my lineage has invested me?"[13]

For three days, they made a great display of courtesy while listening to him. He was even asked to lead the daily prayers. But when he tried to speak of the Qá'im, they found ways of changing the subject because secretly, they planned to kill him. Zaynu'l-'Ábidín Khán knew, though, that if Vaḥíd were harmed, the Bábís would seek revenge and launch a full-scale assault.[14]

One morning, Vaḥíd attempted to leave the camp, but soldiers stationed outside his tent prevented him.* He was their prisoner. One of his companions was able to get out and return to the fort, where he informed the Bábís that Vaḥíd was being held in the camp.** A group of Bábís, anxious for his safety, rushed out of the fort toward the camp, but the soldiers easily repulsed the disorganized attack.† The army commanders immediately went to Vaḥíd to protest the attack, saying it was a violation of their agreement. After pointing out that he was being held prisoner—a charge they denied—Vaḥíd agreed to write a note stating that they had reached a peaceful solution and that the companions should leave the fort and return home.[15]

Vaḥíd wrote the requested note. He wrote a second, secret note, though, in which he told the companions not to believe the first one

---

* Nabíl-i-A'ẓam, *The Dawn-Breakers,* 363, states that Vaḥíd was in the camp for "three days and three nights." Several sources state that he tried to leave the morning after his arrival in the army camp (Afnán, *The genesis of the Babi and Baha'i Faiths in Shiraz and Fars,* 54; Jání, quoted in Rabbani, *The Bábís of Nayríz: History and Documents,* c. 6, 11; Hamadání, quoted in Rabbani, *The Bábís of Nayríz: History and Documents,* c. 9, 15).

** This detail is not in Nabíl-i-A'ẓam, *The Dawn-Breakers,* Shafí', *Narrative of Mulla Muhammad Shafi' Nayrízí,* or Nicolas, *Seyyed Ali Mohammed dit le Bab.*

† Ḥájí Mírzá Jání, quoted in Rabbani, *The Bábís of Nayríz: History and Documents,* c. 6, 11. This detail is not in Nabíl-i-A'ẓam, *The Dawn-Breakers,* Shafí', *Narrative of Mulla Muhammad Shafi' Nayízí,* or Nicolas, *Seyyed Ali Mohammed dit le Bab.* Though this attack is not in those sources, it seems to the authors to be a probable scenario to explain why Vaḥíd later agreed to send a note to the Bábís. Some sources state that the attack reached the camp and dispersed the soldiers or killed many (Afnán 54, *The genesis of the Babi and Baha'i Faiths in Shiraz and Fars*; Hamadání, quoted in Rabbani, *The Bábís of Nayríz: History and Documents,* c. 9, 15).

and to make a surprise attack on the camp that very evening. He told his trusted companion Ḥájí Siyyid ‘Ábid to deliver the two notes.[16]

Ḥájí Siyyid ‘Ábid’s heart, though, had turned away from Vaḥíd. He had already accepted gifts and promises of land from the governor. So he went directly to him with the two notes, sealing the fate of Vaḥíd and the Bábís.[17] The governor told ‘Ábid to deliver only the first note. Then he ordered his troops to get ready.

Reading the note, the Bábís were very confused. Nevertheless, since it was from Vaḥíd, they obeyed it. They prepared to leave the fort. Some discarded their weapons. That night they left the safety of the fort and filed out into the darkness.[18]

Zaynu'l-‘Ábidín Khán knew the Bábís would obey a letter from Vaḥíd. Once the last Bábí had left the fort, his soldiers moved in behind them, cutting off any possible retreat. Then other soldiers came up quickly in front and on the sides. The defenseless Bábís were surrounded. The soldiers raised their guns and fired. The Bábís ran forward trying to break through the line to reach town. Those who still had their swords swung furiously at the soldiers while others fought desperately with sticks and stones. Gunfire lit up the darkness. One Bábí after another fell.[19]

Some of the soldiers went to the Great Mosque in the Bábí neighborhood, climbed onto its roof and up into its minarets. They loaded their guns and waited for any Bábís who might come to the mosque to use it for defense.[20] From these high minarets and roof, the soldiers could scan the whole neighborhood and shoot any Bábís who came near.

The Bábís who broke through the line of soldiers ran all the way to town. Injured and weary, they wanted to reach the security of the Great Mosque. As they neared, the soldiers hiding in the minarets pulled their triggers.[21]

❋ ❋ ❋

With the fort emptied and its defenders dead or dispersed, Zaynu'l-'Ábidín <u>Kh</u>án now had to figure out how to get around his oath to Vaḥíd. He could not simply execute him, because he had sworn an oath for his safety. But he wanted Vaḥíd dead, and the clergy of <u>Sh</u>íráz had issued a fatwa for the execution of Vaḥíd and his principal companions.[22]

In their camp, in the area known as "red mountain" outside of Nayríz, Zaynu'l-'Ábidín <u>Kh</u>án and his advisors conferred. One of the military commanders stepped forward to volunteer his services, saying he had not participated in the oath. He called on anyone whose family member had been harmed in the conflict with the Bábís to come forward and participate in punishing Vaḥíd.

The brother of Mullá Báqir, who had carried a message for reinforcements but had been caught and killed by the Bábís, eagerly volunteered. Several others followed, including the governor's nephew whose father had also been killed. Hungry for revenge, they walked up to Vaḥíd and yanked his turban—the sign of his lineage—off his head and wound it around his neck.[23] Blow after blow struck Vaḥíd. He crumpled to the ground.

They then tied his turban to a horse and dragged him through the streets.* The excited townspeople crowded in, hurled insults, and threw stones. Women danced around him. Somewhere in the frenzy, amid the exultation and the tumult, in the dust and the heat, and the shouts and the screams of violent passion reverberating on the mud-brick walls of Nayríz, Vaḥíd left this life.

---

* According to <u>Sh</u>afí', *Narrative of Mulla Muhammad Shafi' Nayízí*, 11, he was dragged by his feet.

His body was beheaded, his head skinned, and the scalped skin filled with straw.* The feet were fastened to a horse and dragged through streets and alleys for people to desecrate the corpse. This ghastly scene reached the door of the Nazar-Biykí mosque, close to the governor's house in the bazaar quarter.[24]

Women from the Sádát quarter danced to the sound of drums and cymbals and made joyful and mocking noises in celebration.** They would have torn the corpse limb from limb, had it not been under a pile of the rocks they had thrown. The townspeople turned away to go pillage Vaḥíd's home. The frenzy gradually waned, and the streets emptied. The moon rose and spread its silver blue light on the corpse abandoned in front of the mosque.[25]

The following day, a few Bábís gathered up the headless corpse and placed it in the earth near the wall of a local shrine.† The desecration of Vaḥíd's body distressed some of the local people, including Bibi Khánum, the mother of a wealthy man in the bazaar quarter, who considered herself a good Muslim. After all, Vaḥíd had been a siyyid—a

---

* There is no precise account of his actual death, only general descriptions of his martyrdom. Shoghi Effendi, *God Passes By* (43), states that Vaḥíd's head was sent to Shíráz; there is also reliable local lore that a Muslim woman in the bazaar quarter recovered his head. This scenario described by the authors in this account seems the most plausible to them given these sources and what we know about the fate of other Bábí martyrs: that his head was skinned, the scalped skin stuffed with straw and carried to Shíráz, and that the skull was recovered by the servant of the Muslim woman.

** Nabíl-i-A'ẓam, *The Dawn-Breakers*, doesn't specify that it is women from the Sádát quarter, only that they were Nayrízí women. Rouhani, *Lam'átul-Anvár vols. 1 and 2, c. 7.* doesn't mention women from the Sádát quarter; he only describes the group as a "wild mob."

† The shrine was that of Siyyid Jalálí'd-Dín 'Abdull'áh. It was in the heart of the bazaar and had been visited by Muslims for centuries.

descendant of the Prophet Muḥammad. So she ordered her servant to find and bring back the head. When he returned, she washed it, covered it in silk fabric, and then hid it in a box for a few days. Once the violence in town had quieted down, the head was taken to the shrine and placed reverently next to the body in the unmarked grave. Bibi Kh́ánum kept the box as a sacred object.[26]

Before his execution, Vaḥíd had spoken these final words:

> "Thou knowest, O my beloved, that I have abandoned the world for Thy sake, and have placed my trust in Thee alone. I am impatient to hasten to Thee, for the beauty of Thy countenance has been unveiled to my eyes. Thou dost witness the evil designs which my wicked persecutor has cherished against me. Nay never will I submit to his wishes or pledge my allegiance to him."[27]

Siyyid Yaḥyáy-i-Dárábí, one of the most prominent clerics of his time who had given up all social position and prestige purely on faith; who was then renamed "the peerless one," *Vaḥíd,* by the Báb and declared by Him to be one of the two witnesses of the Cause of God; was beaten and beheaded on June 29th, 1850. He was forty years old.

Bahá'u'lláh revealed a Tablet of Visitation in memory of Vaḥíd, blessing him for his certitude and his courage and for having responded to the divine call. This Tablet declared Vaḥid's tomb to be a sacred resting place where people could receive succor if they asked.*

* Provisional translation by Ṭahiríh Ahdieh, Nabíl Hanna, Abir Majíd, Rosann Velnich available at http://www.nayriz.org.

Ṭubá, Vaḥíd's daughter in Nayríz, was deeply depressed by the news of his martyrdom. She was consoled by a dream in which she saw the Báb and her father walking hand in hand with rows of Bábís following them while kings and clerics ran away, their crowns and turbans falling to the ground.[28]

Ten days after the martyrdom of Vaḥíd, the Báb was executed in a square in Tabríz, along with a young man who had begged to be with Him always. Two regiments of soldiers fired hundreds of bullets at Him Who was the Gate to God, and His young follower.

The Báb's mangled body—His face untouched—was then thrown into a ditch outside of town.*

* For a thorough summary of various eyewitnesses and the differences in the accounts of the martyrdom of the Báb and the disposal and retrieval of His body, see Nicolas, *Prophet in Modern Times*, 31–33 and 38–39.

8

PUNISHMENT

In the warm air of an early summer morning, Mírzá Maḥmúd, the British agent for the province of Fárs, sat in his office in Shíráz writing reports to the British government about the conflict in Nayríz. In his first report for the month of June, 1850, he noted that reinforcements had been sent from Shíráz on the 19th and 20th of May, to help defeat the Bábís in Fort Khájih. On June 23rd, Mírzá Maḥmúd reported hearing that the Bábís had been defeated in Nayríz. Those who were still alive would be sent to the prince in Shíráz. The following day, another thirteen heads arrived in Shíráz and were paraded through the streets and then hung from the city walls. The prince in Shíráz was known to have sent an executioner to Nayríz on June 25th to behead Vaḥíd. Mírzá Maḥmúd reported that when the executioner got to Nayríz, Vaḥíd had already been killed "by soldiers." On June 26th, "Two Ghoolams (assistants) arrived from Mehr Ally Khán," and said that Vaḥíd had surrendered. It was rumored that soldiers were plundering Nayríz.[1]

Mírzá Maḥmúd's report and most of the rumors he heard were true. After the fall of Fort Kh̲ájih, many Bábís had been decapitated, their severed heads skinned, the scalps stuffed with straw and mounted on spears. These were brought back to Sh̲íráz as proof of the triumphant victory over the Bábís and as gifts to the governor of the province, Prince Fírúz Mírzá. The Bábí men had been made to walk in chains while the women, clothed in tatters, had been tied onto the bare backs of camels. The foot soldiers had marched behind them to the sound of drums and trumpets. The victorious commanders had ridden proudly at the head of the procession. Near Sh̲íráz, three of the Bábís had collapsed to the ground, unable to walk any further due to their injuries. Several soldiers had then walked over, unsheathed, lifted, and swung their swords down, beheading them. The heads had been raised on spears, the remains left behind on the ground. The caravan had moved on. That spot would come to be called "Qabr Bábí," the Bábí's burial.[2]

The victorious army, with thirty men and fifty women and children captive, arrived at the gates of Sh̲íráz on July 10th. In his report, Mírzá Maḥmúd noted that the soldiers were carrying many precious items, which they had looted from the Bábí homes in the Ch̲inár-Súkh̲tih quarter.[3]

The day of this triumphant entrance had been declared a day of celebration for the whole city by the governor in Sh̲íráz. The townspeople were encouraged to make merry and carouse. There was the sound of music playing and of local women shouting and making joyful noises. The bazaar was festooned with flags.

Then the gruesome processional entered the city—bedraggled men in chains, half-naked, exhausted women tied onto bare camel backs like bundles, and terrified young children.* Around them, the

* 'Abdu'l-Bahá, *A Traveler's Narrative*, 258, n. H; Edward Granville Browne, *A Year Among the Persians* (317) mentions little children among the captives.

soldiers carried straw-stuffed heads mounted on spears. As soon as the spectators saw this nightmarish and sad sight, their mood soured, and many returned to their homes frightened and ashamed by what they had seen.[4]

A chief of one of the nomadic tribes in the province witnessed the arrival of the army and the Bábí captives in Shíráz:

> "After they had slain that honored person [i.e. Vaḥíd], they came to take camels from our tribe, intending to set the captives on barebacked camels. I was distressed at this, but could not resist the governor's order. I therefore rode away from the army's camp at night and came to Shíráz, that at least I might not be among my tribe and have to endure the insolence of the soldiers. When I was come within half a farsang of Shíráz, I lay down to sleep for a while to be rid of my weariness.* When I awoke, I saw that the people of Shíráz had come out in large numbers with minstrels and musicians, and were sitting about in groups at every corner and cross-road, feasting and making merry with wanton women. On every side I noted with wonder drunken brawls, wine imbibing, the savor of roasted meats, and the strains of guitars and lutes. Thus wondering I entered the city.
>
> After a while, unable to endure the suspense, I determined to go out of the city to see what was taking place. As I came forth from the city-gate, I saw much feasting and rejoicing as I had never before witnessed. The men were engaged in making merry and toying with their lecherous and wanton women. After a little while I saw the camels approaching, whereupon there were set

* Roughly 2.4–3 kilometers.

some forty or fifty women. Many of the soldiers bore on their spears the severed heads of the men they had slain. Until this time, the townsfolk had been busy with their carnal desires, but no sooner did their eyes fall on the severed heads borne aloft on spears and the captives set on barebacked camels than they inconsolably burst into tears and sobbing.

Thus they brought the illustrious captives into the bazaar, which had been decorated and adorned, and though it was no great distance from the bazaar to the governor's ark (i.e. the governor's seat), yet such was the throng of spectators who purposely retarded the passage of the captives that it was after midday when they reached the Governor's palace. The Navváb Prince was holding a pleasure party in Kuláh Farangí and the garden adjoining it, he sitting on a chair, and the nobles and magnates of the city standing. A curtain was drawn in front of the other chambers of Kuláh Farangí, behind which the women of the Prince's household were ensconced. And the captives were led in this plight to the accompaniment of cymbals and trumpets into the garden and brought before the Qájár Prince. Then Muhammad-'Alí Khán, Mírzá Na'ím, and the other officers recounted their exploits and their glorious victory, with their various versions and many embellishments, to the Qájár Prince, who in his part kept inquiring as to the names and family of the captives, and throwing in an occasional, 'Who is this?' and 'Which is that?'

And all the captives were women, with the exception of one child five years of age who was with them.

After that, those illustrious beings were excused from the presence [of the Prince] and housed outside of the City in a ruined caravanserai that dated back to the time of Karím Khán Zand."[5]

The prisoners limped into the governor's summer meeting hall with its hat-shaped roof, marble-walled rooms and fountain. In this luxury, the officials feasted and celebrated the victory over the Bábís. The prisoners were brought before them. The military commanders—including Mírzá Na'ím, who would attack the Nayríz Bábís again in 1853—presented them to Prince Fírúz Mírzá. This prince then had Vaḥíd's faithful servant, Ghulám-Riḍá Yazdi, the main Bábí commander, and Shaykha, the executioner from Fort Khájih, hideously tortured and executed.* Other men were tortured as well, including Mírzá Mihdí, the uncle of 'Alí Sardár, the leader in the second Nayríz conflict in 1853. He died later in prison of his extreme physical suffering.[6]

The women were brought to a caravanserai outside the Iṣfáhán gate next to a military barracks, where they were at the mercy of local soldiers.[7] The remaining men and the severed heads were put elsewhere.**

Bábí prisoners were brought out each day into the streets to be humiliated. Khadíjih Bagum, the widow of the Báb, lived in Shíráz at this time:

> "One day I noticed that the City of Shíráz was particularly perturbed and the people were exceedingly jubilant, with the sound

* According to the reports of the British agent Mírzá Maḥmúd, this happened on October 6th, much later than Mázandarání's account: "On the same day two Bábees were delivered by Mehr Ally Khán to H.R.H. (Prince Firuz Mírzá of Shíráz). One of them was the executioner, and the other a Sirdar (officer) of Siyyid Yahyáh. Both were beheaded." Ghulám Riḍá Yazdí was one of the main Bábí leader-soldiers under Vaḥíd.

** Browne states that all the men were slaughtered at this point, but Rouhani (v. 1, 90) states that the remaining men were housed, with the bags containing the severed heads, in the caravanserai, while the women were placed in a house next to the soldiers.

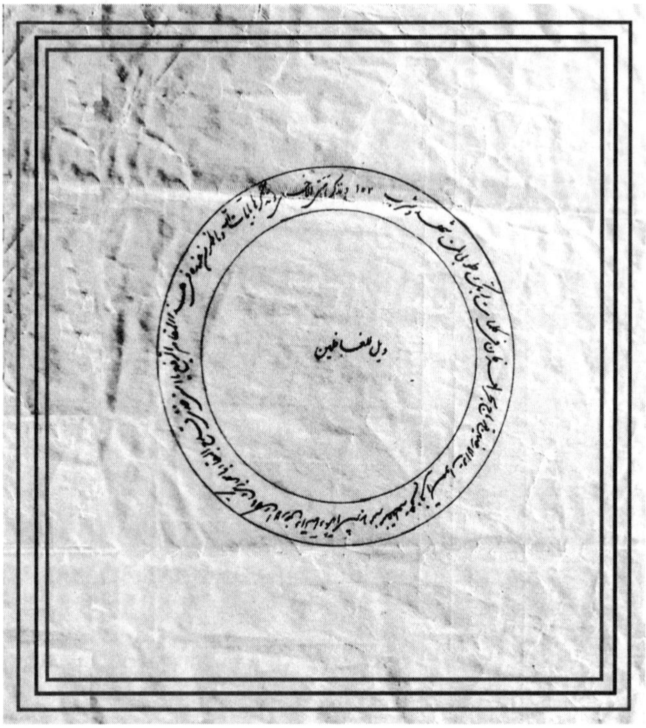

Tablet to Fáṭimih.

> of trumpets and horns heard on every side. I learned that the heads of the Bábí martyrs of Nayríz were brought into the City on that occasion and in the same manner the captives of Nayríz arrived and conducted to their prison. I longed to meet at least one of the kinsmen of the martyrs! But, alas, it was not possible. One day, however, two of them came to our house begging. Even, then, it was not possible to speak to them."[8]

As the Bábís grew weaker under this torment and the local people lost interest in this daily spectacle, some were released into the streets, traumatized and penniless, to try to survive on their own.

Others were returned to Nayríz as prisoners. The governor of Nayríz, Zaynu'l-'Ábidín Khán, was in a state of fury because eleven Bábís from his city had tried to reach the shah with a petition asking for protection against him. They had slipped out of Nayríz on the night when the homes of the Bábís were being raided and had gotten as far as a few station stops from the capital when they were caught by a group of officers, brought back to Shíráz, and executed. One individual, though, got through to Ṭihrán. He was able to present a petition for the protection of the Bábís of Nayríz.* It was then that the original Bábí prisoners who had been sent back from Shíráz arrived in Nayríz.[9]

Zaynu'l-'Ábidín Khán vented his anger on the newly arrived prisoners. He had Shaykh Yúsuf's ears cut off, had another Bábí bridled and others severely beaten. Some of them died as a result of such punishment, including Karbalá'í Mírzá Muḥammad, who had been the gatekeeper at Fort Khájih.[10]

The governor was in the midst of an orgy of violence against all Bábís.

Zaynu'l-'Ábidín Khán began to round up local Bábís and seize their lands and homes. He hired several thousand soldiers—including tribesmen in the region who were loyal to him—to capture those associated with Vaḥíd, and those who had opposed the governor's rule. The Bábí houses in the Chinár-Súkhtih quarter were demolished, and the wooden parts of Fort Khájih were burned. Whatever the Bábís possessed of any monetary value was stolen.[11]

---

* The petitioners were Karbalá'í Abú'l-Ḥasan, Áqá Shaykh Hádí, uncle of the wife of Vaḥíd, Mírzá 'Alí and Abú'l-Qásim Ibn Ḥájí Zayna, Akbar Ibn 'Abid, Mírzá Ḥasan, and his brother Mírzá Bába (Nicolas, *Seyyed Ali Mohammed dit le Bab,* 409).

Bábís who were found were brought into the street in front of their neighbors for all to see their torment. Weeds were placed under their nails and then set on fire. Hot irons were pressed into their skins. Holes were cut into their noses and a cord run through them. Soldiers yanked on the cord to parade them through the streets. Many townspeople stood by, enjoying this, contributing to the suffering and humiliation of their own neighbors.

Zaynu'l-'Ábidín Khán kept the wealthy Bábís captive in Nayríz so he could force them to sign the deeds to their lands over to him. He became a much richer man.[12]

All around Nayríz, famine and widespread poverty had set in. The army sent from Shíráz had lived off the local people, using up the grain supply. Zaynu'l-'Ábidín Khán hoarded large amounts of the grain, selling it at high prices, but, as the situation worsened, he was forced to distribute it at fair market value. He took advantage of this distribution to humiliate the more prominent Bábís by making them sit at the entrance to the site where townspeople came for their rations. Those who wanted grain were ordered to spit on their faces. Some people refused to do this out of respect for these individuals and, as a result, they did not get their share.[13]

Two individuals who underwent public humiliation and torture were Áqá Siyyid Ja'far Yazdí and Ḥájí Muḥammad-Taqí Nayrízí.* Zaynu'l-'Ábidín Khán singled them out as the principal supporters of Vaḥíd, so a special order was issued for their arrest.

Aqa Siyyid Ja'far Yazdí had been one of the leading citizens of Nayríz, a high ranking cleric who had owned a large home in the

* Both men were recipients of Tablets from Bahá'u'lláh.

bazaar quarter. In Yazd, he became a follower of the Báb, for which he had to give up his position and the privileges that came with it. Back in Nayríz, he actively taught the new Faith, and many in the bazaar quarter accepted the claim of the Báb. Zaynu'l-'Ábidín Khán responded by having Siyyid Ja'far debarred from his own home. Siyyid Ja'far then joined Vaḥíd in Fort Khájih and was one of his close advisors. After Vaḥíd's martyrdom, Zaynu'l-'Ábidín Khán held Siyyid Ja'far primarily responsible for the conversion of so many Naryízís to the Bábí Faith.* After his capture, his turban, the symbol of his noble lineage as a descendant of the Prophet Muḥammad, was burned, and so began his torment.[14]

In a biography of him, there is a graphic description of his suffering and his acceptance of it:

> ". . . this once revered man of learning stood by the door of the barn while hundreds of men and women spat upon his blessed face as they filed through that door, looking at him with bitter hate and prejudice.
>
> In the face of this dire humiliation, Áqá Siyyid Ja'far's feelings were not those of disgust, intolerance or indignation. On the contrary, he remained calm and resigned throughout his ordeal and manifested a spirit of sublime joy and love and thankfulness towards those who offended him.
>
> Once during the ordeal, it is authoritatively stated, he noticed several people who hesitated to come forward for their share. Apparently the ghastly deed of spitting upon his face kept them

* One of Áqá Siyyid Ja'far Yazdí's descendants is Dr. Táhirih Ahdieh, wife of Dr. Hussein Ahdieh.

> away. With a face beaming with heavenly joy he beckoned them and said: "You had better come and get your share before it is too late; it won't matter if you spit upon my face; I'll wipe it off with my handkerchief . . ."[15]

Siyyid Ja'far also endured the bastinado. He was brought outside, and his feet were tied to a wooden plank which was raised up horizontally so that the bottom of his feet were facing upwards. Then his soles—the end point of the body's nerves—were repeatedly struck with a rod, causing agonizing pain throughout his body, as well as breaking the small bones in his feet and tearing the tendons. Another time, he was beaten in front of the home of a wealthy citizen. It would only stop when the citizen or passers-by paid ransom money to the soldiers. This scene would then be repeated in another location in town. This went on for nine months. His legs became so swollen and sore that he could not walk.[16]

Ḥájí Muḥammad-Taqí Nayrízí was a young, wealthy merchant known for his honesty. Local people deposited their money with him for safekeeping. He married the daughter of Mullá 'Abdu'l Ḥusayn, one of the Bábís killed in 1850. When Vaḥíd was on his way from Runíz, Taqí had been one of the Nayrízís who had gone out to meet him. He accepted the Faith of the Báb immediately upon hearing the new teachings, and he hired town criers to let Nayrízís know about Vaḥíd's public meetings. When the authorities grew violent, Taqí joined the other Bábís in Fort Kh͟ájih and paid for the fort's expenses. As winter came on, Zaynu'l-'Ábidín Kh͟án decided to have one of the captive Bábís whipped each day and thrown into a pool of ice cold water. Taqí asked to be thrown in place of the others as he was younger and stronger. His blood turned the water red. This was repeated for several days, but he survived. It resulted in his being permanently disfigured and nearly blind. After this treatment, he was taken around town and further humiliated so money could be extracted from passers by.[17]

Throughout this time of violence, Zaynu'l-'Ábidín Khán's wife, who knew both men and was personal friends with their families, did not sleep easily, as she had had a disturbing dream. In it, figures dressed in black clothing descended from heaven, warning Zaynu'l-'Ábidín Khán about his treatment of the descendants of the Prophet Muḥammad. She interpreted this dream as a bad omen and told her husband about it. But he did not relent. So his wife contacted the head of the Sádát district, who was a friend of hers, and asked him to get five donkeys ready outside the city gate that night. Then, she had her attendant go and get Ja'far and Taqí out of the prison and bring them to the secret location. They were put on donkeys and conducted to the town of Harat, which was just beyond Zaynu'l-'Ábidín Khán's jurisdiction. They remained there for several months to recover from their terrible wounds and injuries.[18]

With an insatiable desire for more wealth, Zaynu'l-'Ábidín Khán continued stealing the properties of the Bábís.

Áqá Siyyid Abú-Talíb, a wealthy chieftain of one of the quarters of Nayríz, was known to the king, but this could not save him from becoming another victim of the governor's greed. The governor put him in chains and sent him in secret to Ma'dan, a nearby mine, because he wanted to take possession of his land. The authorities in Shíráz asked about Abú Ṭalíb's whereabouts. Zaynu'l-'Ábidín Khán did not want to turn him over to them because they would most likely execute him for his role in the conflict. Khan lied and told them that Abú Ṭalíb had died, but a local religious figure, who saw Abú Ṭalíb as the source of all the trouble with the Bábís and who bore him a personal grudge, had him murdered with poison.[19]

Zaynu'l-'Ábidín Khán also seized the wealth of the family of Mullá Mírzá Muḥammad Nayrízí by force. Mullá Muḥammad, the famous calligrapher who was one of the original seventy-two Bábís in the fort and who had been injured there, had been recuperating in Iṣṭahbánát when the Bábís were defeated. Returning to Nayríz, he discovered to his horror the fate of his family. In front of their mother, Zaynu'l-'Ábidín Khán had tortured his younger brother with a hot iron. Khán demanded that the deeds to their properties be signed over to him in return for stopping. Terrified, the family turned over ownership to their properties—too late, though, to save the younger brother, who died soon after from his suffering.[20]

Many Bábís escaped the governor's clutches and found safety in the surrounding wilderness.[21] They took no possessions or provisions with them, but they would survive to participate in the coming, and much bloodier, conflict of 1853.

The remaining prisoners in Nayríz were tortured to death, and their corpses dumped into a well dug in the prison courtyard which was then filled in with earth.[22]

Overcome with grief by the fate of his family, Mullá Muḥammad Nayrízí decided on a new course of action. He would avenge his family's treatment by going to Ṭihrán to confront the one man whom he held most responsible for all of their suffering—the king of Persia.

9

ATTEMPT ON THE LIFE OF THE KING OF PERSIA

With the Báb executed, most of His apostles dead, and many devoted followers killed at the battles at Fort Tabarsí, Zanján, and Nayríz, many Bábís are discouraged and a few decide on desperate action . . .

. . . The care-worn Nayrízí mother, traumatized by seeing her young son tortured and by losing her family's lands, wraps a pearl necklace and what few valuables she has left of the family fortune, and gives them to her eldest son, Mullá Mírzá Muḥammad, before he leaves Nayríz in the spring of 1851. In Shíráz, he meets some other like-minded Bábís, and they continue to Ṭihrán.* A Bábí leader organizes them for violent action . . .*

* According to Shafí', *Narrative of Mulla Muhammad Shafi' Nayízí* (12), the other two were Ḥájí Qasím and Ḥusayn, the son of 'Alí Naqí. Shafí', though, places Mullá Muḥammad's leaving for Ṭihrán much later. Shafí' (12) places the movement of these three men—and the suicide of two women—two years after the end of the

. . . One day, the Bábí plot leader visits Jináb-i-Bahá. He tells Jináb-i-Bahá of their plans. Jináb-i-Bahá warns him emphatically not to go through with this, that it was contrary to the Báb's teachings, and that he would have absolutely no part in such an immoral act. He tells the plot leader that such an act would bring catastrophe to the remaining Bábís . . .[1]

. . . A new prime minister, Mírzá Áqá Khán-i-Núrí, has been put into office. He writes to Jináb-i-Bahá, whose family he knows personally, a warm letter expressing the hope of reconciliation with the Bábís . . .[2]

But the wheels of the plot are already in motion.

The following notice appears in the Ṭihrán Weekly gazette of August 12, 1852: "Since the weather in Rudbar is cool and there are plenty of partridges in Ushan, His Majesty's intention is to depart during the next few days for these locations (outside his summer residence)."[3]

A few days later the following story appears in the newspaper: "A short distance from the Prime Minister, the most holy threshold (the king) had issued instructions for the attendants to mount their steeds when suddenly one of the accursed from Nayríz of Fárs who had garbed himself as a villager, bravely ran forth crying: 'I have a supplication!' A few of the servants observing him came forth to see what the vagrant had to say, but before they could apprehend him, he pulled a gun and

---

first incident. Mázandarání (v. 4, 22) places the three going to Ṭihrán a year and a half later but states that the three were "sent" to Ṭihrán by Zaynu'l-'Ábidín Khán as a result of the attack on his men in the Bálá-Taram mountains; Mázandarání inaccurately accounts for the death of Ghulám Riḍá Yazdí as a result of this incident as well. Nicolas, *Seyyed Ali Mohammed dit le Bab* (407), has the three men escaping to Tihrán from Shíráz after being taken captive as a result of the fall of Fort Khájih.

* Azim was his name.

fired upon the monarch. However by divine grace, the bullet missed its mark."[4]*

In the following week's newspaper: "Mírzá Muhammad Nayrízí who had participated in all the battles of Nayríz, Zanján, and Mázíndarán, and bore many cuts from those past battles, was shot to death by the attendants, armed guards, servants and officers of the royal forces, and thereafter his body was beaten with rocks and sticks until it became one with the soil."[5]

❋ ❋ ❋

The retribution for attempting to kill the king of Persia in August of 1852 was swift, violent, and pervasive. A much more fierce and widespread persecution of the Bábís than ever before now took place, just as Jináb-i-Bahá had warned one of the plot leaders. The treasonous action gave the clergy the excuse needed to make a renewed push to exterminate the new Faith once and for all and to appropriate the properties and belongings of its followers.[6]

An Austrian officer stationed in Ṭihrán was so appalled by what he saw that he resigned his position:

> ". . . the bazaar is illuminated with unhappy victims, because on the right and left people dig deep holes in their breasts and

---

* Nabíl-i-A'ẓam, *The Dawn-Breakers* (440), lists two men as attempting the assassination: Sádiq-i-Tabrízí and Fathu'lláh-i-Qumí. Amanat, *Resurrection and Renewal* (205), names four individuals—Mullá Muḥammad Nayrízí, Sádiq-i-Tabrízí, and Fathu'lláh-i-Qumí as attacking the king, and Ḥájí Qasím-i-Nayrízí being involved in the plot as well. The various reports from European representatives at the time list from three to six plotters (Momen, *The Bábí and Bahá'í Religions*, c. 7).

> shoulders and insert burning wicks in the wounds. I saw some dragged in chains through the bazaar, preceded by a military band, in whom these wicks had burned so deep that now the fat flickered convulsively in the wound like a newly-extinguished lamp . . . As for the end itself, they hang the scorched and perforated bodies by their hands and feet to a tree head downwards, and now every Persian may try his marksmanship to his heart's content from a fixed but not too proximate distance on the noble quarry placed at his disposal. I saw corpses torn by nearly 150 bullets . . . At present I never leave my house, in order not to meet with fresh scenes of horror. After their death the Bábís are hacked in two and either nailed to the city gate, or cast out into the plain as food for the dogs and jackals . . ."[7]

Though he had not been hurt, the king was very shaken emotionally, and the ferocity of the attack would stay with him for years.[8] He knew that several recent assassination attempts in Europe had succeeded. He suspected plots among his advisors, wondering if some of them were in collusion with prominent Bábís or if the foreign powers were meddling in the affairs of his kingdom again. He even suspected his new prime minister because his mother, an enemy of the prime minister, suggested to him that he might be involved. She saved most of her venom, though, for the most prominent Bábí: Jináb-i-Bahá.

Jináb-i-Bahá, despite offers of protection from the Russian minister, the prime minister, and other high officials, rode to the headquarters of the imperial army, demonstrating His innocence, His repudiation of such violence, and His obedience to royal authority. He was then turned over to the authorities and was forced to walk to Ṭihrán in chains, with no covering against the sun. He was abused by people along the route. One old woman wanted to throw a stone at Him;

when she was prevented, He said, "Suffer not this woman to be disappointed. Deny her not what she regards as a meritorious act in the sight of God."[9] Then He was thrown into a subterranean, dark, germ-infested dungeon filled with criminals. During His incarceration, He was weighed down with a heavy chain around His neck that left lifelong scars on His body.

'Abdu'l-Bahá, His son, whose title means the "Servant of Bahá," was brought to visit Him one day: ". . . He was allowed to enter the prison-yard to see His beloved Father when He came out for his daily exercise. Jináb-i-Bahá was terribly altered, so ill He could hardly walk, His hair and beard unkempt, His neck galled and swollen from the pressure of a heavy steel collar. His body bent by the weight of His chains, and the sight made a never-to-be-forgotten impression on the mind of the sensitive boy."[10]

While Jináb-i-Bahá was held in the dungeon, He had a significant dream: "One night, in a dream, this all-glorious word was heard from all sides: 'Verily we will aid Thee to triumph by Thyself and by Thy pen. Grieve not for that which hath befallen Thee, and have no fear. Truly Thou art of them that are secure. Ere long shall the Lord send forth and reveal the treasures of the earth, men who shall give Thee the victory by Thyself and by Thy name wherewith the Lord hath revived the hearts of them that know.'"[11]

God anointed Him as the One Whom the Báb had promised, the One for Whom the Báb had opened the gate. Soon He would be forced to leave for Baghdád, and He and His family would begin a life of exile in fulfillment of the divine plan of which He was the instrument—a life of exile from which they would never return.*

* Jináb-i-Bahá's exile began January 12th, 1853.

NAYRÍZ, 1853

10

UPHEAVAL IN NAYRÍZ

Zaynu'l-'Ábidín Khán, the governor of Nayríz, eagerly rose to do his part in wiping out the Bábís of Persia. He would rid his city of these heretics who might overthrow him by allying themselves with his extended family, and then he could enrich himself by pillaging their properties. Many of the surviving Bábís had fled into the mountains where they hid in fear. Much of the Chinár-Súkhtih quarter—where most Bábís lived—was in ruins after the devastation that followed the fall of Fort Khájih. But a new resistance was forming.[1]

The governor received news that Bábís had attacked one of his grape syrup-making facilities on the mountain slopes, killing a few of his men.* He heard rumors of plots. The numbers of Bábís in the Chinár-

* Mázandarání places this event six months earlier. As the time for the grape harvest would be late summer and because these oral memories were all taken down many decades after the events, the authors think it makes sense to place the attack on the grape factory in August as a part of the escalating violence following the attempted assassination of the sháh.

Súkhtih quarter seemed to be growing again. Afraid, he surrounded himself with a number of gunmen for security when he went out in public.[2]

He would have been much more nervous if he had known that, in the fall of 1852, a Bábí renowned for his extraordinary bravery had slipped back into town: 'Alí Sardár.

Sardár was born in 1823, from two distinguished families of the Chinár-Súkhtih district—the Dah-Bradaran and Zarmaghali families.[3] Recognizing his courage and leadership skills early on, Zaynu'l-'Ábidín Khán had originally given Sardár the responsibility of overseeing two of his villages, Rastáq and Qaṭrúyih. In those days, a wealthy family might own land on which there were entire villages; peasant farmers would till the land and pay taxes to the landlord. Sardár had gained local fame when he and his childhood friend, Ḥasan Mírzá, had captured seventy highway robbers. These bandits had pleaded for mercy asserting their innocence, and Sardár had set them free rather than bringing them to the governor for punishment. After that, the villagers greatly admired him for his fairness and bravery.

Though he had been favored by the governor, Sardár had grown increasingly disgusted with him. He knew the governor had gained his position by having his own brother—the rightful heir to the governorship of Nayríz—murdered. So when Vaḥíd arrived in town and proclaimed the Message of the Báb, which included a call for just government along with the new spiritual teachings, Sardár became a follower. When severe persecutions followed the fall of Fort Khájih, he escaped to hide in the neighboring mountains, returning to Nayríz in the fall of 1852 to serve the local Bábís.[4] A group of resistance leaders now formed, composed of 'Alí Sardár, Khájih Quṭbá, Ḥájí 'Abdu'l-'Alí, Vaḥíd's father-in-law, and his two sons, Mullá 'Abdu'l-Ḥusayn and his four sons, and nine others—a group of nineteen, a

"Vaḥíd"—the holy number in the Bábí religion. They decided that Ḥájí 'Abdu'l-'Alí and Mullá 'Abdu'l-Ḥusayn would visit local Bábís and educate them about the teachings of the Báb, of which many had only a slight knowledge. Sardár and Quṭbá went through the mountain area to locate those still in hiding and encourage them to return to Nayríz, where a renewed Bábí community could give the governor greater resistance. With this encouragement, Bábís began returning to Nayríz.[5] Sardár went secretly to the homes of the Bábís who were destitute to bring them provisions, clothing, kerosene for light, and encouragement.* Mullá Ḥasan Lab-Shikarí also provided support of this kind.** The numbers grew, and a community was coming back to life by the winter of 1852–53.

Meanwhile, the governor began making plans for a general attack on these Bábís.

Feeling such an attack by the governor to be inevitable, a group of Bábís whispered the word *assassination* more and more frequently. In the Shí'a Muslim tradition in which they were raised, these Bábís understood religion to be God's will and, because it was Truth, it could be defended by force. They believed the Qá'im would lead an army to establish righteousness, a belief similar to that of the Jews of the first

* Nicolas, *Seyyed Ali Mohammed dit le Bab* (410), states that Zaynu'l-'Ábidín Khán arrested Sardár but was unable to charge him with anything, so he let him go. Nicolas, *Seyyed Ali Mohammed dit le Bab* (410), and Shafí', *Narrative of Mulla Muhammad Shafi' Nayízí* (14), state that five men swore to kill Zaynu'l-'Ábidín Khán: Karbalá'í Muḥammad with his three sons, Khájih Maḥmúd, Khájih Ḥasan and Khájih 'Alí, and Ustád Qásim. According to these sources, they were greatly encouraged by Quṭbá, a close companion of Sardár who would figure prominently in the coming conflict, who nightly exhorted them to take revenge on Zaynu'l-'Ábidín Khán. According to Rouhani, *Lam'átul-Anvár* (v. 1, 171), and Faizi, *Nayríz Mushkbiz* (89), Mullá Ḥasan Lab-Shikarí was involved with the plot as well.

** From a conversation with Mrs. Nura (Shahídpúr) Jamer (March 2010/166 BE).

century CE, who believed the Messiah would return and lead an army against the Romans. The Báb, though, did not condone warfare, as seen by His rejection of the offer of the governor in Iṣfáhán to provide Him with an army.[6]

But this group of Bábís did not understand that the actions they were considering violated the teachings of the Báb. They were angry at the governor and others in Nayríz for killing the revered Vaḥíd, traumatized by their own experiences, and concerned for their own family members and properties; now they were in fear for their lives and felt they needed to act preemptively in self-defense. There was no one of Vaḥíd's stature to educate them, guide them, or give them a spiritual perspective because most of the original Bábí leaders had been killed.

In the early spring of 1853,* the governor gave orders for the Bábís from the Chinár Súkhtih quarter to be rounded up, imprisoned, and tortured.** He also planned to eliminate Mullá Ḥasan Lab-Shikarí, who was protecting local Bábís and who had been very close to the brother whom he had murdered, as well as Sardár, Quṭbá, and others. Someone close to the governor, who knew of this decision, secretly informed the Bábís. His orders could not be carried out in time . . .[6]

On a Friday evening, Zaynu'l-'Ábidín Khán told his attendants to prepare the baths for his visit the following morning.[7]† The bathhouse was an old building with an outer room in which the bather undressed

---

* It would seem that this is true based on the Shafí' and Rouhani sources.

** Shafí', *Narrative of Mulla Muhammad Shafí' Nayrízí* (14), states that Zaynu'l-'Ábidín Khán ordered seventy Bábís from this quarter to be rounded up so he could "put them all in a pot and boil them."

† According to Nicolas, *Seyyed Ali Mohammed dit le Bab* (410), and Shafí', *Narrative of Mulla Muhammad Shafí' Nayízí* (13), the assassination took place on a Friday. Momen, (*Bábí and Bahá'í religions*, 147), gives the date as March 26, 1853, which is a Saturday.

and received a towel before going into the hot bath in the main room. There an attendant would wash him, and he would go into a separate pool to submerge himself. This water, though, was used by everyone and was therefore quite dirty.*

The following morning, Zaynu'l-'Ábidín Khán walked with his attendants and soldiers to the bathhouse. Before entering the baths, he told his gunmen to go up on the roofs and the towers of his house, located across the street from the baths, to be on the lookout for anything suspect.

The bathhouse had been emptied for his private use. What he didn't know was that in the early morning, five men had entered the bathhouse without being seen. They lurked in the dark recesses of the bathing rooms, waiting. Zaynu'l-'Ábidín Khán and his attendants stepped inside. He began to disrobe, looking forward to his bath, when several men appeared out of nowhere and rushed at him, shouting, with knives in their raised hands. He felt a knife go into him. His servant shrieked. His other attendants ran in and lunged at four of the attackers, stabbing them. The governor was bleeding profusely but still standing. He heard the last attacker** screaming, "O accursed one . . ." With those words reverberating in his ears, Zaynu'l-'Ábidín Khán crumpled over and fell onto the stone floor. The next day he died.[8]†

* Bahá'u'lláh later forbade the use of such a pool.

** Ustád Qásim.

† Ábádi'í, quoted in Rabbani, *The Bábís of Nayríz: History and Documents, Witnesses to Bábí and Bahá'í history vol. 2* (c. 13, 2), states that there was one assassin who had posed as a construction worker so he was not suspected of being a Bábí. The Bábí was then gunned down.

❁ ❁ ❁

One man who did not mourn Zaynu'l-'Ábidín Khán was Mírzá Na'ím, the cousin and brother-in-law of the new prime minister.* Mírzá Na'ím had worked as paymaster for the troops in the Province of Fárs and had great power there. He had been actively involved in the first Nayríz conflict. His cousin, the new prime minister, separated the governorship of Nayríz from the responsibilities of the governor of the province of Fárs because of how poorly the Bábí situation had been handled and, in 1852, gave it to Mírzá Na'ím.** He instructed Mírzá Na'ím to be considerate to the Bábís, to give them a sense of safety, so he could ensnare them at a later time. Even though Mírzá Na'ím had let Zaynu'l-'Ábidín Khán and his family run the day-to-day affairs of Nayríz, he had not liked that Khán acted independently of the authorities in Shíráz, often making situations worse.[9]

After the Khán's assassination, Mírzá Na'ím immediately sent his uncle, Mírzá Bábá, to Nayríz at the head of a company of soldiers to prevent any further violence. A few weeks later, Mírzá Na'ím himself arrived with a much larger contingent.[10] To show their respect for the

---

* Mírzá Taqí Khán, the prime minister who had been responsible for ordering the execution of the Báb, was dismissed from power by the king in November, 1851, for overstepping his authority. He was then stripped of all his titles and positions. As he faced death at the hands of the sháh's executioner, he is said to have expressed remorse over the killing of the Báb and the persecution of His followers (Mázandarání, *Zuhúr al-Haqq*, v. 4, 26). Mírzá Áqá Khán-i-Núrí became the new prime minister in November, 1851.

** The governor of Fárs was Ṭahmásb Mírzá who was the grandson of Fatḥ 'Alí Sháh and replaced Firuz Mírzá in May, 1853; he would stay in this position until 1858 (Momen, *The Bábí and Bahá'í Religions, 1844–1944, Some Contemporary Western Accounts*, 485).

new governor, 'Alí Sardár and other Bábís came out to greet him; they were looking forward to a time of much greater peace and tranquility.

The wife of the murdered Khán, however, had revenge on her mind. She approached Mírzá Na'ím about avenging her husband's death on her family's behalf; she offered him all of her jewels and any of her other possessions he might want.[11] She suggested inviting the Bábís to come and air their grievances as a way of trapping them.

So Mírzá Na'ím sent out word that any Bábís who had complaints against the government, or who had lost property and goods, should come to him on a designated day to receive compensation. The Bábís were not sure what to make of this offer—such generosity seemed very suspicious after three years of persecution. They decided to accept the invitation as a way of honoring his gesture, but they would not accept any compensation. Rather, they would let divine justice punish those who had killed their friends and relatives.[12]

On the chosen day, 'Alí Sardár, Quṭbá, and others approached the governor's mansion with a sincere wish for reconciliation. The soldiers had been instructed not to allow a single Bábí to escape. The large group of Bábís stepped into the governor's courtyard. As soon as the last man had entered, the soldiers locked the exits and began arresting all of them. A scuffle broke out and several Bábís were beaten. About one hundred and fifty of the more prominent of them were imprisoned, including 'Alí Sardár and Quṭbá.* The Bábí women despaired when they heard the news of this deceit and capture.[13]

Mihr 'Alí Khán, the military commander posted in Nayríz, wrote to the prime minister, praising Mírzá Na'ím's capture of so many of

* Rouhani, *Lam'átul-Anvár* (v. 1, 176), puts this figure at 130.

the Bábís without the shedding of blood. The prime minister, in turn, showed this message to the shah, who was very pleased to hear of this success and asked that the prisoners be sent to him in Ṭihrán.

Mírzá Na'ím left Nayríz for Shíráz on other pressing business now that he felt secure that he had brought the Bábís under control.[14]* He left his uncle, Mírzá Bábá, in charge, with a list of Bábí prisoners to hold as captives until they could be transferred to Ṭihrán. Mírzá Bábá was soon challenged by the villagers of nearby Qaṭrúyih, who were refusing to pay new taxes being imposed on them. Faced with the stubborn refusal of these villagers, and not knowing what to do, he approached 'Alí Sardár for help.

Sardár had originally been responsible for administering Qaṭrúyih under Zaynu'l-'Ábidín Khán and was respected and feared by its inhabitants. Mírzá Bábá offered Sardár some gifts—a decorated robe in honor of his service and the promise of restoring properties to the Bábís. For the sake of the Bábís and good relations with the authorities, Sardár agreed to carry out the task with some of his companions. The villagers, hearing that Sardár was coming for this purpose, retreated, and the taxes were paid. In gratitude, Mírzá Bábá released the other Bábí prisoners and treated them with greater respect.[15]**

In Shíráz at this time, the shah's officials arrived on their mission to escort the Bábís in Nayríz back to the capital. Mírzá Na'ím added some of his own men to the expedition going to pick up the prisoners.

---

* Some sources, such as Rouhani's *Lam'átul-Anvár,* attribute the following events to Mírzá Na'ím. Shafí', *Narrative of Mulla Muhammad Shafí' Nayrízí,* is clear that Na'im had departed from Nayríz and left his uncle in charge.

** Another version (Ma'ani, *Against Incredible Odds,* 229) of these events recounts that after successfully quelling the tax revolt in Qaṭrúyih, Sardár and the other Bábís were invited to Na'ím's mansion for their compensation. Sensing a trap, they declined, saying they had to visit their families first.

Shíráz, the birthplace of the Báb, had high ranking authorities who were sympathetic to the Bábí Faith, and others who wanted to destroy it to protect their priviledged positions. Thus, while prominent clerics in Shíráz were actively denouncing the Bábí Faith and its followers, some important Shírázís* may have informed the Bábís of Nayríz that soldiers were on their way to Nayríz to get them. Mírzá Faḍlu'lláh, the British agent in Shíráz, may also have sided with the Bábís. In his October 1853 report, he blames Mírzá Na'ím for falsely accusing people in Nayríz of being Bábís, for using criminal elements in Nayríz to mistreat the citizens—thereby contributing to social unrest—and for plundering the properties of innocent people.**

---

* The Afnáns, who were the family of the Báb and Shaykh Abú Turáb, the head Ímám of Shíráz (Faizi, *Nayríz Mushkbiz,* 106).

** A section of his report reads: "Meerza Naeem having falsely accused the people of Neireez of being Bábees, obtained an order from the Government to seize one hundred and seventeen of the inhabitants, put them in chains and sent (sic) them to Tihrán to be punished. Thus empowered he proceeded to Neireez with a number of people and there he pillaged and plundered the houses of the people and committed every kind of excess. The Neireezees fled, some to the mountains and others to various places, and a large body of them took sanctuary a few days ago in a Shrine outside the city. Meerza Naeem then bribed the worthless characters who frequent the city to assist his people in seizing the Neireezees and dragging them from their place of sanctuary, and at night he sent his people thus aided to effect this. A dreadful uproar ensued and in the confusion one young lad was seized and conveyed to Meerza Naeem's house, where he was beaten with the bastinado until he died. Hajee Kavam, the Vezeer of Shíráz on learning this, sent people to prevent the seizure of the rest of the Neireezees. In truth Should Meerza Naeem be permitted to remain here he will drive the people into rebellion, for they are quite annoyed at the conduct of the Government in acting in this manner at the instigation of a man like this" (Momen, *The Bábí and Bahá'í Religions, 1844–1944, Some contemporary Western accounts,* 147–48, footnotes).

He was fired when his report on the events in Fárs was read by the prime minister, who was Mírzá Na'ím's relative.[17]

Having been secretly advised of the arrival of the government troops, the Bábís in Nayríz decided to defend themselves by dividing up into three groups. The clerics gathered in a local mullá's home, while the riflemen, led by Sardár, were in another house.

The third group, led by Quṭbá, hid in a vineyard south of town, where many Bábí families owned vineyards and orchards.[18] Typically, these properties were demarcated by walls of various heights. Behind such walls, the Bábís could find cover. Trellises, thickly woven with vines, provided shade from the sun.

Every hour, messages were exchanged between the different groups to keep each other informed.

Mírzá Bábá feared the wrath of the shah if he did not deliver the Bábís. So he tried tricking them by sending a messenger to say their help was needed to quell a rebellion in a neighboring village—as Sardár had done earlier. When the Bábís refused to help, Mírzá Bábá sent another messenger, who was also rebuffed. Becoming desperate, he arrested some local Muslim gunmen from a nearby village who were unaware of these events. He contemplated sending them in place of the Bábís but was cautioned not to do this, as this might get him in trouble.[19]

Mírzá Bábá now found himself in a real quandary. He realized he would have to use force to make good on the promise of sending captured Bábís to Ṭihrán. So he ordered his troops into action.

It was the fall of 1853. The second Nayríz conflict had begun.

11

BATTLE IN THE VINEYARD

Mírzá Bábá's soldiers approached the vineyard nervously, knowing that Bábís, who had a reputation for being fierce, were inside. They surrounded the vineyard, but only a few would venture in. Immediately a group of Bábís counterattacked with swords, sticks, and stones, calling out, "God is great," and chased them out.

The Bábí clerics and fighters, who were gathered in houses in town, heard the tumult, emerged from their locations, and ran out towards the vineyard to help their friends. The defensive force was now much more formidable. The battle intensified.[1]

A lone sword-wielding Bábí dressed in white—a funerary color worn to show one's readiness for death—rushed at cavalrymen near the vineyard. They fled, the lone Bábí in pursuit. The chase went all the way to the governor's mansion, where the soldiers overcame and arrested their pursuer.*

---

* His name was Muḥammad, son of Mírzá Aḥmad (Shafí', *Narrative of Mulla Muhammad Shafi' Nayrízí,* 17).

Hundreds of shots were now being fired in the vineyard. The two hundred or so Bábís fought the soldiers, who surrounded them on all four sides. Throughout the afternoon, the shooting continued, stopping only because of darkness.[2]*

Several Bábís were captured when they were going towards the vineyard, brought back into town and thrown into a dungeon beneath the tower of the former governor's mansion.** Locked in and not knowing what fate awaited them, they thought of ways to escape.

Soon, in the pitch black of the dungeon, the sound of knives could be heard, digging into the wall. The prisoners were attempting to make an opening through which they could crawl. But one prisoner, Kh͟ájih, betrayed the rest by letting the governor know about this escape attempt.[3] He claimed that a mistake had been made, that he wasn't a Bábí.

The authorities told him that he would have to prove that he was not a Bábí by beheading the other prisoners.[4]

The prisoners were brought out to the entrance of the Nazar-Biykí Mosque, in front of which Vaḥíd's body had been abandoned three

* As mentioned in an earlier footnote, Shafí', *Narrative of Mulla Muhammad Shafi' Nayrízí* (17), states that the Bábís were fighting from behind the wall of an aqueduct, but there were no aqueducts in Persia. So if the wall had to be connected to a structure having to do with water, it would have to be the wall of a mill. There were several mills in the area south of Nayríz. The biggest were the Zardos͟ht mill, due south, and the Kh͟obar mill, southeast of town near Fort Kh͟ájih. The other possibility is that they were fighting behind the wall of the vineyard, and the water ran through irrigation canals into the vineyard, which is the more likely scenario because these walls would have been higher than those at the mill.

** This group of prisoners by the end of the day consisted of Mullá Muḥammad-'Alí Ghabez; Muḥammad, the son of Mírzá Aḥmad; Maḥmúd, the son of Ḥaydar-Bayk; 'Abdu'lláh, the son of 'Askar S͟habán; Aḥmad, the son of Mas͟hhadí Ismá'íl; 'Alí Murad-i-Sírjáni; Riḍá, from the Qanqárí region of Bávanát; and the traitor, Kh͟ájih Ghafar (Shafí', *Narrative of Mulla Muhammad Shafi' Nayrízí*, 17; Ahdieh, *Nayrízi-Shurangiz*, 115).

years earlier. Once there, a guard pulled one of the prisoners out of the group and shot him to begin the executions. Kh͟ájih, the betrayer, was then given a sword. One by one, the other prisoners were forced to kneel. Kh͟ájih swung the sword down onto each innocent neck. In a few minutes, he stood holding the bloody sword in front of the lifeless bodies of his former companions, their severed heads strewn about in the dirt.

Kh͟ájih had shown his true nature. His father, profoundly ashamed of his son's treachery, later disowned him in front of others by referring to him as a "bastard."[5]

Once the soldiers surrounding the vineyard had gone back to camp for the night, the Bábís decided they needed a safer location. Under cover of darkness, they moved to the orchards by the spring at Bid Bukhun, in the foothills several kilometers south of town.[6] Most of the fruit trees there had been planted by Vaḥíd's own hands. Two days passed, during which more Bábí men came out from Nayríz. Now they numbered around four hundred.

The Bábís knew they would eventually face martyrdom. Some of them, lacking the wise leadership of Vaḥíd, wanted to avenge the deaths of their friends and family members and punish the Nayrízís who had caused them so much suffering. This was the season for tending the fruit trees out on the slopes, so local Nayrízís were out working. Coming through the orchards, Bábís surprised and attacked one such Nayrízí as he tended his trees . . . and then another . . .

❁ ❁ ❁

A call for reinforcements went to Sh͟íráz, while villagers summoned to join the fight against the Bábís grabbed their rifles and anything that could be used as a weapon.[7]

Through the dark streets of the Chinár-Súkhtih quarter, hundreds of Bábí women in their black chádurs carried what they could and held their children's hands as they followed their men out to the mountain south of town.* Hearing of their plight, a young Bábí who was away visiting the town of Harat came rushing back.** Mullá Ḥasan Lab-Shikarí stayed in Nayríz to continue supporting the Bábís who remained behind. Because of his marriage to the governor's sister, he would be safe for the time being.†

In Shíráz, the British agent wrote in his report:

> ". . . the people (Bábís) returned and having withdrawn their families from the place, again fled to the mountains where they have conveyed provisions, enough to maintain them for three to four months. Meerza Naeem has demanded and received from the new Governor, who knows nothing of the matter, a force amounting to four hundred soldiers, two guns with artillerymen and ammunition, and he has started for the purpose of seizing these poor people and sending them to the Capital. The Governor has also given him orders to receive aid from the different Districts in the vicinity. But the Neireez people have fixed upon a very strong place in the mountains for their quarters and there is only

---

* Shafí' numbers the women and children at 600 arriving in the mountains on the sixth day. Mázandarání, *Zuhúr al-Haqq* (v. 4, 36), and Nayrízí (quoted in Rabbani, *The Bábís of Nayríz: History and Documents*, c. 12, 5) also give this number though in the month of peace which follows the first battles at Darb-i-Shikáft.

** Mullá Muḥammad Taqí, a son of Mulláh 'Abdu'l Ḥusayn, had gone to Harát, a town near Yazd, to visit Áqá Siyyid Ja'far Yazdí (Shafí', *Narrative of Mulla Muhammad Shafí' Nayrízí*, 19).

† From a private conversation with his great-granddaughter, Mrs. Nura (Shahíd-púr) Jamer in May 2010 CE / 166 BE.

one road to it, so it is believed that the troops will not be able to seize them . . ."[8]

Cannon, soldiers, cavalry, and Khamseh tribesmen came over the road from Shíráz that wound through the stark brown mountains. Mírzá Na'ím led the large force; he had been given the authority to conscript many more men from the region's villages and towns.[9]

When the opponents drew nearer to each other, skirmishes began. For protection, the Bábís moved further up the mountain to an area called Darb-i-Shikáft, where there was a large shallow cave and an open area with orchards and makeshift dwellings of stones and branches made by farmers.[10] Simple defenses were improvised with boulders put across the path coming up the mountain. From that area, there was also a pass to the highest ridge of the mountain, by which they could escape to a higher altitude if necessary.

Thousands of men appeared from every direction to join the attack on the Bábís.

A thousand gunmen came from Iṣṭahbánát in the east, and another thousand came from Íraj in the south. Village chiefs and their men arrived from the Dúr-i-Qalat direction, and a thousand more gathered by the sheriff of Nayríz joined the attack. Mírzá Na'ím's troops from Shíráz camped near Darb-i-Shikáft.

The Bábís were surrounded on all four sides.[11]

12

THE BLOODY MOUNTAIN: DARB-I-SHIKÁFT AND BÁLÁ-TARAM

No sound could be heard but the wind and the cry of a bird when the crackle of a rifle shot suddenly cut the silence and set off a barrage of gunfire. The Iṣṭahbátáni gunmen were attacking, having been encouraged by their clerics who promised them salvation for wiping out these infidels. Four mullás from their ranks, though, went over to the Bábí side, carrying weapons and ammunition.* The attackers advanced quickly, capturing one makeshift defense after another until the Bábís had only a few positions left to defend. The two groups faced each other at close range.**

* The four mullás were Mullá Faḍlu'lláh, the son of Mullá Abu'l-Qásim, the judge of Iṣṭahbánát; Mullá Muḥammad 'Alí, the son of Mullá Muḥammad-Báqir; Karbalá'í Safar; and Muḥammad-Ismá'íl (Shafí', *Narrative of Mulla Muhammad Shafi' Nayrízí*, 19).

** This choice description is taken directly from Nicolas, *Seyyed Ali Mohammed dit le Bab* (415).

From his hiding place behind a boulder, an Iṣṭahbátáni sharpshooter lowered his rifle, squinted to focus on one of the Bábís, and pulled the trigger. The rifle spit the bullet through the air, piercing the body of the Bábí, who fell over. The sharpshooter focused and fired, then fired again. Three Bábís collapsed on the mountain slope; again he fired, and then one more time. Two more Bábís lay dying. He eased the trigger back again, but this time, it only clicked. Now, a Bábí was rushing over at him, and he could do nothing. The Bábí brought his sword down with such force that his head was cleft in two.[1]

As the fighting intensified, 'Alí Sardár came back to his fortification exhausted and asked for some food. He was given some dried bread and a few walnuts. A man brought him a water pipe to smoke while he tried to regain a little strength. Before 'Alí Sardár could take a hold of it, the water pipe fell over. A bullet had struck the man serving him. Sardár lept up, grabbed his sword, and ran out. Other Bábís, wielding their swords, immediately followed in his footsteps. Frightened by the onslaught, the hapless soldiers fell back, then ran down the mountain, pursued by Sardár and his companions. Twenty-one soldiers were captured, while the rest fled all the way to the village of Íraj. The prisoners were taken to the cliff at the top of the mountain and thrown off.[2]

In the lower part of the mountain, Mírzá Na'ím, unaware of what was happening above, prepared a message to be sent to all those under his command, telling them to take positions for an assault on the Bábís from each direction. Once he finished writing out the details, he rolled up the paper and handed it to a messenger, who left the tent and went up the mountain to find the troops.* Instead, the Bábís took him by

* Nicolas, *Seyyed Ali Mohammed dit le Bab,* 416. The messenger's name was Mas͟hhadí Djafir.

surprise. They found the note and executed him on the spot.* Now with knowledge of Mírzá Na'ím's plans, the Bábís prepared to defend themselves.

Several hundred attackers appeared near the Bábí positions. As they looked out at the Bábí encampments, some of them saw their own wives on the opposing side and wondered why they were there. They shouted:

"Why have you brought our wives to this mountain?"

But these women had understood the new teachings and were willing to die for them. They had relinquished the bonds of marriage to the husbands who had rejected the Message. They would now live by the Báb's holy laws.

Some Bábís responded: "They are no longer your wives, as you and they are no longer permitted to one another."

"How is it that you have recognized the Lord, and we have failed?"[3]

"You have failed in your recognition the same way that Salman and Abú-Dhar recognized the Prophet of Islám while the Arabs and Jews with all their divines remained deprived."[4]

While this conversation was shouted back and forth, Sardár was instructing a group of riflemen to encircle their attackers, so the Bábís

---

* Nicolas, *Seyyed Ali Mohammed dit le Bab,* 416. Rabbani, *The Bábís of Nayríz: History and Documents, Witnesses to Bábí and Bahá'í history vol. 2,* c. 11, 16. The Ahdieh translation does not say that the messenger was killed. In Mázandarání, *Zuhúr al-Haqq* (v. 4, 34), the messenger is killed, and a message is written in blood on his body, which is sent back to Mírzá Na'ím's camp. The authors think the scenario described in the text is the most likely given the situation—the need to preserve the secrecy of finding the note and the danger that would have been brought on by doing such an act as writing a message in blood for which there is no other example in Bábí behavior.

could open fire on them from several directions. Once he had finished, a young man led the riflemen out without being seen. Each man took his place with the attackers clearly in view. At a given moment, the Bábís opened fire, startling and frightening their attackers, who dropped their arms and provisions and ran to save themselves.

The Bábís picked up what the attackers had left behind—bread, clothing, lead, gunpowder, rifles, and swords. Exhausted, they stumbled back to their defenses. They had snatched victory from a day begun with defeat.[5]

The sun dropped low in the sky. A sentinel who had been watching from the mountain pass came running towards the Bábí defenses. He reported that Mírzá Na'ím was at the Darb-i-Shikáft pass, which led to where the Bábís were camped. From the note that had been intercepted, they knew the plan had been to attack the Bábís from four directions. They discussed their options. Some wanted to wait until the sun was up and launch an attack, but Sardár encouraged them to do it that very night and rout the enemy. Then they would rest.[6]

Sardár organized two groups of nineteen men each; he would lead one, and Quṭbá would lead the other. One group would position itself over the Darb-i-Shikáft pass, and the other group would go to the Asbergun heights and wait for the soldiers to fall asleep. They made preparations for the night attack.

The sun had now completely disappeared, and the moonlight made deep shadows on the mountain side. Dark figures moved down between the rocks and crags like panthers. One, though, had weak eyesight. As he brought his foot down, he dislodged several rocks that tumbled down.[7] The soldiers jumped up and reached for their weapons. The Bábís immediately began their assault.

"God is great" echoed in the darkened canyons as the Bábís jumped out from their hiding places at the soldiers who panicked and ran about, disoriented. The Bábís put the soldiers' temporary dwellings to the torch. Flames leaped up and lit a scene of men trying to overcome each other in a confusion of shouting, grunting, swords clashing, and guns firing.* The Bábí women who had come out to the mountains, stood on rock outcrops watching, throwing stones and ululating encouragement. The soldiers—carrying Mírzá Na'ím—turned and ran in a jumble through the pass, their backs lit by the orange firelight.[8]

A large black cannon sat abandoned in the midst of the debris of the struggle. The Bábís took off its wheels and attached ropes to it. They dragged it up the slope. When they reached a cliff, men went to the top and together hoisted it up. The great black cannon was dragged up one end at a time, knocking on the rock face, the ropes creaking and whining in the night wind.[9]

❋ ❋ ❋

As the mid-November winter cold began to seep into his office, Mírzá Faḍlu'lláh, the British agent in Shíráz, sat down with some hot tea and wrote his report:

> "I wrote you last month that Meerza Naseem had proceeded with Sirbaz [i.e. soldiers] and Guns, and a body of villagers to exterminate the Neereezees. On reaching the foot of the mountains, where the enemy lay, Meerza Naeem incited and urged the Sirbaz, villagers, and artillery to ascend the single pass that leads

* According to Nayrízí, *"The Account of Siyyid Ibrahim concerning Nayriz"* (4), the burning of the yurts happened in a previous battle, but the Shafí' manuscript is closer in time to the events described here, so the authors use his version.

into the heart of the mountain, (along which the Neereezees had erected a few towers, and in each one planted a number of men armed with firelocks), and having reached the interior, to cut all the people to pieces. Yielding to the pressing importunities of Meerza Naeem, the army ascended, and, as luck would have it, they reached the first tower about Sunset—the garrison (located therein) were perfectly quiet—not a Sound was heard—so still did they remain that one would have thought the tower deserted and empty: —the troops gaining confidence pressed onwards to number two tower, where they found the same stillness prevailing, and having passed them all they entered the mountain itself. (No sooner had they done so than) the Neereezees, who were in the van of the Troops, backed up by those who were in the rear of the Towers, fell upon and commenced slaughtering the men of the unfortunate and ill-starred army: —there being no mode of escape, and the disaster having come upon them thro' the ill-management of their commander, the Neereez women clambered up the rocks, and, beating their mouths with their hands, vented forth cries of exultation. Night was succeeded by darkness—the troops were scattered over the mountains, and one of their guns fell into the hands of the Enemy [i.e. the Bábís].

Being desirous that so severe a calamity should be kept secret, a story was put in circulation that two of the Gulpaeeganee Sirbaz had been killed in the fray, and some few had gone astray in the mountains, who would shortly return.

From the villagers, who accompanied the forces, however, it became known that many were killed, that the Neereezees had carried off the horses, and everything pertaining to the army: in short that Meerza Naeem and his army had been shamefully discomfited. The new Ruler proposes sending a fresh commander with fresh troops. Report has it that Mírzá Naeem had been in two or three engagements prior to this one, and in one and all was he defeated."[10]

Mírzá Na'ím had failed completely to dislodge the Bábís from the mountains south of Nayríz. The troops had dispersed, but 'Alí Sardár knew they would be back. So he looked towards the Bálá-Taram heights of the mountain from where they would be better able to defend themselves.

Bálá-Taram was at the top of the mountain but could be reached by crossing the mountain on a foot path from Darb-i-Shikáft. Several imposing cliffs stood there, and there was also a spring for water. From these heights, one could survey the mountain and the valley below.

The Bábís set about adding to their defenses by building nineteen solid fortifications from the Darb-i-Shikáft pass all the way up to the Bálá-Taram heights. Many men were moved into the upper area of the mountain.* Eighteen Bábís defended each fortification—the nineteenth was the Báb, Whom they believed to be with them in spirit as they gave their lives for Him. Above each fortification, a red flag fluttered. Seven men went between the different locations to coordinate their actions. Sardár was the overall commander because he

* Shafí', *Narrative of Mulla Muhammad Shafi' Nayrízí* (19), states that there were forty fortifications which had been built whereas Nayrízí, *"The Account of Siyyid Ibrahim concerning Nayriz* (4), the other eyewitness, remembers the number of fortifications being to the "number of Vaḥíd," meaning nineteen, a number special to Bábí theology. Local lore and the remains of the fortifications lean towards nineteen being the correct number. The number forty may be accounted for because of the numerous makeshift dwellings and smaller defenses that were built up when they first entered the mountain area. The government newspaper issue #148 put the number at 200–300 (Faizi, *Nayríz Mushkbiz,* 118).

knew a lot about warfare, and Quṭbá, highly respected by the Bábís, was his second in command.* A chronicle and records were being kept by Mullá 'Alí-Naqí, the son of Mullá 'Abdu'l Ḥusayn, so that what happened in these mountains would be known and remembered.[11]

The first fortification in the line of defense, which the Bábís named "the mother of Samí," was guarded by women who acted as lookouts. The group, led by a darvish from Mashhad, defended the Darb-i-Shikáft pass. Fortifications were also assigned to Quṭbá, Mírzá Ismá'íl, Háj Qásim, and Mullá Sháh 'Alí.[12]

'Alí Sardár's fortifications commanded the heights of the Bálá-Taram ridge.

From there, he could see the grey smoke of many small fires over which their devoted women—mothers and daughters, providers and caretakers—prepared food. Their black forms moved about uncomplainingly in the early winter cold.

With so many young women and men, marriages were organized in the "Samí" fortification uniting the young people in the Báb's Covenant.[13] A few verses were read in the presence of Shaykh 'Abdu'l 'Alí, and the simple ceremonies concluded with the chanting of verses from the new Revelation.

To announce a gathering, a cannon would be fired. Shaykh 'Abdu'l 'Alí and Mullá 'Abdu'l Ḥusayn tried to educate the Bábís in their Faith. They taught them from the holy writings and encouraged patience and forebearance in the suffering to come.[14]

---

* The seven courageous men were Báqir, the son of Mír Aḥmad; Karbalá'í 'Askar Bíraq-Dár, the flag-bearer; Ḥájí, the son of Aṣghar; 'Alí, the son of Aḥmad, known as Garmsiry; Ḥusayn, the son of Mashhadí Ismá'íl; Ḥusayn, the son of Hádí Khayrí; and Ḥasan, the son of Mírzá (Shafí', *Narrative of Mulla Muhammad Shafi' Nayrízí*, 19).

A number of the Bábís, though, decided to take advantage of the retreat of the troops and exact revenge from other Nayrízís. The pain and anger at the shocking desecration of the corpse of Vaḥíd, the pillaging of their homes, and the killing of many of their relatives after the fall of Fort Khájih smouldered in their hearts. They had grown up in a Shí'a culture that permitted the use of violence in certain religious matters, and they were only beginning to understand this new Revelation, which forbade it. They did not have Vaḥíd's presence to moderate their desire for revenge. So, almost one hundred Bábís descended the mountain and made their way by night into the Sádát section of the bazaar, where the mullás and their families lived.

Bábís had come to town before to get provisions, but in much smaller numbers. This had always resulted in some conflict, but this time the conflict would be much worse because these men were motivated by revenge. They searched the neighborhood for the women who had jeered and thrown stones at Vaḥíd's body, and killed thirty-five of them.* The Bábís caught Mírzá Ḥusayn Rawḍih-Khán and Ḥájí Siyyid 'Abid, who had been so treacherous towards Vaḥíd, and executed both of them. They set upon a barracks of soldiers. In the fighting, two Bábís were killed. Fear spread throughout the neighborhood, and many residents fled in the direction of Kirmán.** The large group of Bábís headed back to the mountains, satisfied that some measure of justice had been extracted for Vaḥíd and their own torment and loss.[15]

---

* Mázandarání gives the number of Bábís as ninety-five. Nicolas puts it at one hundred.

** Nicolas, *Seyyed Ali Mohammed dit le Bab* (417), states the direction as the city of Zanján.

Mírzá Na'ím knew he needed more help. His reputation was suffering from his inability to bring these Bábís under control. This time, he would have to pay for the help.[16] Mírzá Faḍlu'lláh wrote:

> "Neereez has to pay of Revenue 5,500 Tomans: —the Governors and Revenue Collectors were wont in former days to levy 10,000 Tomans at the very least. But so completely had Mírzá Naeem ruined the Country, and that too out of pure selfish motives, that expectation of payment of Revenue hereafter must be out of the question altogether. Hosts of the inhabitants have been slain and many yet will follow . . .
>
> On the 15th of Mohurrun (18th of Oct., 1853) 600 of the Kashkaee Sirbaz [i.e. soldiers], 200 Shíráz Sirbaz and Two Guns, with complement of Gunners and ammunition, the whole under command of Luṭf Alee Khán Sirteep, were in orders to proceed to the assistance of Meerza Naeem in Neereez."[17]

13

DEATH OF THE COMMANDER

Mírzá Na'ím was desperate and sent another plea to Shíráz for troops and with it, a substantial contribution—over $250,000 in today's money.[1]

The Prince in Shíráz received the request and understood its urgency; after all, the conflict was happening in his province. The large sum of money greatly increased his willingness to help. So he chose one of his best army generals for the task: Luṭf 'Alí Khán, son and successor of the leader of the large Qashqá'í tribe.[2]

On October 18th, 1853, Luṭf 'Alí Khán received orders to march on Nayríz with six-hundred soldiers and two cannon. In addition, the authorities sent out an order of general conscription to villages and towns throughout the region, to raise a much larger group of men than before. Men came on horseback and on foot from Gulpáyigán and Sarvistán, Iṣṭahbánát and Íraj, Panj-Ma'ádan and Qaṭrúyih, Bashnih and Dih-Cháh, Mushkán and Ghúry, Rastáq and Maharlú, and outlying regions such as Dahmurid, Khájíh Jamáli, Chár-Ráhy,

Qárání, Lashtí, and tribes such as the Bahárlú, and Aynálú. They were commanded by those who had been defeated in the first mountain battles.* By late October, twelve thousand men were assembled, milling around in the foothills, waiting for a decisive assault.[3]**

Mírzá Na'ím regained his courage when he saw the reinforcements. He and some other important Nayrízís brought Golpáyigání soldiers and sharpshooters within sight of one of the major Bábí fortifications. Once they had set up camp, the soldiers began blowing bugles and thumping drums to intimidate their opponents, and firing cannon and rifles to let them know they were well-armed and ready for a serious fight.

As the days went by, the Bábís remained calm in the knowledge of their coming martyrdom and did not respond to the provocations. Mírzá Na'ím became bolder and moved his men to a field near the Darb-i-<u>Sh</u>ikáft passage, close to the main Bábí fortification, and built a defense there.

Nearby, Bábís collected fresh water from the Yaqútí spring. Several paths crossed at this spring—one led up the mountain to Darb-i-<u>Sh</u>ikáft and then on to Bálá-Taram, another went around the mountain to the other side and then up to Bálá-Taram, and another led down to the Bid Bukhun area.[4]

Mírzá Na'ím ordered his best soldiers to surround the spring and prevent the Bábís from reaching it. Sardár and his companions watched this movement from behind their barrier. When they saw that the way to the spring had been cut off, they knew they had to act. He gathered fourteen of his bravest men, including Karbalá'í 'Askar, the flag bearer,

---

* The commanders were Aḥmad Khán, <u>Kh</u>án Mírzá, and Ma'súm <u>Kh</u>án Qúrt.

** Rouhani, *Lam'átul-Anvár* (v. 1, 184), places the number at 10,000.

and those who had been in charge of communicating between Bábí groups. They picked up their weapons, came out of the safety of their fortification and, crying out "God is great," descended on those guarding the spring.

Seeing the Bábís charging them, a soldier lowered his rifle, aimed it at the flag bearer, and fired. The bullet tore through Karbalá'í 'Askar's right hand, but he managed to plant it in the ground. With his left hand, he swung his sword at the soldiers. Then another Bábí, Mírzá Zaynu'l-'Ábidín, ran towards them, picked up the flag in one hand as he passed, and dove into the fight. The soldiers lay in disarray, wounded or dead on the ground.[5]

From the direction of the village of Íraj south of Nayríz, a large contingent of Bahárlu sharpshooters—known as the best in the whole kingdom—made their way up the mountain. They encircled the two fortifications commanded by Ḥájí Qásim and Quṭbá. When they were securely in place, they fired a barrage of bullets and then rushed at the defenses, killing Bábís and capturing their positions.[6]

The numerous, well-armed soldiers were advancing steadily up the mountain.

❁ ❁ ❁

With thousands of soldiers coming up the mountain, Sardár knew that their day of martyrdom was now close. He sent a message to the Bábí leaders in the other fortifications to come to him.[7]

Once they were all gathered, he spoke to them of the days ahead. Their supplies were running out, he said, and they could not hold out much longer against so many soldiers. If anyone wanted to leave, now was the time. Unanimously, the Bábís proclaimed their desire to fight with him to the death.

Sardár praised them for their courage and fortitude. Then he lifted his hand and showed them the ring on his finger. If he were decapitated, he told them, they would recognize his body from this ring; if the hand or finger was cut off, they could identify him that way. He asked that his body be brought back and buried near this fortification.

The women and children, though, might survive and return to their lives, and they would need funds. So money and jewelry were collected and placed in a copper pot, which was then buried in the ground. The survivors could come back to this spot and dig up this aid from those who had given their lives.[8]

Meanwhile, the fighting continued on the mountain slope. The Bahárlú sharpshooters positioned themselves out of sight behind trees and large boulders from which they could shoot the Bábís who tried to make an outing.[9] From these positions, they fired at will. Skirmishes peppered the vast mountainside.

The following day,* the soldiers paraded around on their horses and sang songs mocking the Bábís to goad them into coming out of their defenses into direct confrontation.** 'Alí Sardár said good-bye to the Bábís in his fortification, mounted his horse, gave it a kick, and was gone. Several other Bábís followed him out.† They approached the

---

* In Shafí', *Narrative of Mulla Muhammad Shafi' Nayrízí,* it seems to be the same day. In Nicolas, *Seyyed Ali Mohammed dit le Bab* (418), it is described as "one day."

** Nicolas, *Seyyed Ali Mohammed dit le Bab,* writes that they were having horse races. Shafí', *Narrative of Mulla Muhammad Shafi' Nayrízí* (22), describes it as singing humiliating songs and trying to provoke them.

† According to Shafí', *Narrative of Mulla Muhammad Shafi' Nayrízí* (22), they were Mírzá Muḥammad, the son of Á<u>kh</u>únd Mullá Musá, and Áqá Siyyid 'Alí, the son of Mírzá 'Abdu'l-Ḥusayn.

cavalrymen without being seen and stopped at a spot where they were not expected. When the cavalrymen were near, the Bábís charged. Swords flashed like sparks in the air.[10]

From their hiding place, the Bahárlú sharpshooters trained their rifles on Sardár and the Bábís and opened fire. Sardár was hit in the leg. As he bled, he aimed his rifle. It malfunctioned. He threw it down, drew out his pistol and pulled the trigger. It only clicked. Again he was hit. He grabbed his sword handle and pulled, but it was stuck in its scabbard. Hit again by the sharpshooters' bullets, he slumped over, wrist relaxed, fingers uncurled, reins slipping out. He fell from his horse, fatally wounded, his body resting close to those of his companions.[11]

From an outlook higher up the mountain, a Bábí watched this scene unfold. He recognized Sardár, and, overcome with grief, jumped out from his observation post and ran down the mountainside. He wept as he threw himself on the corpse of his beloved leader. But the soldiers took no pity and shot him. His lifeless body rolled over onto the ground; he joined his commander in the next life. Three years earlier, it had been this young Bábí's own brother who had died by the side of Vaḥíd outside of Fort Kh̲ájih.[12]

One of Sardár's companions, Siyyid 'Alí, who lay on the ground bleeding from the cut in his throat was unconscious but, miraculously, still alive. He heard a voice tell him to go let the Bábís know of Sardár's death, and that his own martyrdom would come months later when he reached Ṭihrán.

Up in the fortifications, the Bábís knew nothing of Sardár's death. They thought he had gone after the soldiers and victoriously routed them, as he had so many times before. But this time he was not returning.

One of the Bahárlú leaders stepped out from his hiding place and walked over to the scene of the carnage.* When he recognized the face, he thought of the reward he might get, unsheathed his sword and brought it down with full force onto the corpse's neck. He grabbed the severed head by its hair and ran towards Mírzá Na'ím's camp. Arriving at the camp, he came in front of Mírzá Na'ím and raised the severed head. The Nayrízí guides who were accompanying the army confirmed that this was indeed Sardár's head. Extremely relieved to see his much-feared opponent dead, Mírzá Na'ím covered the Bahárlú chieftain with a robe of honor—an overcoat made of fine fabrics—and gave him a large number of coins.[13] Now Mírzá Na'ím could sleep more easily, and the Bahárlú chieftain walked away a wealthier man.**

As night came, the Bábís up in Sardár's fortification were greatly concerned. Suddenly, they saw Siyyid 'Alí—who had ridden out with Sardár earlier that day—stumbling and lurching toward them through the darkness. They ran to help him, and as they got closer, they saw the blood on his clothing from his many wounds. Barely able to speak, he told them of being shot at and pelted with stones. Then he uttered

* Khán Mírzá Bahárlú was the Bahárlú chieftain who is purported by some to have shot 'Alí Sardár and cut his head off (Shafí', *Narrative of Mulla Muhammad Shafi' Nayrízí,* 23; Nicolas, *Seyyed Ali Mohammed dit le Bab,* 419).

** This rendition of the cutting off of Sardár's head and its identification is a combination of two versions: the Shafí' manuscript and Nicolas. One story is that all the heads were cut off and recognized later that day by the Nayríz guides who travelled with the army. The other is that the Bahárlú chieftain shot Sardár and, knowing the importance of the person he had killed, cut off the head and went to try to get a reward. This combination seems the most plausible and explains why one of the three companions was not beheaded and was able to get up later and go back up to the fortification. This companion did survive the conflict and was martyred later in Tihrán. We know this was how he died, so any account of Sardár's death has to account for this companion's survival.

words which they couldn't bear to hear, that Sardár had been killed, or, as Ḥájí Muḥammad Nayrízí later wrote, the "bird of Sardár's spirit has been released from the prison of self."[14]

❋ ❋ ❋

The Bábís received a message from the commanders of the troops near their fortifications stating that their goal had been to kill Sardár, and, now that he was dead and the Bábís did not have the strength to fight the government's forces, it would be better for the Bábís to take their families and leave. The message further noted that every day an additional thousand reinforcements were arriving, while the number of Bábís was dwindling, and the weather was turning bitter cold. They had no chance, so why not give up?[15]

Quṭbá and the other Bábí leaders knew that the time of their martyrdom had come. But they would not give in just to save their own lives. They were fighting for a higher Cause the only way they knew how. No, they would not simply capitulate. They responded by asserting that this whole conflict had been unnecessary, and then asked the commanders to back their soldiers away from the immediate area, so that they could retrieve the bodies of their fallen companions and give them a proper burial.[16]

Their reply was sent. After a while, the Bábís saw soldiers picking up their weapons and materials and moving to other locations further down the mountain. Once the immediate area was clear, Bábís walked out to the places where skirmishes had been fought and lovingly lifted up the bodies of their brethren. Some bodies had clothes caked in dried blood; other bodies were naked, the clothes being taken by the attackers. Many had been beheaded. The bodies were carefully laid in one common grave.

The women wailed at the site of the bodies. The colors of the flags on the fortifications were changed from red and green to black, the color of mourning.[17]

Quṭbá decided to send the women and children to the Asbergun orchards, further down the mountain, and the men would relocate themselves to the rock defenses right above those orchards.

Asbergun, where rock was quarried, was up the path from Darb-i-Shikáft. From there, two paths led back to Nayríz—one went up to Bálá-Taram and then down around the mountain the long way, while the other went down the steep, and much more direct, Bísámán path. It took about an hour by donkey from Bálá-Taram to Asbergun.[18]

Women and children were gathered from the different fortifications and temporary dwellings on the mountain and led down the path to the Asbergun orchards. Then the men moved with their weapons, donkeys, and few possessions, and took their places in the defenses above.[19]

A message was sent back to the military commanders: "It is true that you killed our Sardár, kindly suggested that we should run away, and you moved back. For this we thank you. But you do not seem to understand that we have been waiting for four years for martyrdom and have accepted the captivity of our families. The sooner we are martyred the greater an achievement. You are assigned to kill us; do not disobey your orders. If you do not kill us, someone else will. Bring back your troops. If you desire to treat us kindly, be compassionate toward our families after our death."[20]

The temperature was dropping into winter depths. At night, the stone made for a bitterly cold shelter. Only some rice, figs, and donkeys remained for food. The women ate a few figs a day and prepared the rice for their men who would need energy for the fight. A donkey had to be sacrificed each day for meat.[21]

There was a nearby source of water but its few drops were not nearly enough to slake the thirst of the hundreds of Bábís. So a group of brave women took their pots and walked towards the Yaqútí springs—about a forty minute walk north down the mountain. There were soldiers guarding it again. The women approached the spring. They had only their pots with them, though some carried the standard, showing their willingness to fight. The guards showed no mercy. Once the women were near, the soldiers shot at them. One woman was hit, and the soldiers took her captive while the others fled. A few days later this woman died.

The frayed clothing on the Bábís could not protect them against the cold. Food ran out, water was scarce, even the donkeys began dying.[22] The ammunition was almost gone.

Luṭf 'Alí Khán moved in his cannon, cavalry, and infantry, including sharpshooters from Iṣṭahbánát and Cháhr-Bulúk, and built fortifications facing those of the Bábís. The Bahárlú gunmen soon joined the attacking force as well.[23]

One day, the cannon and guns were let loose on the defenses. The cannonballs pounded the rocks, splintering them and sending stone chunks in all directions. The Bábís did not respond, so as to conserve what little ammunition they had. The soldiers beat their drums and blew their bugles.

The next day, the cannon and rifles opened up again, firing repeatedly at the defenses, cannonballs cracking the rock face. Bábís heard the constant drumming and bugling of the soldiers, but none gave up.

The following day, the cannons again blasted the Bábí fortifications, and the sharpshooters tried to find targets. But still, there was no surrender.

More soldiers were arriving.

Quṭbá exhorted the Bábís to exert themselves while they could and rejoice in the knowledge of their coming martyrdom.

The rock shrapnel injured several Bábís. Without nutrition of any kind, they were weakening.

Luṭf 'Alí Khán realized that firing weapons and making loud sounds would not drive them out. He decided to try the same deception that had been used with Vaḥíd. A message was sent to the Bábís: "If your claims are the truth, we will accept it. Come under the banner of the king, and we will mediate for your safety. We are sure that the king will forgive you."[24]

One of the most learned and spiritual of the Bábís volunteered to go to the army camp and explain the Faith, though the Bábís knew this was just a ploy. He left the Bábí stronghold and walked to Luṭf 'Alí Khán's camp. Once there, the commanders of the army listened to him tell them about the the Báb's claims and teachings. They seemed to listen respectfully, and when he was finished speaking, they were all in agreement that it was time for peace. His duty discharged, he rose and left.

Once the Bábís heard the news of peace, they watched to see what the soldiers would do. Some time went by, but there were no signs of the army breaking camp. On the other side, Luṭf 'Alí Khán and his commanders watched for any movement among the Bábís, thinking they would come out of their defenses after the declaration of peace and the commanders could give the order to massacre them. But no Bábís came out.

Instead, the Bábís called out: "We are not seeking peace. The only thing we claim is that the Truth has appeared. If you want to continue to fight, we are ready. If you do not wish to fight, then leave this spot."[25]

This was followed by a bugle rousing the troops into battle. A thousand soldiers and sharpshooters from Iṣṭahbánát and other places took up positions behind trees and boulders and readied their rifles for the kill. Other soldiers began marching towards the Bábí position. The din of bugles and drums swirled in the air, encouraging them. They lowered their rifles.

The Bábís appeared. The soldiers kept moving. Both sides were closing in on one another. But the views were obstructed by the many trees in that immediate area. A slow drizzle began to fall and a thick fog rolled in. Only the sound of a man's voice could identify him now. The Bábís took out their swords and ran forward shouting. The soldiers, who had marched a few hundred feet from their camp, began to retreat. Though barely able to see, the Bábís kept charging.

Suddenly, a firestorm of bullets from the soldiers waiting in ambush cut through the humid fog. The Bábís turned around and struggled to get back to the safety of their fortification. Bullets were coming at them from all directions. They fought their way through fog and the frightening confusion of enemies hidden behind trees firing at them, one Bábí struck down, then another, and another until some reached the safety of their defenses.

They looked around, counted the missing and collapsed from exhaustion. Fifty had not made it back. After two hours, a group of Bábís set out to find the bodies of their fallen companions so the wild animals of the mountains would not feed on them. Quietly they moved among the trees in the damp and cold. One body after another was lifted up by the still living, to be carried back for burial. They struggled to carry their fallen brethren through the forest and up the rocky incline without being detected.

The last night of their earthly lives began for most of the Bábí men. There was great hunger but little food. If they lit fires, the sharpshooters' bullets would find them. So they shivered in the cold dark air. The mountain echoed with the soldiers' songs about what was going to happen to the Bábí women after the coming defeat. The injured lay in pain, and whenever one regained consciousness, he would cry out for warm water. But none could be made, and he would lapse back into unconsciousness. Whatever blankets could be found were spread over their bodies like mercy. Quṭbá consoled them with words about the coming glory of their martyrdoms. Two or three Bábís, though, greatly fearing what was to come, snuck away into the mountains.

Dawn came, accompanied by the sounds of beating drums and shrieking bugles. Soldiers were mobilizing for an assault. The Bábís pulled themselves up. They came out exhausted but resigned to facing battle one more time. Thousands of soldiers opened fire on them, and they began falling. One group of Bábís summoned all their remaining strength and tied themselves to one another for a final charge led by Mullá 'Alí Naqí. As they ran into the soldiers' fire, a bullet went through Naqí's skull; soon the others were struck down also. In the rear of the fighting, another group of fifteen or sixteen Bábís, seeing that the women were being rounded up, attacked, but soldiers surrounded them and gunned them down.

Soon the Bábí men were all dead or captured. The injured were beheaded. The Bábís who had snuck away the night before were either found by soldiers and killed, or got lost in the cold mountain night and perished.[26]

14

SACRIFICE OF THE FAITHFUL

The Bahárlú tribesmen began rounding up the women and children.[1] They brought them out of the Asbergun orchards and marched them to Mírzá Na'ím's camp. The elderly, the very young, the pregnant, the still nursing, trudged along, shell-shocked by weeks of fighting, wasted away from lack of food and water, bereft of their fathers, husbands and brothers, and now, without their male protectors, completely exposed.

Two elderly men who had been unable to fight were singled out.* Frail from age and hunger, they were brought forward to be executed. The officer who was in charge of the Nayrízí troops lifted his gun and, without a thought, shot one of them. The old man's body crumpled. A soldier beheaded the corpse. The elderly man's family members watched in horror. The officer picked up the bloody head and forced a

---

* The two men were Mullá Musá Namad-Mál, the felt-maker; and Ma<u>sh</u>hadí Báqir Sabbágh, the dyer (Shafí', *Narrative of Mulla Muhammad Shafi' Nayrízí,* 27).

terrified Bábí child to carry it to Mírzá Na'ím's camp as a gift.* He then had a black veil put over the face of his elderly victim's granddaughter and sat her on his horse as the hundreds of captives were marched away to be shown off to the army leaders.**

At his camp on Bísámán mountain, Mírzá Na'ím sat on a large rock in the middle of a garden. His officers and he were celebrating and dancing when the officer in charge of the Nayrízí troops rode up, jumped off his horse, pushed the little girl with the veil forward onto the ground and threw the severed head of her grandfather at their feet.[2]

"O Emir, whatever you wished has come true. The Bábís have been wiped out," boasted the officer in charge of the Nayrízís.

"Praised be to God!" exulted Mírzá Na'ím as he smiled broadly, looking around at his officers with cruel satisfaction. It was now time to punish these loathsome people who had cost him so much.

There was a large trench nearby, and the women and children were told to get in it.

Among the captives was Mullá 'Abdu'l-Ḥusayn, one of the most distinguished clerics of Nayríz who had become a Bábí three years earlier and had been the first one to be injured in the 1850 conflict. Many people in his neighborhood had come to believe in the Báb's claim out of respect for his wisdom and knowledge. Mírzá Na'ím had this elderly Bábí brought before him and asked him scornfully: "You are a sage. Why, with all your knowledge and wisdom and a life of

---

* Nicolas doesn't have this detail.

** There are varying numbers given for the women and children: Rouhani, *Lam'átul-Anvár* (v. 1, 190), gives 700; Nicolas, *Seyyed Ali Mohammed dit le Bab* (422), and Shafí', *Narrative of Mulla Muhammad Shafi' Nayrízí* (27), give 603; Mázandarání, *Zuhúr al-Haqq* (v. 4, 51), Ahdieh, *Nayrízi-Shurangiz* (118), and Faizi, *Nayríz Mushkbiz* (112), all give the number 600.

hard work, have you accepted that your sons be killed and your wife captured?"

Mullá 'Abdu'l-Ḥusayn replied, "I do not have the strength to answer. The only thing I can tell you is that all the divine laws of the past have been abrogated."[3]

He meant that the past was now fulfilled. This was the time of a new Divine Revelation, so all Islámic laws were now superseded by those of the Báb, the new Manifestation of God and divine lawgiver.[4]

Mullá 'Abdu'l-Ḥusayn's bold statement and courage angered Mírzá Na'ím, who wanted even more now to humiliate and break the old man. So he ordered soldiers to take fistfuls of dirt and fill his mouth with it. If he wasn't going to be contrite and beg for mercy, he wouldn't say anything. Another soldier took out a pistol and shot at Mullá 'Abdu'l-Ḥusayn, but the bullet only grazed his head, and Mírzá Na'ím shouted for him not to shoot. As one of the senior clerics of Nayríz, Mullá 'Abdu'l-Ḥusayn had to be brought alive to the authorities in Ṭihrán.

A Nayrízí who was with the troops recognized an important townsman among the prisoners. Wanting to impress Mírzá Na'ím, he picked up his club, went after the defenseless captive, and beat him in view of Mírzá Na'ím.[5]

The time had come to lead the men, women, and children back to Nayríz, along with Mírzá Na'ím's prized trophies—some two hundred severed heads which had been hacked off by his soldiers.*

---

* There are varying numbers regarding how many heads were taken by Mírzá Na'ím into Nayríz and then to Shíráz: Shoghi Effendi, in *God Passes By* (79), writes "no less than two hundred"; Mázandarání, *Zuhúr al-Haqq* (v. 4, 50), gives 180; Rouhani, *Lam'átul-Anvár* (190), gives 200; Shafí', *Narrative of Mulla Muhammad Shafi' Nayrízí* (28), gives "about 180"; Shafí', *Narrative of Mulla Muhammad Shafi'*

His men loaded the heads into pairs of open baskets, usually used for transporting fruit that were slung over the packsaddles of the donkeys.*

To get back, they took the steep path down the mountain.** Farmers had made this path as a shortcut to the upper part of the mountain. To help keep their footing on the steep incline, some wooden logs had been pushed into the ground for makeshift stairs.† The women did their best to clamber down, but many lost their footing and fell, or could go no further and collapsed.‡

Once out of the mountains, they went toward the mill.[6]

A fourteen-year-old boy walked behind his mother with his hand tied to her waist.*** He asked why he was tied to her; she told him that if the soldiers took him and killed him, she wanted to be there so she wouldn't spend the rest of her life wondering and waiting. She carried her other, much younger, son in her arms. Following the advice her husband had given to her before being killed, she had put on her

---

Nayrízí, lists 157 martyred men by name; Mázandarání, *Zuhúr al-Haqq,* gives 166; and Rouhani, *Lam'átul-Anvár,* gives 159 (v. 2, 451).

* These baskets are called "loudehs" (Binning, *A journal of two years' travel in Persia, Ceylon, etc, Volume 1,* 243).

** Shafí' refers to this mountain as "Bísámán." Local Nayrízís who were interviewed describe a "Bísámán" trail that curves up the slope, so while it took longer, it was easier to walk. The quicker—but much steeper trail—mentioned in the main text was used for animals and men who could climb more easily.

† From a private conversation with Mrs. Jahántáb (Sardári) Jazabi, January, 2010 CE. The word for this steep path is "sakesh."

‡ According to Rouhani, *Lam'átul-Anvár* (v. 2, 457), sixty women died on their descent from the mountain.

*** Muḥammad Shafí', the author of the manuscript that forms the basis of much of the information in these chapters. According to his manuscript, he was nine during the events of 1853, but given other events in his life, it is more likely that he was fourteen, as Mázandarání, *Zuhúr al-Haqq* (v. 6, 870), states.

plainest, coarsest clothes in anticipation of being captured by soldiers. On her younger boy, though, she had accidentally left a hat with little ornaments on it. A cavalryman rode up, leaned down and snatched it off with such violence that her boy was thrown from her arms, his small body landing on the hard ground some distance from her. She ran to him in a panic and picked him up. He was unconscious, a bald spot where his hair had been torn out by the violent grab. She cradled him in her arms, trying desperately to revive him, kneeling on the ground—enveloping his little body just like she had at his birth—when he stopped breathing.[7]

❋ ❋ ❋

The large Qa<u>sh</u>qá'í tribe, named after their Turkic language, and made up of nomadic clans, drove their flocks across the province of Fárs to seasonal pasture lands when winter turned to summer and back again. Their colorful and highly prized rugs were sold in the markets of <u>Sh</u>íráz, and their multicolored clothing was easily recognizable in the countryside. Passing through <u>Sh</u>íráz, the capital of Fárs, they had become involved in the politics of the region. The tribal leaders worked with the Persian rulers in controlling and ruling the province.[8]

Luṭf 'Alí <u>Kh</u>án was one such Qa<u>sh</u>qá'í leader who served as a brigadier general for the Persians. He had been hired to fight the Bábís in the mountains of Nayríz. With overwhelming numbers of men and several cannon, he had subdued them for his Persian overlords.

He and his men camped with Mírzá Na'ím by the mill and conducted clean-up operations.* They had beheaded all young male prisoners.

* In the sources, there are several stories of cruelties perpetrated against the Bábís after the last mountain battle. It is unclear from the sources in what order these

Now he announced to his men that there would be a reward for anyone who brought him a Bábí, dead or alive; Qa<u>sh</u>qá'í fighters swept up the mountain paths with daggers and swords and rifles, looking behind boulders, slashing into groves, entering into dark caves, looking out from rock outcrops, climbing higher and higher . . .[9]

In another place, a group of women, their children, and some men hid in the darkness of a cave and just hoped that they would be passed by. But they were found. Soldiers piled the entrance high with hay, twigs, branches, poured kerosene all over, and lit it. Soon the opening of the cave was completely sealed by a wall of roaring fire which turned the mountain rock black and the inside of the cave into a smoke-filled oven.[10]

Somewhere else, three Bábí brothers were in a hiding place when three tribesmen appeared and leapt on them. As they fought, one of the brothers was pinned down. But he grabbed the dagger of the attacker and used it to free himself. He and his two brothers escaped.[11]

Down below, as his fellow Qa<u>sh</u>qá'í and other soldiers scoured the mountains for Bábís, Luṭf 'Alí <u>Kh</u>án sat outside his tent with his commanders and celebrated their victory. By evening they were usually drunk, and had Bábí prisoners brought before them. A prisoner's beard would be set on fire, and they entertained themselves by watching the desperate jerking movements made by the prisoner as he tried to put out the fire.[12]

---

occurred and which can be attributed to Mírzá Na'ím and which to Luṭf 'Alí <u>Kh</u>án. In the Shafí' manuscript, it seems that Mírzá Na'ím and 'Alí <u>Kh</u>án lead two different groups: Mírzá Na'ím taking women, children, and severed heads into Nayríz soon after the last battle, and Luṭf 'Alí <u>Kh</u>án staying outside of town at the mill. The authors have put together their best guess about the order of events and which leader was responsible for which actions.

A prisoner was brought over to one of the cannon that was being rolled back to Nayríz.[13] A soldier fastened him to the cannon's mouth with rope and lit the fuse. The iron ball exploded out of the mouth of the cannon, tearing the young man's body to pieces.

The piles of severed heads of Bábí prisoners grew. Soldiers and villagers set about skinning them. This was done quickly, then the skin was stuffed with straw and left to dry in the sun.[14]

The sun sank below the mountaintops as they prepared to go the final distance into Nayríz. Torches were prepared for the coming darkness. The severed heads were again loaded onto the donkeys, which then lumbered forward, with hundreds of captives dragging behind them.[15]

Mírzá Na'ím mounted his horse and proudly led the way.

Luṭf 'Alí Khán had discharged his duties to his overlords. The British agent in Shíráz wrote in his report: "On the 6th of Suffur [8 Nov. 1853] His Royal Highness [Prince Tahmásb Mírzá, the governor of Fárs] wrote word to Luṭf Alee Khán nephew of the Eel Khánee 'Now the affairs of the Neereezees have come to such a pass, you must by no means return to Shíráz, but proceed to Laristan and the Sabaijat, and there await my arrival.'"[16]

❋ ❋ ❋

The final short distance—no more than a large city square—to Nayríz was to be a slow, painful processional for the Bábís.[17] Townspeople came out of their homes to watch and heap abuse on their fellow Nayrízís, whom they had been taught by their clerics to fear and despise.

In one instance, thorny brush was strewn on the ground, and barefooted women were forced to walk on it, tearing up the soles of their feet.

As the procession came to a pond, some women were pushed into the frigid water. Local men stood around the pond ululating while their women picked up mud and threw it at the Bábí women.[18] Then the Bábí women were made to march in the winter night with wet clothes.

A tired older woman carried two small children. She held them tight as the soldiers pushed her into a canal swollen with water. The cold of the water shocked her. She desperately struggled to keep her footing and hold on to her children while Nayrízís watched and jeered at her.[19]

After six hours, the procession came into the bazaar district, the area of town most hostile to the Bábís. In the middle of the night, the captives were crowded into the dilapidated caravanserai near the Ímám Zádih shrine. The small building could not hold the hundreds of women and children, who found there only cold floors, rats, and brackish water. They huddled together to warm each other. As they shivered in the dark, they worried about what would happen to them next.

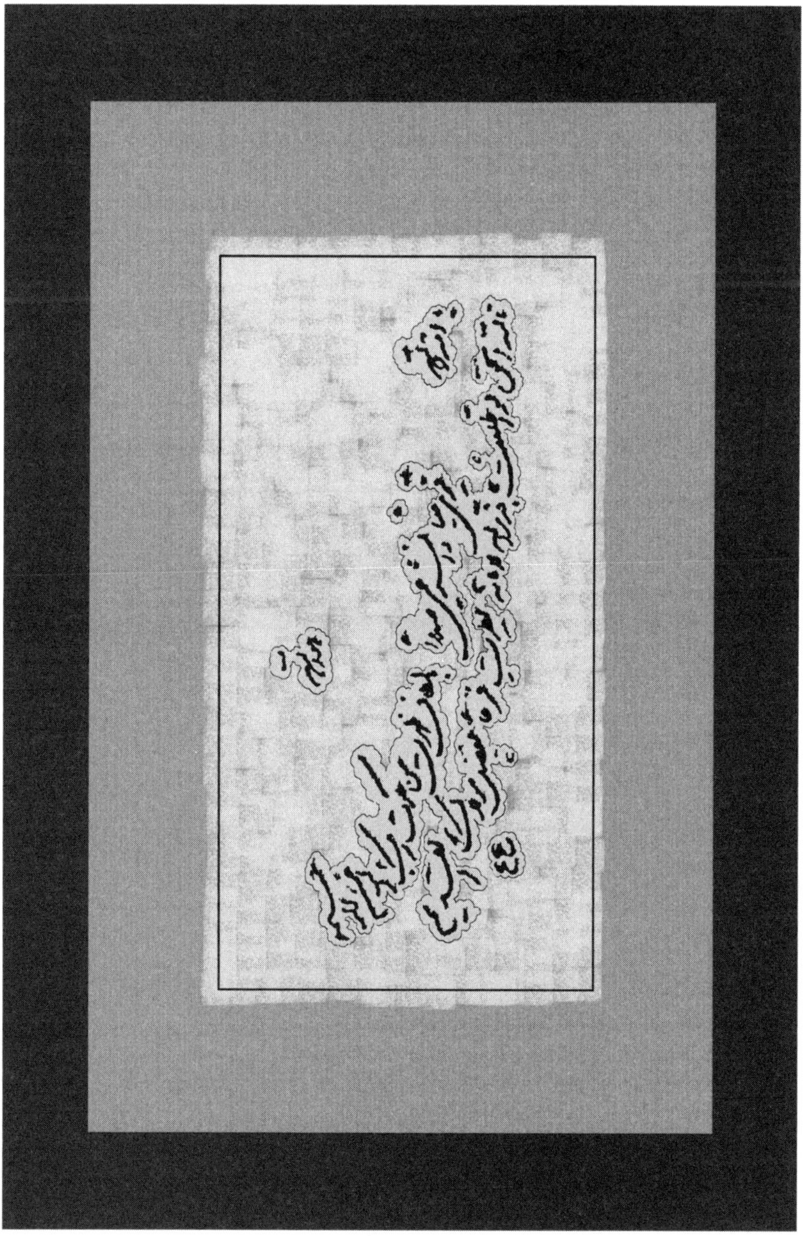

Tablet from 'Abdu'l-Bahá to Khávar Sultán

15

THE LONG ROAD INTO CAPTIVITY

As night receded, the outline of the shoulders, heads, and backs of the prisoners emerged from the gloom. All around the stone yard and rooms of the caravansera, the silent mass trembled. Feeble cries of infants rose up into the cold air, only to give up and fall back down into the morass of exhaustion and hunger.

Guards came into the yard and called the prisoners to attention. They lifted each other up against the protests of their weakened bodies. They were going to be led out of the madrisih to another location.

Outside, a mob had gathered. The Bábí women took their torn clothing and tried to cover their faces and arms as best they could—faces and arms that had never been seen by strangers—and as they came out of the caravansera gate, feelings of shame engulfed them.

Stepping into the street, they saw the faces of their fellow townspeople contorted in anger, their mouths shouting insults, baring teeth. A volley of small stones, dirt, and spit showered the prisoners. They placed their arms over their children to shield them.

They were led up the street, battered on all sides by taunts and jeers, until they arrived at a local school, the Madreseh K͟hán, which had been built earlier in 1815 by the governor of the city.[1] The cold day wore on, but no food was brought. The desperate prisoners used stagnant water in the schoolyard's pool to quench their thirst.

Elsewhere, the order had gone out from Mírzá Na'ím that the prisoners would be sent to S͟híráz. A few kilograms of cornbread now appeared each day at the school. Some prisoners refused anything given to them from the hands of their oppressors, resorting instead to eating discarded pomegranate skins and date seeds off the ground.[2]

Day after day, dry crumbling cornbread kept starvation at bay by a bare mouthful.[3]

One day, soldiers came for S͟hayk͟h 'Abdu'l-'Alí, Vaḥíd's father-in-law and one of the elders who had inspired the Bábís, and took him out with his two teenage sons. He was made to watch as his two boys were beheaded. Then the soldiers turned on him for his close association with Vaḥíd, and brutally killed him.* Left behind was his wife. Her relatives helped her escape that evening, but her brother refused to take her in.** She found shelter in the home of her servant, but later that night she died, traumatized by what she had seen.[4]†

---

* The authors conjecture that this is the reason for his execution, as another prominent cleric—Mullá 'Abdu'l Ḥusayn—was spared so he could be presented as a valuable prisoner to the Prince in S͟híráz.
** Ahdieh, *Nayrízí-Shurangiz* (60), states that she went to her "brother's wife."
† The servant's name was Karbalá'í Riḍá.

South of the school where the Bábí women were being held, soldiers roamed the streets of the Chinár-Súkhtih quarter, looking for more prisoners to take to Shíráz. As they searched the homes, Bábís were rounded up. The Gulpáyigání soldiers had been able to capture many who escaped after the last battle.

As the day to leave approached, the women prisoners in the school were brought out. An official looked them over, perhaps to choose the ones who could survive the march to Shíráz.[5] He selected about half the women and sent the others back to their homes in the Chinár-Súkhtih quarter. Women and children waited in dread as he decided their fates. The sound of wailing filled the sky whenever his choice took mother from daughter, sister from sister, and grandmother from grandchild, but nothing stopped the sorting.

A fifteen-year-old boy, the son of Quṭbá, 'Alí Sardár's close friend and one of the main Bábí leaders, and his mother were rescued by an uncle but, shunned by other family members, would quickly descend into poverty, living in a small dark dwelling with trash thrown at its entrance.[6]

The day of departure came, and the prisoners were assembled and readied.[7] The severed heads were piled into the baskets, the women were tied in pairs to ride on donkeys, while their children had to keep up on foot. The men were bound together in groups of ten. When all was ready, the large contingent of hundreds of prisoners, of donkeys carrying gruesome loads, of frightened children, of soldiers, and of officers on horseback, lurched forward to the edge of town. There, a large group of Nayrízís waited to gawk at them and hurl a final insult.

So began many days for the captives of trudging down the road to Shíráz through the cold, being fed only enough to keep walking, and spending nights with villagers whom the soldiers paid to house them.

. . . children, some motherless, who could not continue in the cold without food or warm clothing, fell by the side of the road,* and so did several mothers . . .[8]

. . . the young son of a woman named Fáṭimih, grandniece of the leading mullá of Shíráz, starved to death . . .[9]

. . . an elderly man, Mullá Muḥammad-'Alí Qábid, grew too weak to walk and collapsed by the side of the road. Soldiers beheaded him and threw the head into one of the baskets . . .[10]

. . . at another stop, the heart of one of the soldiers softened after seeing the suffering of the prisoners. He gave them two pieces of sheepskin, which they broiled and ate. Mírzá Na'ím found out about this and had the soldier beaten to warn soldiers not to help the prisoners . . .

. . . Mírzá Muḥammad 'Ábid died from hunger and was beheaded.[11] When the caravan of suffering moved on, his body was left discarded on the ground. Local tribesmen who came along later buried the corpse . . .**

The prisoners finally reached the last stop—a village seventeen kilometers from Shíráz.† Word was sent to the prince in Shíráz that the procession had arrived. A reply came that there would be a citywide celebration, and the procession could enter.‡ In the morning, the

---

* Mázandarání, *Zuhúr al-Haqq,* (v. 4, 53), states that some children had been separated from their mothers.

** This was the Báyír tribe that raised cattle in the area (Shafí', *Narrative of Mulla Muhammad Shafi' Nayrízí,* 32). These last two anecdotes are taken from the section in Shafí''s diary, which covers a procession to Shíráz led by Luṭf 'Alí Khán. However, as stated in an earlier footnote, the authors believe that the prisoners went in one group.

† Shafí', *Narrative of Mulla Muhammad Shafi' Nayrízí* (33), states that this stop was three fársangs from Shíráz. A fársang is roughly five and a half kilometers.

‡ Faizi, *Nayríz Mushkbiz* (114), states that the governor in Shíráz asked that the heads be put on spears. Mázandarání, *Zuhúr al-Haqq* (v. 4, 53), states that it was Luṭf 'Alí Khán who ordered the heads to be mounted on spears.

women were put back on donkeys, the men were lined up, the heads were taken out of the baskets and impaled on the tips of long spears, which were then hoisted high in the air by the soldiers.* Mírzá Na'ím rode to the front, and the procession moved down the road.

He was ready for his triumphal entry into Shíráz.

❋ ❋ ❋

Behind the wall that enclosed Shíráz, the word had gone out from the prince that this day would be one of celebration. Shírázís made their way excitedly through the narrow streets and alleys between the walls of the inward facing homes that made up the city's compact jumble of one- and two-story houses. Wealthy women in their homes and women in the public baths were staining their hands and fingernails in the dark orange toffee-colored henna patterns.[12]

On any normal morning at the bazaar, boys would have been carrying cups of tea on trays, and early morning shoppers would have been threading their way through the already crowded brick halls. Merchants would have been rushing in and out of their shops, which were set into the walls every few feet, displaying eggplants, pomegranates, onions, sour pickles, and nuts. The merchants would have been pouring out mountains of spices used for chicken, fish, and stews, for passers-by to see. The aromas of cinnamon, peppermint, turmeric, lavender, cumin, and pilau would have blended into the air, and the voices of people

---

* According to Shafí', *Narrative of Mulla Muhammad Shafí' Nayrízí* (32), the group led by Luṭf 'Alí Khán came into Shíráz three hours after sunrise; Mázandarání, *Zuhúr al-Haqq* (v. 4, 53), states that it was two hours after sunrise. Since no other time is given for Mírzá Na'ím's group and since the authors conclude that there was only one group, this time frame is used in this narrative.

bargaining would have echoed off the pointed stone arches above. The teahouses in the bazaar would already have had S͟hírázís taking a break or preparing for the day by sitting together and sipping steaming tea, hard sugar between their teeth.

But that would have been normal, and this was not a normal day, so the long halls of the bazaar were dark and empty. The prince had ordered all stores closed for the city-wide holiday.

S͟hírázís of all social classes came out into the main street to see the dreaded Bábís enter through the south-facing Saʻdí gate. It was 1850 all over again. They saw first a proud leader—this time Mírzá Naʼím—riding triumphantly, his sword hanging by his side. They looked up and pointed excitedly at the severed heads moving aloft on spears. Below these, a large group of men struggled forward in front of more than a hundred donkeys carrying poorly clad women and dirty, hungry children. Among them could be seen elderly men still able to move forward. The prisoners' faces showed the two months of struggle they had endured in the cold mountains. S͟hírázís vented their fear of the Bábís by shouting at them, though the sight of all the suffering hurt the hearts of some.[13]

The women and children were marched through town to the S͟háh Mír-ʻAlí Hamzih caravanserai by the north-facing Iṣfáhán Gate on the outskirts of S͟hiráz. The men were led to a prison. In the darkness of the prison cells, they met Bábís from Nayríz who had been languishing there since the struggle at Fort K͟hájih, three years earlier. The severed heads were dumped in another location to be kept for the last leg of the journey to Ṭihrán.[14]

At the caravanserai, bread rations arrived in the evening. The women immediately fed their starving children. At night, in the dark of the caravanserai's stone rooms, the cold intensified. Women huddled with

Shrine of Shah Mirhamzeh in Shiraz

Shrine of BibiDokhtaran in Shiraz

their children, hoping their body heat would help warm them. Their small teeth chattered as they drifted in and out of sleep.[15]

The next morning, the order came from the prince that the Bábí men were to be brought to him. He asked a local tough from Nayríz, Jalál, whom Mírzá Na'ím had brought with him, to tell him who the different men were and what their part had been in the conflict. The first to be unbound and brought in was Mullá 'Abdu'l-Ḥusayn, the elderly cleric who had been a respected guide to the Bábís for three years. Jalál immediately indicated him as the most troublesome of the Bábí leaders. Now, he stood before them, and though he appeared a physically wrecked and frail old man, an indomitable spirit lived on in him.

He was asked about his deeds. He responded that he had summoned people to the new Revelation and pointed to the willing suffering of the Bábís as proof of its truth.[16]

The prince ordered him to curse the Báb. He refused. The prince called for others to be brought to him. He ordered them to recant. They refused. Five men were immediately taken out to the square close to the prison. Spears were driven into three of them, and two others were beheaded.[17] The prominent clerics among the Bábís would be spared so they could be presented in Ṭihrán.

An important tribal leader urged the prince to be merciful toward these unfortunates. He had previously been critical of Mírzá Na'ím for recreating the famous scene of the killing of Ímám Ḥusayn in Karbilá, revered by all Shí'a, a drama reenacted every year and of deep emotional meaning. This time, though, it was the Bábís who appeared as the faithful and the Shí'a as the persecutors.[18]

For the women and children, these days were spent in public ridicule. With each cold night that passed, the children grew weaker. One mother tried to warm her infant son by cradling him in her bosom.

Her two girls curled up to her as close as possible. She embraced them with her other arm and tried to cover them with whatever clothing she had. But their lives were ebbing away, and there was nothing she could do to stop that. Hunger and the winter cold took her girls and the children of others.[19]

Every day, the Shírázís passed this scene of hungry ill-clad women and children being humiliated. The cruelty of what had happened became more apparent as the excitement at Mírzá Na'ím's triumphal entry faded. Gradually, their hearts softened.[20]

But the ordeal for many Bábí women would never end. It was decided that the women would be given as rewards to soldiers and other authorities. The men came to the caravanserai, looked over the captives and claimed the ones who pleased them, forcing some to become their wives. All others were simply let go with their children into the streets to fend for themselves.[21] In the months and years to come, some were able to make it back to Nayríz, while others were reduced to begging.

In another part of town, Khadíjih Bagum, the widowed wife of the Báb, now living in her sister's house, heard of the tumult in the city and the suffering of the Bábís of Nayríz but could not go out to see them. Since the departure of her husband, she had lived in constant uncertainty, rarely receiving information of His whereabouts or condition; even the news of His martyrdom and that of His uncle, in whose home she had played as a child, had been kept from her for a time. How she longed to see these Bábís of Nayríz who were the spiritual sons and daughters of her husband, their sacrifice the signs of His station! Soon, it became possible to have a few of the freed women come regularly to a friend's house and visit with her. A few of these women even became a part of her household. She gave each a fine linen scarf. One of them, a young widow whose husband's head had been displayed on a pike, had given birth out in the fields on the journey to Shíráz. Khadíjih Bagum gave the baby the name Humáyún, which means *blessed.*[22]

At the prison, the Bábí men were sorted. It was determined that sixty of the more prominent among them who had not fought in the conflict should be allowed to go free.[23] Seventy-three men were bound and readied for the long march to the capital, to be presented to the King of Persia.

❋ ❋ ❋

Tied together and accompanied by soldiers, the Bábís began their march to Ṭihrán, the capital of the kingdom of Persia, over nine hundred kilometers to the north. Donkeys carrying the severed heads followed. They left through Shíráz's northern Iṣfáhán gate and headed into the dry rocky hills. It was midwinter, and a cold wind buffeted them as they walked. Left behind were their loved ones, destitute or captive in other homes, if they had survived at all. What lay ahead for them was the unknown.

Soon the brown landscape with its flickers of greenery flattened out. The winter wind lashed the prisoners as they crossed the flat land. When a man could go no further, he fell by the wayside. Soldiers would behead each one who fell and leave the corpse on the side of the road.

One of them was the elderly and venerable cleric, Mullá 'Abdu'l-Ḥusayn, who had been the first injured in 1850. He lost a son in the Fort Khájih struggle and four sons in the mountain battles. In his eighties, his body gave out, three day's journey from Shíráz. He was decapitated and his body abandoned on the ground.[24]

After some days, they arrived at the last major town in Fárs province, Ábádih, an important stop on the migratory route of the Qashqá'í tribe. Local people, urged by their clerics, came out to mock and heap abuse on the prisoners, assured that they would receive special blessings for doing so. The procession was met in Ábádih by a messenger from the court of the King of Persia, who told them to leave the heads behind before continuing their journey to the capital. The local people refused to have the heads buried in their cemetery, for fear of its being desecrated by the presence of the Bábí remains. So an abandoned field outside town was selected. Soldiers dug large pits and dumped the heads of the Bábís into them.[25] As the Bábí prisoners were forced to resume their journey, they left this field in Ábádih behind them.

This desolate field on the outskirts of Ábádih would remain untouched for ten years.

In the future, the One Whom God Shall Make Manifest, promised by the Báb, would reveal Himself, new Bábís would settle in to Ábádih, and a Bahá'í community would be born. Half a century after the burial of the martyrs' heads, Bahá'ís stood in the presence of 'Abdu'l-Bahá in the Holy Land, and he asked them the name they had given this field. "Garden of the Martyrs' Heads," they replied. 'Abdu'l-Bahá stood up, and revealed a tablet to be recited on his behalf by a believer.[26] 'Abdu'l-Bahá gave this place a new name; it would hence forward be called "The Garden of the Merciful."

❋ ❋ ❋

The prisoners continued the long march, at times barely able to put one foot before the other. They trudged through the former great capital, Iṣfáhán. Still they moved forward, through the clerical city of Qum with its evaporating lakes on the eastern side of the road. Some twenty-two prisoners fell by the wayside.[27]

They finally saw the capital of the kingdom. Entering it, they were brought into the presence of the king. His Royal Highness ordered

هو الله

ايا نفحات الله انتشري في تلك البقعة النوراء و بلّغي وله قلبي و شوق
فؤادي و انجذاب نفسي و شدّة ولعي الى تلك البقعة التي توارت
فيها رؤوس مكلّلة بالشهادة الكبرى مجلّلة بجواهر مشرقة على القرون
والاعصار بما افترقت عن الاجساد في سبيل الله و قولي النور الساطع
اللامع من الملكوت الابهى يشرق على تلك المقبرة النوراء و نسيم
الهاب من رياض الجنة العليا تمرّ على تلك البقعة الغراء الحديقة
الغنّاء و الروضة العليا التي تشرفت بكم ايها الرؤوس المقطوعة في
سبيل الله و الوجوه المنورة بضياء شمس الهدى و الاعين القريرة بمشاهدة
انوار الله و الآذان الواعية الصاغية لنداء الله و الادمغة المنتعشة من
الانفاس طيب هدايات الله و الاذواق المستحلية كل مرّ في محبت الله
روحي لكم الفداء و كينونتي لكم الفداء و حقيقتي لكم الفداء ايها الوجوه
النورانية و النفوس الروحانية و الرؤوس المقطوعة السبحانية و النجوم
الفرزانية و الجنود الربانية طوبى لكم بخّ بخّ لكم احسنتم احسنتم على
ما فعلتم بما فديتم اموالكم و اولادكم و ارواحكم في سبيل البهاء حبّاً بالجمال
الاعلى سبحان ربي الابهى بما خلق و سوّى و بعث هولاء من مرقد
النفس و الهوى و حشرهم تحت لواء الحمد اذ قامت القيامة الكبرى
فانتبهوا عند ما زلزلت الارض زلزالها و حدّثت اخبارها و استبشروا

Tablet of Visitation from ‘Abdu’l-Bahá to be read at the burial place of the heads of the martyrs of Nayriz, in Ábádih.

عندما ارتفع نداء الله في اوج العلى وسمعوا الست بربكم الاعلى و
قالوا بلى يا رب بلى وفدوا ما لهم وعليهم في هذا المنهج البيضاء و
اصبحوا اربابا بيد الاشقياء وطرحت اجسامهم على الغبراء ثم قطعت
رؤسهم المتهاديه على القنا واسر اهلهم الى البقعة المباركة التي كانت
موطن النقطة الاولى ثم ارسلت رؤسهم مرتفعة على الرماح الى هذه
الارض الطيبة الغيناء فدتكم روحي ونفسي وذاتي ايها النقباء النجباء
الشهداء في سبيل الله السعداء في الآخرة والاولى وعليكم البهاء
وعليكم الثناء وعليكم العون والعناية من ربكم الاعلى. ع ع"

fifteen of them to recant. They refused and were executed.* In prison, twenty-three more died.**

After three years, thirteen were released, but most died soon thereafter, their bodies simply giving out. Four were known to have made it all the way back to Nayríz.[28]

They would become part of the birth of the Nayríz Bahá'í community.

---

* Shafí', *Narrative of Mulla Muhammad Shafi' Nayrízí* (35), remembers the following names: "'Áqá Siyyid 'Alí, the one who was badly injured in the mountains of Nayríz and was left unconscious. He had dreamt that he must go to Tihrán and be martyred there; Karbalá'í Rajab Salmání; Sífu'd-Dín; Sulaymán Karbalá'í Salmán; Ja'far Fardí; Murád Khayrchí; Ḥusayn Karbalá'í Báqir; Mírzá Abú'l-Ḥasan; Mírzá Taqí, who was beaten with clubs for becoming a Bábí by Ḥájí Mírzá 'Abdu'l-Vahhab to please Mírzá Na'ím; and Mullá Muḥammad-'Alím, the son of Áqá Mihdí."

** "One was 'Alí, the son of Mír-Shikár Báqi (Shafí', *Narrative of Mulla Muhammad Shafi' Nayrízí*, 35).

16

THE TRANSFORMATION OF THE BÁBÍS INTO BAHÁ'ÍS

Months rolled away.[1] In Sh̲í̲ráz, those who survived the ordeal of 1853 were released into the streets. The Bábís trickled back into Nayríz, built new lives, married, had children, started businesses, worked the land, and faced new torments. Among them . . .

- The young grandson of Mullá 'Abdu'l-Ḥusayn,* named Mullá Muḥammad Shafí‘, and his mother, were rescued by the head mullá of Sh̲í̲ráz, S̲h̲ayk̲h̲ Abú Turáb, who earlier had protected the Báb. Shafí‘'s five brothers had been killed in the mountain battles. S̲h̲ayk̲h̲ Abú Turáb took care of the two and sponsored Shafí‘'s schooling. The boy showed great ability in his studies.[2]

---

* The father of the boy, and son of Mullá 'Abdu'l-Ḥusayn, was Mullá 'Alí Naghi.

- The thirteen-year-old sister of 'Alí Sardár, who had been with him in the mountain battles, was sent to Shíráz as a captive. After great suffering, she was released. She married a man named Ḥusayn and had three children who would greatly aid the community in the persecutions that were still to come.[3]

- The mother of Humáyún, after receiving aid from the Báb's widow, returned to Nayríz with her young daughter. She was asked for her hand in marriage by a man who later broke the Covenant, meaning that he became a Bahá'í only to later challenge the authority of Bahá'u'lláh. He traveled with Bahá'u'lláh to Turkey, and Bahá'u'lláh attempted to guide him, but to no avail. He was expelled from Bahá'u'lláh's presence and later killed in 'Iráq by thugs whom he befriended. But their son, Mullá Áqá Bábá, did not follow his father's path and instead became a teacher of the Faith in Shíráz.[4]

- Karbalá'í Muḥammad, commander of one of the nineteen fortifications on Bálá-Taram, and his two sons evaded capture after the mountain battles.* All three returned to Nayríz. Karbalá'í Muḥammad's first son, Ḥájí Ibráhim, married a woman who was not a Bábí but who, in time, became a sincere believer; they had three children.**

---

* According to Mázandarání (*Zuhúr al-Haqq,* v. 4, 57–59), he had three sons, the third being "Luṭfu'lláh."

** Their three children were Mu'min, Fáṭimih, and Muḥammad-'Alí. His second son, 'Alí, had three children, Luṭfu'lláh, who fought alongside him in the mountains in 1853, Badí'u'lláh, and Amru'lláh. 'Alí would die young, and his children would later suffer persecution (Rouhani, *Lam'átul-Anvár,* v. 1, 280).

- A sixteen-year-old girl, Fáṭimih, was freed in Shíráz, along with her mother. Her father, who had fled to another city, was so grieved to hear of the imprisonment of his wife and daughter that he passed away. The young Fáṭimih, after her return to Nayríz, married Khájih Ismá'íl. She would have three children and spend much of her time practicing traditional medicine to assist the sick and destitute in the community.[5]

- A young mother and her ten-year-old son, Khájih Muḥammad, were released in Shíráz. Their father, Karbalá'í Báqir, had been killed in the conflict. They returned to Nayríz with no resources and lived in poverty. But the mother guided her boy and, once grown, he would make a living trading cotton and lift his mother and himself out of poverty. They would experience persecution again.[6]

- Three brothers had escaped captivity after a struggle with soldiers in the mountains.* One, Amír, traveled all the way to Baghdád. Another, Muḥammad Báqir, returned to Nayríz to support the Bábís and teach the Faith. He married Núríján, and they would have three sons and two daughters. All these children would suffer greatly in the times to come. The third brother, Muḥammad Kázim, would remain steadfast in his faith and continue to support the community. He would have two sons and two daughters.[7]

* These three brothers don't appear on Mázandarání's list (*Zuhúr al-Haqq*, v. 4, 57–59).

- A very young woman, whose name has been lost to history, survived the battles of 1853, and was able to get back from Shíráz to Nayríz. She married Mírzá Ismá'íl, who worked as a shoemaker, and they had a son, Mírzá Akbar, who would be martyred in the persecutions to come. Her husband would die early, and she would remarry and have another son who would serve the Bahá'í community devotedly.[8]

- Another young woman who had lost her husband, Ḥájí Muḥammad, was taken captive to S͟híráz with her young sons, Muḥammad Ismá'íl and Muḥammad Ibráhim, both of whom would perish in the later persecutions along with one of Ismá'íl's sons, 'Alí.[9]

- A young boy, Áqá Siyyid Muḥammad-Báqir, lived with his mother and tended the few sheep he and his mother owned in the countryside outside the C͟hinár-Súk͟htih quarter. Their father, Siyyid Mírzá Muḥammad 'Abid, had been killed in the conflict. They stayed for some time with her Muslim relatives in another quarter of the city but left the comfort and protection of that home to move to the Bábí quarter, where they lived in poverty, eking out a living from these sheep.[10]

- A young mother, Fáṭimih, and her son, Karbalá'í Muḥammad-Sálih, were released in S͟híráz and made their way back to Nayríz.* She raised her boy to have a deep love for the Faith. He

* He does not appear on Mázandarání's list (*Zuhúr al-Haqq,* v. 4, 57–59).

grew up to marry Zahra, the daughter of S͟hayk͟h Yúsuf, who had stood by Vaḥid and been severely tortured after the fall of Fort K͟hájih. Karbalá'í Muḥammad-Sáliḥ and Zahra would have two children,* both of whom would later suffer persecution.[11]

- In the late 1850s, S͟hafí' returned to Nayríz. He was appointed prayer leader of the Great Mosque by S͟hayk͟h Abú Turáb, the leading mullá of S͟híráz.[12] In Nayríz, he helped Bábís who were in need, feeding those who were hungry, and brought others back to Nayríz and gave them employment.

- Vafa, the son of Mullá Báqir, the head mullá of the Great Mosque in Nayríz who secretly considered himself a Bábí, married one of the women prisoners in Nayríz, Fáṭimih, whose husband had been killed in the 1853 conflict. They had a child named K͟hávar Sultán.[13]

- Fatḥ 'Alí K͟hán, the governor of Nayríz, felt compelled to avenge the murder of his father, Zaynu'l-Ábidín K͟hán, for the family's honor. He hired men to kill Mullá Ḥasan Lab-Shikarí, one of the plotters and a prominent citizen who had been able to protect Bábís. Lab-Shikarí has escaped retribution and persecution because of his relation to the K͟hán's family. Now that the mountain battles were over and the Bábí community scattered, Fatḥ 'Alí K͟hán decided to move on him. When Lab-Shikarí visited the walled village of Sayf-Ábád on the northeast edge of Nayríz, the K͟hán's men found him and killed him.[14]

---

* The two children are Amru'lláh and Fáṭimih (Ahdieh, *Nayrízí-Shurangiz*, 159).

❋ ❋ ❋

While the Bábís gradually return to Nayríz, other developments are taking place across Iran. Jináb-i-Bahá, widely seen as the spiritual leader of the Bábís after the Báb's martyrdom, is exiled with His family to Baghdád by the Persian government. His jealous half-brother stirs up conflict there among the Bábís, so He goes into self-imposed seclusion in the wilderness of the mountains of northern 'Iráq. Now He returns to Baghdád and begins to rebuild and gather together the Bábís. He pours out sacred writings—the Book of Certitude, the Hidden Words, the Seven Valleys, the Four Valleys, the Tablet of the Holy Mariner—and the Bábís begin flocking to Him.[15]

Shafí' sets out for Baghdád in 1859 to visit Jináb-i-Bahá. He travels with his fellow-believer, Karbalá'í Muḥammad-Sálih; each rides a donkey for the long trip. Along the way, one of the donkeys is stolen. Out of deference to the other, neither man will ride the donkey, so both end up walking. In Baghdád, Jináb-i-Bahá provides them with funds to buy a second donkey for the long return trip. Instead of spending on this though, they use it to host Bábí gatherings.* Even though Jináb-i-Bahá has not made His Declaration that He is indeed the One foretold by the Báb, Shafí' recognizes His station. Both become totally devoted to Jináb-i-Bahá and begin to educate the Bábís of Nayríz in His Writings.[16]

Jináb-i-Bahá's influence spreads well beyond Baghdád, and the Bábí community is now revived and growing. Alarmed by this, the Persian Foreign Minister writes to the Persian Ambassador in Constantinople with a message for the Sultan of the Ottomans:

---

* From a private conversation with Hussein Ahdieh, December, 2010.

"Excellency,

After the carrying out of those energetic measures on the part of the Persian Government for the . . . extermination of the misguided and detestable sect of the Bábís . . . their roots were torn up . . . But by chance, and through the ill-considered policy of former officials, one of them, to wit Mírzá Ḥusayn 'Alí of Nur', obtained release from the Anbar prison and permission to reside in the neighbourhood of the Shrines, . . . he is in Baghdád, and at no time hath he ceased from secretly corrupting and misleading foolish persons and ignorant weaklings . . . it would be a proof of the most complete negligence and lack of prudence on the part of the Persian Government . . . not to set itself to seek some means to remedy or remove them . . . instruct you without delay to seek an appointment with their most glorious Excellencies the [Ottoman] Prime Minister and Minister of Foreign Affairs . . . to request . . . the removal of this source of mischief from a place like Baghdád, which is the meeting-place of many different peoples and is situated near the frontiers of the protected provinces of Persia . . . that Mírzá Ḥusayn 'Alí and such of his followers and familiars as are the cause and root of the mischief should be arrested in such manner as is requisite, and handed over at the frontier to the officers of the aforementioned Prince and that the Government should . . . deport and detain that mischief-maker [i.e. Bahá'u'lláh] and his several intimates from Baghdád to some other place in the interior of the Ottoman kingdom which has no means of communication with our frontiers, so that the channel of their mischief-making and sedition may be stopped.

Written on the 12th of Dhu'l-Hijja, A.H. 1278" (May 10, 1862)."[17]

In the desert south of Ṭihrán, there is a shrine to a descendant of one of the Ímáms, the Ímámzadeh Ma'sum with an abandoned building near it. Inside, there is a wall built by a Bábí. Behind the wall, there is a one-meter-long wooden casket, containing a cloth wrapped around the earthly remains of the Báb. It was to remain a secret location. But word spread among the faithful, and, unable to resist, more and more of them come to the desert location.[18]

Ḥájí Muḥammad-Taqí Nayrízí, the wealthy young merchant who sacrificed everything in the conflict of 1850 and was severely tortured afterwards, journeys on foot from Yazd, where he had been recuperating, to Baghdád with his family. Though almost crippled he makes it. While living there in the joy of Jináb-i-Bahá's presence, his son is killed. Jináb-i-Bahá reveals a Tablet in the boy's honor. Taqí accepts his son's death with aquiescence. He passes away in Baghdád three years later. Jináb-i-Bahá participates in his funeral procession. He gives Taqí's grief stricken widow a boy to be raised by her who is the same age as her own deceased son. He reveals the Suriy Sabr, known as the Lawh Ayyúb, on His first day in the Garden of Riḍván in Baghdád, in which He gives Taqí the title *Ayyúb,* meaning *Job,* the figure in the Hebrew Bible whose very name has come to mean 'patience.' Bahá'u'lláh remembers the terrible suffering of Taqí and other Nayrízís in a Tablet to the Nayrízís.[19]

Before He leaves in early May, 1863, for His banishment to Constantinople, Jináb-i-Bahá gathers His fellow Bábís in a garden outside of Baghdád and announces that He is the One for Whom the Báb had prepared the way—Bahá'u'lláh, meaning the *Glory of God.* The Bábís are overcome with joy. The chronicler Nabíl remembers: "Every day, ere the hour of dawn, the gardeners would pick the roses which lined the four avenues of the garden, and would pile them in the center of the floor of His blessed tent. So great would be the heap that when His companions gathered to drink their morning tea in His presence, they would be unable to see each other across it. All these roses Bahá'u'lláh would, with His own hands, entrust to those whom He dismissed from His presence every morning to be delivered, on His behalf, to His Arab and Persian friends in the city."[20]

Bahá'u'lláh now outlaws the use of violence in the spreading of the divine teaching. On the first day of His public declaration in the Garden of Riḍván, He writes:

> """On the first day of His arrival in the garden designated the Riḍván, the Ancient Beauty established Himself upon the Most Great Throne. Thereupon, the Tongue of Glory uttered three blessed verses. First, that in this Revelation the use of the sword is prohibited."""[21]

In the words of His son, 'Abdu'l-Bahá:

> "If ye be slain," said He, "it is better for you than to slay. It is through the firmness and assurance of the faithful that the Cause of the Lord must be diffused. As the faithful, fearless and undaunted, arise with absolute detachment to exalt the Word of God, and, with eyes averted from the things of this world, engaged in service for the Lord's sake and by His power, thereby will they cause the Word of Truth to triumph. These blessed souls bear witness by their lifeblood to the truth of the Cause and attest it by the sincerity of their faith, their devotion and their constancy. The Lord can avail to diffuse His Cause and to defeat the froward. We desire no defender but Him, and with our lives in our hands face the foe and welcome martyrdom."[22]

This was the Day, Bahá'u'lláh writes, in which "all created things were immersed in the sea of purification" and "the breezes of forgiveness were wafted over the entire creation."[23]

News of His Declaration reaches Nayríz.

Vafá writes poetry in praise of Bahá'u'lláh, and a series of questions in poetic form. He receives a tablet in return:

> "O Vafá! Render thanks unto thy Lord for having aided thee to embrace His Cause, enabled thee to recognize the Manifestation of His Own Self and raised thee up to magnify Him Who is the Most Great Remembrance in this glorious Announcement.
>
> Blessed art thou O Vafá, inasmuch as thou hast been faithful to the Covenant of God and His Testament at a time when all men have violated it and have repudiated the One in Whom they had believed, and this notwithstanding that He hath appeared invested with every testimony, and hath dawned from the horizon of Revelation clothed with undoubted sovereignty."[24]

Shafí''s efforts help to repopulate the Chinár-Súkhtih quarter with survivors of the 1853 conflict and their descendants, and the Bábís of Nayríz transform themselves into a Bahá'í community.[25]

Pilgrims stream to see Bahá'u'lláh in Turkey where He and His family have been banished. They are now the "people of Bahá" and replace the greeting "Alláh'u'Akbar" ('God is Great') with that of "Alláh'u'Abhá" ('God is Most Glorious'). Bahá'ís move into new countries to spread the Teachings. Bahá'u'lláh reveals many tablets during this period, including one to a believer, Aḥmad, who longed to reach him but couldn't and had to turn back. Bahá'u'lláh reassured him: "O Aḥmad! Forget not My bounties while I am absent. Remember My days during thy days, and My distress and banishment in this remote prison. And be thou so steadfast in My love that thy heart shall not waver, even if the swords of the enemies rain blows upon thee and all the heavens and the earth arise against thee."[26]

Suffering the ill effects of a poisoning by a jealous family member, Bahá'u'lláh now declares His Station and Mission to the kings of Persia, the Ottoman Empire, France, Russia, and Prussia, and the Pope, summoning them to turn to Him and warning them of the consequences of ignoring His Call:[27]

> "Adorn the body of Thy kingdom with the raiment of My name, and arise, then, to teach My Cause. Better is this for thee than that which thou possessest. God will, thereby, exalt thy name among all the kings. Potent is He over all things. Walk thou amongst men in the name of God, and by the power of His might, that thou mayest show forth His signs amidst the peoples of the earth. Burn thou brightly with the flame of this undying Fire which the All-Merciful hath ignited in the midmost heart of creation,that through thee the heat of His love may be kindled within the hearts of His favoured ones. Follow in My way and enrapture the hearts of men through remembrance of Me, the Almighty, the Most Exalted."[28]

Khájih Muḥammad's cotton trading business has grown, and the authorities in Nayríz ask him to serve as the head of one of the neighborhoods in town. He keeps his home open for Bahá'í gatherings.[29]

One day in 1867, a few Bábís approach the gate of Ṭihrán with the casket containing the sacred remains of the Báb. The number of pilgrims had brought too much attention to the previous location. At the gate, they fear its contents will be discovered by the guards. Suddenly a severe thunderstorm erupts, and everyone on the road runs through the gate in a jumble. The Bábís get through unnoticed with the casket. The remains will now spend over two decades hidden under the floor of the inner sanctuary of the Ímámzadih Zayd shrine in Ṭihrán.[30]

In 1868, Fatḥ 'Alí Khán, the governor of Nayríz, orders the assassination of Fáṭimih Bagum's husband, Ḥájí Muḥammad-Ismá'íl. The governor thinks the husband is returning with Fáṭimih Bagum to claim her father's properties which had been illegally seized by the assassinated governor, Zaynu'l-'Ábidín Khán, after the conflict of 1850. She is the daughter of Áqá Siyyid Ja'far Yazdí, the distinguished cleric who had stood by Vaḥíd and been publically humiliated after the Fort Khájih conflict. He had owned extensive properties in the area before being forced to sign them over. Shafí' sends several young men to go accompany her and her children from the village of Qaṭrúyih back to Nayríz. Fáṭimih is able to support her children on her own after a while. She was taught by her father to write Persian and Arabic. She teaches other Bahá'í women and her Muslim friends about the Faith. Bahá'u'lláh acknowledges her contribution. Her brother, Siyyid Muḥammad, comes to Nayríz to help and ends up marrying and settling in Nayríz. He establishes long-running classes on the Faith for children and youth; Bahá'u'lláh sends him at least seven tablets.[31]

❋ ❋ ❋

Shafí' has been educating the Bábís of Nayríz in the precepts of the Bahá'í Faith, and they gradually change their orientation as a community to welcoming greater interaction with their Muslim neighbors. Fatḥ 'Alí Khán, the son of Zaynu'l-'Ábidín Khán, reaches out to the Bahá'í community as the best way to govern the town. Shafí' and he draw up a peace agreement in which Fatḥ 'Alí Khán agrees to leave the Bahá'ís in peace; they, in turn, will drop their grievances regarding their properties and loss of life in their families. He appoints Haj Qasím and Haj Muḥammad, two Bahá'ís who became believers in the Báb through Vaḥíd and participated in the defense of Fort Khájih, to administer certain lands under his control. Fatḥ 'Alí Khán even hired Bahá'ís as guards for his home and lands.[32]

When Shafí''s first wife passed, the leading mullá of Shíráz, Shaykh Abú Turáb, arranged a marriage between him and his niece, Khávar Sultán. Their family grows to seven children including Shaykh Muhammad-Ḥusayn, who will serve on the Spiritual Assembly of Nayríz. All will be persecuted later in their lives.[33]

After his planting is done, Jináb Mírzá Báqir Khoshnevis, also known as Mírzá Áqá, loves to be at home with his Muslim wife and the niece of Sardár, Fáṭimih Khánum, copying the Sacred Tablets of Bahá'u'lláh. In time, he will copy the Book of Laws, the Book of Certitude, and many Tablets for the Bahá'ís to read; this is his great joy. The governor of Nayríz, Fatḥ 'Alí Khán, recognizing the beauty of his calligraphy, has him write important communications to high officials on his behalf. After the death of the governor, Mírzá Áqá will be driven out of Nayríz by the mullás; his Muslim wife will be held there by her family against her will. Mírzá Áqá will continue to produce beautifully calligraphied copies of the Sacred Texts for the friends in Arabic and Persian even as he is chased from Nayríz to Iṣfáhán to Ṭihrán, his works banned and confiscated.[34]

Áqá Siyyid Muḥammad-Báqir has grown up and now owns a small farm. He marries and has four daughters and two sons.[35]

The wife of Quṭbá, who had suffered with her husband through the battles in the mountains, and then through years of poverty, dies in

1871. By this time, her son Mírzá Ja'far, who had shared her suffering, has a successful business engaging in overseas trade. He marries and has three daughters; the four of them will suffer greatly in the coming persecution. Mírzá Ja'far is able to make several trips to see Bahá'u'lláh in 'Akká, the remote fortress town in Palestine and the final place of His exile. Bahá'u'lláh reveals several tablets for him.[36]

A Westerner, writing in 1875, remembers the fate of Mírzá Na'ím, who had led the troops against Sardár and the Bábís in 1853:

> The governor of Fárs at that time, the Zil-es-Sultan, wishing to wring a large fine, and a considerable sum of money supposed to have been appropriated by the paymaster-general, after numerous indignities placed Mírzá Na'ím in a snow chair—the man was seventy-five years of age—compelled him to drink water-melon juice, to produce the well-known diuretic effect, and while the sufferer was frozen to the snow seat, caused a dog to be placed on his lap, thus insulting his aged co-religionist. Although the man had borne these horrible tortures for some hours, he now consented to pay the sum demanded. Of course the result to his aged frame was not long in doubt, he soon succumbed to the effects of the injuries he received.[37]

The Persian Kingdom has been in a steep economic, social, political, and cultural decline. In 1875, at Bahá'u'lláh's request, 'Abdu'l-Bahá writes an essay in which he offers new approaches and ideas to help Persia modernize in a way that will cause it to flourish and lift itself out of its total stagnation. 'Abdu'l-Bahá suggests the harmonizing of scientific advances and spiritual values, learning from other nations that have progressed beyond Persia, freeing themselves from old prejudices and cooperating with other countries:

> We must now highly resolve to arise and lay hold of all those instrumentalities that promote the peace and well-being and happiness, the knowledge, culture and industry, the dignity, value and station, of the entire human race. Thus, through the restoring waters of pure intention and unselfish effort, the earth of human potentialities will blossom with its own latent excellence and flower into praiseworthy qualities, and bear and flourish until it comes to rival that rose garden of knowledge which belonged to our forefathers. Then will this holy land of Persia become in every sense the focal center of human perfections, reflecting as if in a mirror the full panoply of world civilization.[38]

The essay is published anonymously as a gift of guidance to the Persian people and is entitled *The Secret of Divine Civilization.*

Shafí' continues holding weekly classes on the Bábí and Bahá'í writings. He also develops a business association with Áqá Mírzá Áqá Afnán, a relative of the Báb's, which includes other Nayrízís. This results in greater prosperity for the Bahá'ís as well as new business relations with their fellow townspeople, some of whom become Bahá'ís. In addition, these relations help protect the community. 'Abdu'l-Bahá praised him for guiding the Bahá'ís in their loyalty to the Covenant.[39]

Páríján, granddaughter of Mullá Lab-Shikarí, the Bábí leader who had been murdered by Fatḥ 'Alí Khán's men, is born.[40]

From Shíráz, Aḥmad moves to Nayríz where he will live for twenty years, spending much time meditating on the Tablet revealed for him by Bahá'u'lláh.[41]

Khadíjih Bagum, wife of the Manifestation of God, who suffered so deeply for years for her love and loyalty to her Husband, passes away in Shíráz in 1882, heartbroken that she had not been able to visit Bahá'u'lláh in the Holy Land.[42]

Fáṭimih Bagum, daughter of Áqá Siyyid Ja'far Yazdí, the distinguished cleric who had followed Vaḥíd and later been humiliated and tortured, passes away in the mid-1880s. She has raised three children.[43]

The grandson of Mihr 'Alí Khán, the commander who led the forces against Vaḥíd and the Bábís at Fort Khájih in 1850, remembers the fate of his grandfather: "My grandfather, the Shuja'u'l Mulk, when stricken down by his last illness, was dumb till the day of his death. Just at the end, those who stood near him saw his lips move, and, stooping down to hear what he was whispering, heard him repeat the word 'Bábí' three times. Immediately afterwards he fell back, dead."[44]

This grandson becomes a devoted Bahá'í.[45]

❋ ❋ ❋

Standing on the slope of Mount Carmel and looking over its rocky ground and the row of Cypress trees, Bahá'u'lláh, turns to 'Abdu'l-Bahá and tells him this is the spot which will receive the remains of His Herald, the Báb, and on which a shrine must be built for all to come and worship.[46]

In April of 1890, a boat is sailing on the Mediterranean toward Beirut. One of its passengers is an Englishman, Edward Granville Browne, the foremost Persian language scholar of Europe. He had become enthralled with the figure of the Báb and now is venturing east again to find and meet Bábís: "I wish very much that while in Persia I could have seen anyone who had seen the Báb or conversed with him . . . For suppose anyone could tell us more about the childhood and early life and appearance of Christ, for instance, how glad we should be able to know it. Now it is impossible to find out much, but in the case of the Báb it is possible, and I feel that now that it is possible, it may be neglected, and some day, when Bábísm has perhaps become the national religion of Persia, and many men long to know more about its founder, it will be impossible . . ."[47]

After riding south from Beirut, he came to the mansion of Bahjí outside of 'Akká, where Bahá'u'lláh lived now that the conditions of His imprisonment had been considerably loosened. Browne came into his presence:

> In the corner where the divan met the wall sat a wondrous and venerable figure, crowned with a felt head-dress of the kind called taj by dervishes (but of unusual height and make), round the base of which was wound a small white turban. The face of him on whom I gazed I can never forget, though I cannot describe it. Those piercing eyes seemed to read one's very soul; power and authority sat on that ample brow; while the deep lines on the forehead and face implied an age which the jet-black hair and beard flowing down in indistinguishable luxuriance almost to the waist seemed to belie. No need to ask in whose presence I stood, as I bowed myself before one who is the object of a devotion and love which kings might envy and emperors sigh for in vain.
>
> A mild dignified voice bade me be seated, and then continued: "Praise be God that thou has attained! . . . thou hast come to see a prisoner and an exile . . . We desire but the good of the world and the happiness of nations; yet they deem us a stirrer up of strife and sedition worthy of bondage and banishment . . . all nations should become one in faith and all men as brothers."[48]

On the evening of May 23rd, 1892, Bahá'u'lláh gathers family members, servants of His household, Bahá'ís and pilgrims and tells them He is well pleased with them. Six days later, a few hours after midnight, He passes away. Later that afternoon, His body is buried next to the mansion of Bahjí. This message is sent to the Sultan of the Ottoman Empire: "The sun of Bahá has set." Nabíl, the chronicler of the Bábí and early Bahá'í Faith, selects the passages which become the Tablet of Visitation and describes that time: "In the midst of the prevailing confusion a multitude of the inhabitants of 'Akká and of the neighboring villages, that had thronged the fields surrounding the Mansion, could be seen weeping, beating upon their heads, and crying aloud their grief."[49]

Nine days later, in front of nine witnesses and a large group of Bahá'ís which include members of Bahá'u'lláh's and the Báb's families, the Book of the Covenant is unsealed and read aloud. In it, Bahá'u'lláh instructs all—including members of His and the Báb's family—to "turn, one and all, unto the Most Great Branch ('Abdu'l-Bahá)."[50]

Vast numbers of mourners of all backgrounds flock to the mansion. Nabíl can't bear the separation and throws himself into the ocean.

Shafí', at 'Abdu'l Bahá's request, travels throughout the region of Nayríz to spread the Faith and prevent Covenant-breaking.[51]

Shafí' passes away in 1896. He is survived by seven children who will all suffer in the coming persecution. Because of the training he has given to the Bahá'í community, no one in Nayríz follows the Covenant-breakers, not even opening their letters.[52] His wife Khávar Sultán continues to use their home as a center for traveling teachers and other Bahá'í activities. She will suffer persecution in the coming time. 'Abdu'l Bahá composes a tablet of visitation in Shafí''s memory, praising his steadfastness, servitude, and love.*

---

* Provisional translation by Ṭahiríh Ahdieh, Nabíl Hanna, Abir Majíd, Rosann Velnich available at http://www.nayriz.org.

On May 1st, 1896, the King of Persia, Náṣiri'd-Dín Sháh, travels to the ancient city of Rey just southeast of Ṭihrán to offer thanksgiving for his rule at an important shrine.* By the reckoning of the Islámic lunar calendar, the king is approaching the fiftieth anniversary of the start of his reign. In honor of this, he is allowing ordinary people to approach him with a petition. Inside the magnificent blue domed shrine, he prays. When he rises, a poor merchant approaches him, stretches out his hand with a petition, then pulls out a small gun. The poor man, part of the rising tide of discontented people in Persia, fires the gun at point blank range, killing the king who has ruled Persia for half a century.[53]

The remains of the Body of the Báb are moved in secret to private homes of Bahá'ís in Ṭihrán to avoid being found. These are transferred from a wooden coffin into one made of iron. A letter is received from 'Abdu'l-Bahá telling the Bahá'ís that it is time to bring the Sacred remains to the Holy Land. Several Bahá'ís accompany the earthly remains of the Báb on the long journey through Iṣfáhán, Kirmansháh, Baghdád, Damascus, and Beirut . . . the Bahá'ís of Burma have made a sarcophagus of marble . . . half a century after the martyrdom of the Báb, His Remains arrive in Palestine.[54]

In the Book of Laws, Bahá'u'lláh had prophecied of Persia:

> Rejoice with great joy, for God hath made thee "the dayspring of his light," inasmuch as within thee was born the Manifestation of His glory. Be thou glad for this name that hath been conferred upon thee—a name through which the daystar of grace hath shed

* The shrine was dedicated to a religious scholar and descendant of the Third Ímám, Ímám Ḥusayn, Sháh Abdul Azim (786–865 AD).

its splendor, through which both earth and heaven have been illumined.

Erelong will the state of affairs within thee be changed, and the reins of power fall into the hands of the people. Verily, thy Lord is the All-Knowing. His authority embraceth all things. Rest thou assured in the gracious favor of thy Lord. The eyes of His loving-kindness shall everlastingly be directed toward thee.[55]

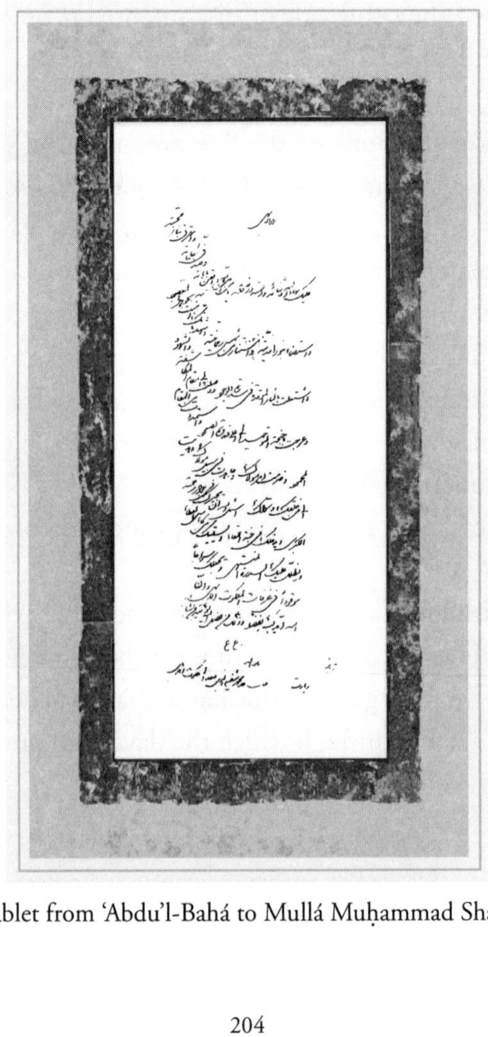

Tablet from 'Abdu'l-Bahá to Mullá Muḥammad Shafí'

NAYRÍZ, 1909

17

THE KINGDOM OF PERSIA IN CHAOS

Descendants of the sháhs were thrust into the most lucrative posts throughout the country, and as the generations went by they filled innumerable minor posts too, far and wide, until the land was burdened with this race of royal drones who owed their position to nothing better than their blood and who gave rise to the Persian saying that "camels, fleas and princes exist everywhere."

Even when a sháh wished to make a just and wise decision in any case that might be brought before him for judgment, he found it difficult to do so, because he could not rely on the information given him. Critical facts would be withheld, or the facts would be distorted by the influence of interested witnesses or venal ministers. The system of corruption had been carried so far in Persia that it had become a recognized institution . . .

(French historian A.L.M. Nicolas, quoted in the introduction to Nabíl-i-A'ẓam, *The Dawn-Breakers,* xxiv)

> "... Under a twofold governing system ... namely, an administration in which every actor is, in different aspects, both the briber and the bribed; and a judicial procedure without either a law or a law court—it will readily be understood that confidence in the Government is not likely to exist, that there is no personal sense of duty or pride of honour, no mutual trust or co-operation (except in the service of ill-doing), no disgrace in exposure, no credit in virtue, above all no national spirit or patriotism."
>
> (Englishman Lord Curzon, quoted in the introduction to Nabíl-i-A'ẓam, *The Dawn-Breakers,* xxvi)

By the early 1900s, the ineptitude, corruption, and backwardness of the Qájár dynasty had fatally weakened it. After his father's assassination, Náṣiri'd-Dín Sháh's son—who had spent his entire life pursuing pleasure without learning anything about statecraft, came to the throne to find the royal treasury completely empty. The kingdom he now ruled was deeply in debt to Russia and England. This did not stop him, though, from continuing his extravagant lifestyle. To pay for everything, he made concessions to foreign countries that would now control large parts of the economy.[1]

A movement aimed at bringing the kingdom under the rule of a constitution, limiting the power of the king, curbing the influence of England and Russia, and establishing the rule of law, took root. At the local and provincial levels, ordinary people had been at the whim of their clerics and government officials who made decisions arbitrarily. Often, any outcome depended on who could pay the most. The constitutionalists and the royalists struggled over the future of Persia and plunged the kingdom into chaos.[2]

Bahá'ís had been guided to stay out of these partisan struggles and always to work toward unity. 'Abdu'l-Bahá explained the Bahá'í teaching in a letter to Edward Granville Browne, who actively supported the constitutionalist cause and did not understand the Bahá'í view: "The aim of the Bahá'ís is the reformation of the world, so that amongst all the nations and governments reconciliation may be effected, disputation and conflict may cease, war and bloodshed may be abolished. Therefore they hasten onward with heart and soul, endeavour hard and spend themselves that perchance the Government and the Nation, nay all groups and nations, may be united to one another. And that peace and reconciliation may enter in."[3]

Bahá'u'lláh, in a Tablet revealed to Queen Victoria in the late 1860s, praised the creation of a representative assembly in governing a kingdom: "We have also heard that thou hast entrusted the reins of counsel into the hands of the representatives of the people. Thou, indeed, hast done well, for thereby the foundations of the edifice of thine affairs will be strengthened, and the hearts of all that are beneath thy shadow, whether high or low, will be tranquilized."[4]

Though some prominent Bahá'ís openly advocated for the constitutional side, the community as a whole followed 'Abdu'l-Bahá's guidance. Still, the Bahá'ís were blamed by pro-constitutionalists for supporting the monarchists and denounced by prominent clerics for supporting the constitutional side. Bahá'ís did have an influence through 'Abdu'l-Bahá's book *The Secret of Divine Civilization*, which proposed improving the Kingdom of Persia through the application of universal spiritual principles:[5]

> Would it seem shortsighted, improvident and unsound, would it constitute a deviation from what is right and proper,

if we were to strengthen our relationships with neighboring countries, enter into binding treaties with the great powers, foster friendly connections with well-disposed governments, look to the expansion of trade with the nations of East and West, develop our natural resources and increase the wealth of our people?

Would it spell perdition for our subjects if the provincial and district governors were relieved of their present absolute authority, whereby they function exactly as they please, and were instead limited to equity and truth, and if their sentences involving capital punishment, imprisonment and the like were contingent on confirmation by the Sháh and by higher courts in the capital, who would first duly investigate the case and determine the nature and seriousness of the crime, and then hand down a just decision subject to the issuance of a decree by the sovereign? If bribery and corruption, known today by the pleasant names of gifts and favors, were forever excluded, would this threaten the foundations of justice? Would it be an evidence of unsound thinking to deliver the soldiery, who are a living sacrifice to the state and the people and brave death at every turn, from their present extreme misery and indigence, and to make adequate arrangements for their sustenance, clothing and housing, and exert every effort to instruct their officers in military science, and supply them with the most advanced types of firearms and other weapons?[6]

With unrest spreading, the king was forced to make concessions in 1906 and allow for a constitution and a national assembly, both of which limited his royal power. A little over a month after doing this, he died of a heart attack. The new king now began to roll back the advances of the constitutionalists by eliminating the assembly, and he abolished the constitution, claiming that it was against Islámic law.[7]

Order broke down. Local power struggles flared up everywhere. Bandits roamed the countryside, and local chieftains took control in the provinces.[8]

In the hottest, most inhospitable part of the southern region of Fárs province lay the small city of Lar, from which a small-time cleric and rebellious opportunist emerged, Siyyid 'Abdu'l Ḥusayn Lárí. Through a combination of charisma and deception, he developed a wide circle of influence and took advantage of the chaos in the kingdom. Stories spread among the susceptible rural and village dwellers that he was gifted with miraculous powers, such as walking on water and healing through the application of the water he used for ablutions, which he sold to his followers. In the kingdom's constitutional struggle, he sided with the reformers so that he could take advantage of the popular discontent and defeat his rivals in the province. One such rival was the important tribal leader and supporter of the king, the Qavámu'l-Mulk, who was based in Shíráz and had important business dealings with the Afnán family, relatives of the Báb. When the king abdicated in the middle of that year, Siyyid 'Abdu'l Ḥusayn Lárí set up his own independent state in Fárs, complete with postage stamps, currency, and a police force. As his power spread through the province, he recruited local toughs to organize mercenary militias for various districts. One of these was Shaykh Dhakaríyyá from the town of Sar-Kúh. He was given responsibility for waging battle against the King's forces in his region.[9]

Unfortunately for the Bahá'ís, one town he set his sights on and which was about to have its calm shattered was Nayríz.[10]

18

THE INVASION OF 1909

In March, 1909, hundreds of fierce mountain tribesmen, loosely under the command of S͟haykh D͟hakaríyyá, arrived on the windy slope of the treeless "Mountain of the Infidels" and looked down at their prey—the town of Nayríz.[1] A few bushes rustled in the wind on the rocky slope; water here was scarce.* These men of the countryside, holding their rifles—some with swords, some on horses, others on foot and dressed in rough village clothing—had followed the S͟haykh in the hope of stealing riches during the coming battle.

The S͟haykh had come to Nayríz following Siyyid 'Abdu'l Ḥusayn Lárí's order to his underlings to go throughout their respective regions and attack government forces.[2] In advance of his coming, he had sent the following note to the leader of the Muslim community in Nayríz, the S͟haykhu'l Islám:

---

* Geographical information from a private conversation with Mr. Shoja'ádin Sardári (September, 2010).

> His Excellency, the Ayatu'llah Aqa Ḥájí Siyyid 'Abdu'l-Ḥusayn has currently ascended the throne, and the constitutional monarch is none other besides him. All must show submissiveness before him by considering his every command their religious obligation. As in accord with the all-sovereign wishes of the illustrious Ayatu'llah, I have arrived in this region today, I hereby charge you that, contingent with the instructions contained in this letter, you chain and send before me all the absolute monarchists so that I may send them under guard to the illustrious Ayatu'llah, the Sultanu'l-Muslimin [the King of the Muslims] that he may punish them in conformity with Islámic jurisprudence.
>
> Moreover you are to purge Nayríz of all members of the wayward and perverse Bahá'í community.
>
> Should anything other than what is commanded in this letter occur, then stand forewarned that I will come forth to Nayríz and will show no mercy.[3]

The order from Siyyid 'Abdu'l Ḥusayn Lárí gave Shaykh Dhakaríyyá the perfect opportunity to settle a score with his rival, the governor of Nayríz; to extend his personal power; and to gain wealth in the process.[4]

The Shaykhu'l Islám had a grievance against the governor stemming from the divorce between his daughter and the governor's son. As a result, the Shaykhu'l Islám had written Siyyid 'Abdu'l Ḥusayn Lárí asking for help against the governor, who sent Shaykh Dhakaríyyá.[5]

Shaykh Dhakaríyyá's men were now busy making crude four-foot stone fortifications.[6] From these positions, they could see the northern part of Nayríz, with its extensive bazaar, the main government buildings, and a bathhouse. On the northern edge of the town lay the Kúchih Bálá neighborhood, which had minor defenses and included the Sádát quarter where many of the clergy lived. To the east lay the walled village of Sayf-Ábád, manned by government soldiers. Many villages had walls around them and could be defended like a fort.

In the hazy distance lay Chinár-Súkhtih, the district where most of the Bahá'ís lived. The only substantial building there with any kind of defense was the Great Mosque at its south end where Vaḥíd had originally proclaimed the Message of the Báb.

Chinár-Súkhtih had recently been a place of great excitement, with the visit of two well-known Bahá'í teachers, Mr. Tarázu'lláh Samandarí and Mírzá 'Alí Akbar Rafsinjání, who had been traveling in Persia for several years lecturing on Bahá'u'lláh and His teachings. They had inspired the Bahá'ís of Nayríz and given them a much deeper understanding of the Faith. The meetings had grown larger as others in town became attracted to this new Faith. Some had to stand on roofs to hear what was being said in the courtyard of the home where Mr. Tarázu'lláh Samandarí was reciting the words of Bahá'u'lláh with a luminous expression on his face. He invited them all to join him as he sang Bahá'í songs in his Turkish accent.[7]

The deep social and emotional wounds caused to the local Bahá'ís by the violence of 1850 and 1853, as well as many other incidents of persecution, had begun to heal by 1909. Families were starting to do business with one another and neighborly relations were warming up. It was but a short time until the Persian New Year, March 21st, a season of celebration.

But this fragile social fabric was about to be torn apart, and the season would soon turn bloody.

On the morning of March 16th, Shaykh Dhakaríyyá ordered several of his men to go into the Kúchih Bálá neighborhood of northern Nayríz and spy on the defensive preparations. His men made it into town unnoticed and were even able to enlist some local people to help out. The town was weakly defended because the disputes between the families of the governor and the Shaykhu'l-Islám, meant they would not work together. There were also Nayrízís who supported the cause of the Shaykh Dhakaríyyá as they understood it.[8]

Darkness fell. Shaykh Dhakaríyyá's men crept down the rocky slope of the Mountain of the Infidels and approached Kúchih Bálá, with its one-story houses like a prey sleeping in the moonlight. Its few defenders were caught completely by surprise. The Shaykh's men walked into the town with no resistance and took over the area.

With morning came the realization that the takeover of Nayríz had begun. The government troops moved towards the Kúchih Bálá neighborhood to attempt to retake it. In the daylight, though, the Shaykh's men could see the soldiers and fired on them. Throughout the day of March 17th, they turned back the government's soldiers, killing many. Shaykh Dhakaríyyá stayed up in his mountain lair and sent his orders into town. Though the invaders controlled most of the neighborhood, sporadic fighting continued for several days.[9]

News of the attack by Shaykh Dhakaríyyá's men spread through town to the Bahá'í quarter. A young girl, Páríján, left her home with her family for a more secure location next to the Great Mosque, the strongest building in south Nayríz.[10]

The following day, March 18th, the 24th of Saffar, the Shaykh's men moved on Sayf-Ábád, the walled village a short distance to the east. Government troops were stationed there, but many of its residents supported the Shaykh. The attack got underway. The soldiers fired back, but without popular support or much personal motivation, their defense quickly disintegrated. Shaykh Dhakaríyyá soon came down the mountain to march into Sayf-Ábád at the head of his men.[11]

Now he invited the leading citizens of Nayríz to come meet him. Once they had arrived at Sayf-Ábád, the Shaykh stood in front of them and proclaimed Siyyid 'Abdu'l Ḥusayn Lárí the ruler of the province of Fárs and himself the defender of the law of Islám. He proclaimed that he had come on the new ruler's orders to overthrow the government forces and cleanse Nayríz of Bahá'ís. He calmed the nervous citizens by speaking of his peaceful intentions toward Muslims and then served his guests dates to show his goodwill. They left the meeting feeling more like his supporters than his victims. Rumors spread that the Shaykh had great powers and that he could perform miracles, such as multiplying dates to feed large numbers of guests. Some even believed that in fighting for him, they were fighting for the Twelfth Ímám, the liberator who would restore Islám.[12]

The Shaykh's men then turned their attention to the wealthy bazaar district to the west where large fortified homes stood empty—their wealthy owners having fled—except for the governor's mansion, where a few defenders remained. The Shaykh moved into the military commander's home, the strongest building in the area. The commander, Muḥammad Ḥasan Khán, and his family had left the city disguised in *chádurs*, the traditional covering for women. The Shaykh's men positioned themselves at the windows and fired across the street at the governor's home. After some initial resistance, the outnumbered defenders ran from the house. Hundreds of the Shaykh's men fanned out throughout the bazaar. Hearing news of the commander's abandonment of the town and the loss of government protection, Bahá'ís quietly began packing necessities and slipping away.[13]

With the bazaar to themselves, the Shaykh's men began looting the homes of the Muslim residents. The Shaykh exercised little control over his men, and they were intent on profiting from their attack on Nayríz.[14]

The Shaykhu'l-Islám's house was the first to be looted. As men ransacked his house, the Shaykhu'l-Islám sat on the stairs, shocked by the betrayal of S͟hayk͟h D͟hakaríyyá. After this home invasion, the S͟hayk͟hu'l-Islám secluded himself in a room, refusing to come out. For the next twenty-four hours, homes of other Muslims were attacked.¹⁵

Alarmed by the violence, wealthy merchants, important clerics, and even a prominent siyyid from Iṣṭahbánát visited S͟hayk͟h D͟hakaríyyá on March 19th.* The siyyid told the S͟hayk͟h that the people of Nayríz supported their religious leader, the S͟hayk͟hu'l-Islám, and would turn against him because of this looting, ally themselves with the Bahá'ís, drive him out, and give popular support to the government forces who would then return. S͟hayk͟h D͟hakaríyyá, an uneducated man from a village, was easily swayed by these more learned men. He apologized for what had happened and assured them that the violence had been the initiative of his men and not done on his orders. He showed the siyyid from Iṣṭahbánát the order that Siyyid 'Abdu'l Ḥusayn Lárí had written. The siyyid told him that to restore trust with the Muslim residents and be seen as a defender of Islám, he should concentrate on attacking the Bahá'í neighborhood and promise that the Muslims would not be attacked again. This also would have to be announced publicly to the Nayrízís. The S͟hayk͟h agreed to this plan.¹⁶

On the day before the beginning of the New Year, the town criers' voices echoed through the streets. They announced the offer of two hundred tumans for any Bahá'í taken alive and one hundred tumans for the severed head of a Bahá'í. Muslims would be safe. Many Nayrízís now turned their backs on their Bahá'í neighbors, even pointing out the homes of Bahá'ís. Some Muslims, though, such as Mírzá Muḥammad Sho'a; Mas͟hhadí Ḥasan S͟hu'á"i; Siyyid 'Alí Heshmatu'lláh Islám and his father, Siyyid Dawhood—two important clerics**—and others,

---

* Siyyid Ja'far Iṣṭahbánátí.
** These two are listed by Ahdieh, *Nayrízi-S͟hurangiz* (130).

helped their Bahá'í neighbors at great personal risk. S͟hayk͟h D͟hakaríyyá offered this bounty on Bahá'ís in part because he knew they were fleeing to the mountains, and he wanted to enlist the Nayrízís in the effort to capture them.¹⁷

Now an exodus from C͟hinár-Súk͟htih, the Bahá'í district, began. Even the governor of Nayríz—disguised in a chádur—had fled Nayríz with the Bahá'í families. In homes all over that area, clothing and food were being bundled up, and weapons of any kind were given to the men for whose lives the women now feared. Many began walking hurriedly towards their orchards in the mountains to the south, twelve went to Iṣṭahbánát, some went to Lashni*—a village on the road to Sírján northeast of Nayríz**—and a large contingent headed in the direction of Sarvistán. To divert attention away from those fleeing, a group of men stationed themselves at the Great Mosque and prepared to fire on S͟hayk͟h D͟hakaríyyá's men.¹⁸

The sounds of the S͟hayk͟h's men shouting and shooting could be heard through the streets of C͟hinár-Súk͟htih. A home was torched. As some of the attackers approached the Great Mosque, shots were fired back and forth. One shot from the street hit Muḥammad Ḥasan, a Bahá'í fighting in the mosque, as he looked through a hole in the upper defenses. The bullet traveled through the hole and into his eye, killing him.† His home was later ransacked and burned. Still a young man, whose livelihood had been to make and sell hats out of sheep's wool, his death left his daughter, Zivar, bereaved.¹⁹‡

---

* The Iṣṭahbánát and Lashni groups are listed in Faizi.

** From a conversation with Shoja'ádin Sardári, July, 2010.

† Rouhani states that the S͟hayk͟h's men came to round up Bahá'ís on the following morning but, given the other sources, and the fact that a Bahá'í was killed on this day, the cited rendition seems more likely.

‡ She married 'Abdu'llah Amjadi. They had five children: Fariboorz, Hussein, Vaḥíd, 'Abbás, and Jalál.

One large Bahá'í family that had to flee was that of Shaykh Muḥammad Ḥusayn,* the son of Shafi', who had married the daughter of 'Alí Sardár's niece, Saheb Jan. Shafí' had inherited his father's position of transcribing legal and religious documents at the Great Mosque. Wishing to leave that line of work, he had founded a dry-goods trading company with a fellow Bahá'í, Kh́ájih 'Alí Izadi. He often acted to protect fellow Bahá'ís and friends in times of difficulty. Now, Shaykh Muḥammad Ḥusayn led a large group out of town with its necessary belongings loaded onto donkeys. The group included his grandmother, mother, four aunts, sisters, young children, youth—nieces and nephews—and brothers-in-law, Mashadí Darvish and Asadu'lláh. A Muslim friend, Asadu'lláh, guided them south to the mountains. But when they came into the foothills, they didn't have the strength to make it up the mountains, so they headed for Tang-i Láy-i Ḥiná, a valley to the west that had several caves that could be used for shelter and as hiding places. Once they had found one for the night, they settled down and rested.[20]

Night came. The Shaykh's men left the hunting of Bahá'ís for the next day. In the dark, the rest of the Bahá'í men over ten years of age and more families fled. Defense of the Great Mosque was abandoned.[21]

Shaykh Muḥammad Ḥusayn's brother-in-law, a Muslim, ran to the cave in Tang-i Láy-i Ḥiná where the family was hiding. He informed them of the events of the day and that all men and boys over twelve were in danger for their lives and must leave the area.[22]

It was March 20th, New Year's Eve.

* Later the name *Ahdieh* became his family's name.

Saheb Jan Khánum

'Abdu'l-Bahá with Shaykh Muḥammad Ḥusayn

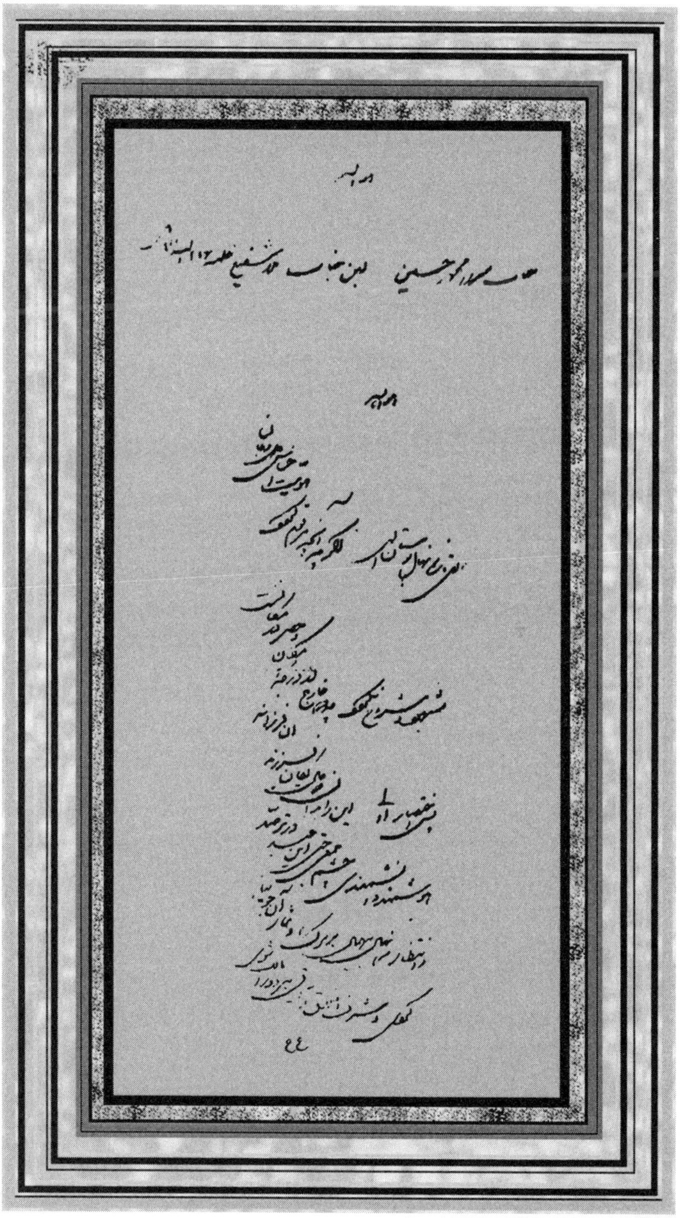

Tablet from 'Abdu'l-Bahá to <u>Sh</u>ay<u>kh</u> Muḥammad Ḥusayn

19

SUFFERING OF THE FAITHFUL

At two in the morning inside a dark cave in the Tang-i Láy-i Ḥiná valley, Shaykh Muḥammad Ḥusayn entrusted the women and exhausted young children in his family to his Muslim brother-in-law who had come to help them. The men would leave the region. The women and children would return to Nayríz under the care of the brother-in-law, but there were boys just over twelve who, lacking nourishment and strength, could not make the long trek through the mountains. So the men dressed the boys in chádurs to hide their faces and bodies so they could return to Nayríz undetected.

The women and children, hungry and frightened, and the men, powerless to protect their families, all longed to stay together but were now forced to separate, leaving each others' comforting presence for uncertainty and danger. Khávar Sultán did her best to be courageous as she let go of her son, Shaykh Muḥammad Ḥusayn. With tears, the two groups parted.[1]

Tablet from 'Abdu'l-Bahá to Mírzá Ibráhím

The New Year's day sun rose on mountains where Bahá'í men hid for their lives and on a Chinár-Súkhtih district empty except for Bahá'í women and children who trembled inside their homes, with a few of their men hiding in the darkest corners, hoping not to be found.

Out in the Bídlang area at the foot of the southern mountains, where the wind blows through the fruit trees and a spring of water bursts out of the ground, a Bahá'í woman, Hajan, the daughter of Karbalá'í Mehdí, was in the orchard making bread for the morning meal. She had argued the night before with her son, 'Abdu'l-Riḍá, who hated the Bahá'í Faith. On this morning, as he prepared to go on a hunt, he again insulted the Faith. She cursed him. Angry, he went to get his hunting rifle, returned, and shot her.[2]

In another part of the foothills, a group of Shaykh Dhakaríyyá's men were looking for Bahá'ís and approached some Nayrízís who were out working. A reward had been offered by the Shaykh for their capture or their heads, and his men wanted that money. Hoping that any reward money might be shared, the Nayrízís pointed back towards the orchards where several Bahá'ís hid.[3]

The Shaykh's men saw three Bahá'ís hiding there, surrounded them, and opened fire, killing their Muslim servant. The other two surrendered, accepting that they would sacrifice their lives. One of them, Mullá Ḥasan, a thirty-one-year-old wealthy cloth merchant, was the grandson of Mullá Ḥasan Lab-Shikarí, who had received a ring from the Báb and helped the Bábís in 1850 and 1853. His fellow prisoner was his own father-in-law, Mullá Muḥammad 'Alí. The two men were bound and pushed forward toward town.[4]

The prisoners walked the five kilometers to Nayríz while being hit and taunted by their captors. Hearing of their capture and alarmed by what would happen to their friends, three respected Muslim citizens, Haj Siyyid Ibráhim and Haj Siyyid Qasím from the bazaar quarter, and

Siyyid Nasru'lláh from the Chinár-Súkhtih quarter, decided to help them gain their freedom. They found the prisoners before they arrived in front of the Shaykh and implored Mullá Ḥasan to recant, but he refused to disguise his faith even though he knew he'd be leaving his wife, Páríján, to care for their two small children, Fáṭimih and 'Abdu'l Samí, alone.* He recited a verse regarding the immortality of the soul. A guard struck him. His three friends then went to offer money to the Shaykh to prevent the execution. The Shaykh accepted the bribe on condition that the two recant.[5]

But still Mullá Ḥasan did not recant. Angered, the Shaykh motioned, and a sword struck Ḥasan's head and face. He fell to the ground. A guard raised his rifle and shot him. With blood pooling around his son-in-law's body, Mullá Muḥammad 'Alí cursed at Shaykh Dhakaríyyá. The Shaykh motioned to one of his men who then pulled out a large knife and in one motion slit Mullá Muḥammad 'Alí's throat. Several men then bound the feet of the barely breathing 'Alí and dragged him through the streets of the Chinár-Súkhtih district to the Great mosque, where they strung his body upside down from a tree. Stones pelted 'Alí, and his life slipped away.** Men piled wood beneath

---

* Fáṭimih later married Mírzá 'Alí Aghsan and had two children: Olya Khánum and Muḥammad Riḍá, both of whom became Bahá'ís. 'Abdu'l Sami married Mírzá Aḥmad Vaḥídi's daughter, T'abandeh Khánum. They had many children: Parivash, Fáṭimih, Ghodsiyyih, Ḥasan, Hooshang, Ruhu'lláh, Muḥammad 'Alí, Bahram, and Bahman, who all served the Faith in Iran and different parts of the world (Ahdieh, *Nayrízi-Shurangiz*, 133).

** He had three children at the time: Khánum Páríján Shahídpúr, Muḥammad Báqir, and Fazlu'lláh. Muḥammad Báqir married Bibi Vafa'i but they had no children. Fazlu'lláh married Khánum Siyaiyeh, daughter of Siyyid Mahd Anvari. They had a son, Ḥájí Áqáyih Rasekhi who married Gohar Khánum; Gohar's father was Jináb-i-Badí'u'lláh Jazzabi.

his corpse and started a fire. The body began burning. A man sliced open the abdomen, and the intestines spilled out into the flames.[6]

A few hours earlier, Páríján had left her hiding place to see what was happening. A neighbor saw her and came over in tears. Páríján asked her why she was crying, and the neighbor told her she had just seen Páríján's father and husband killed. Páríján quickly put her six-month-old son and five-year-old daughter back in the house and raced north up the street towards the bazaar district where the killing had taken place. She ran into a very large crowd. They were watching something. She made her way forward and then saw the body of a man being dragged by his feet. It was her father.

Her mother joined her. Other women, recognizing Páríján and her mother, told them that they had to go and hide, or they too would be killed. Mother and daughter ran back to the Chinár-Súkhtih district and banged on several neighbors' doors, but even friends and neighbors were too frightened to let them in. Having nowhere to hide, they made their way south out of town and found a field with tall bushes. They pushed their way into it, but its owner saw them crouching down and told them to leave. They came to a wall, climbed over it, and fell into a large orchard. They remained there without making a sound. In the distance, they could hear the mob screaming as Páríján's father's body was being hung upside down. Looking up, they saw a man climbing over the wall. He was a friend. He jumped down and told them they could find shelter with him for the night.[7]

❋ ❋ ❋

Shaykh Muḥammad Ḥusayn's extended family finally arrived at an old abandoned house near Nayríz in which they could take shelter. They didn't have the strength to go any further.

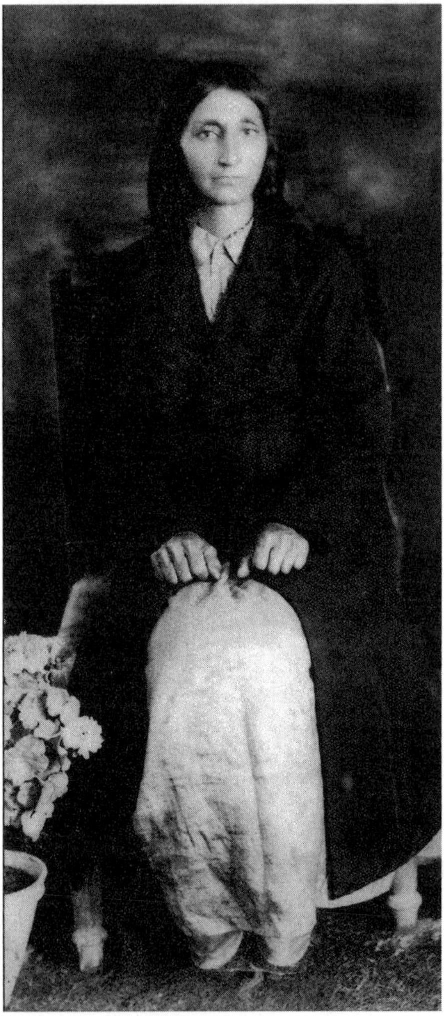

Páríján Khánum

The night before, the children had cried from hunger. In the morning, their guide, Mashadí Ḥasan, had come to lead them to Nayríz. They had approached a small house with smoke coming out of the chimney, hoping they might be able to prepare the small amount of flour they had left. The woman of the house, though, screamed at them to leave. She blamed them as Bahá'ís for the misfortunes that had recently fallen on Nayríz.

So they had trudged on, only able to cover seven kilometres that day. Along the way, some of the Shaykh's men had seen them and, even though Mashadí Ḥasan and his servant were Muslims, had robbed them of all their belongings. The chádur covering the twelve-year-old-boy Rouhani had saved him from being taken captive and killed.

The only nourishment the women and children found were figs strewn on the ground; they eagerly picked them up and ate them. With evening coming on, they decided to stop for the night in an old abandoned house. Mashhadí Ḥasan went to get them water and bread.[8]

❋ ❋ ❋

A thousand miles away from Nayríz, the fifty-nine year long journey of the body of the Báb from hiding place to hiding place was reaching its final moments on the slope of Mount Carmel in Palestine. A group of Bahá'ís, including three men from Nayríz, watched every one of 'Abdu'l-Bahá's movements as the profoundly sacred moment unfolded.

'Abdu'l-Bahá lowered the casket into the marble sarcophagus by the light of a solitary lamp. His hands let go of the wooden casket containing the body of Siyyid 'Alí-Muḥammad, the Báb, who had been the Manifestation of God to all people, the Giver of Laws and the regenerator of all life. So many years had passed, so many Bahá'ís had given their lives, so much suffering had been endured by Him, and so much power had poured out from His Pen before He gave up His own Life . . .

With the casket resting on the bottom of the sarcophagus, 'Abdu'l-Bahá took off his turban, his shoes, and his cloak and ". . . bent low over the still open sarcophagus, His silver hair waving about His head and His face transfigured and luminous, rested His forehead on the border of the wooden casket, and, sobbing aloud, wept with such a weeping that all those who were present wept with Him. That night He could not sleep, so overwhelmed was He with emotion."[9]

Later, 'Abdu'l-Bahá wrote of this day:

> The most joyful tidings is this, that the holy, the luminous body of the Báb . . . after having for sixty years been transferred from place to place, by reason of the ascendancy of the enemy, and from fear of the malevolent, and having known neither rest nor tranquility has, through the mercy of the Abhá Beauty, been ceremoniously deposited, on the day of Naw-Rúz, within the sacred casket, in the exalted Shrine on Mt. Carmel . . . By a strange coincidence, on that same day of Naw-Rúz, a cablegram was received from Chicago, announcing that the Bahá'ís in each of the American centers had elected a delegate and sent to that city . . . and definitely decided on the site of the Mashriqu'l-Askár."[10]

❋ ❋ ❋

In Nayríz that night, a silvery figure made its way through the empty streets of the bazaar. The mutilated corpse of Mullá Ḥasan had been left in a public square of the bazaar. The figure was Mullá Ḥasan's Muslim friend from childhood, 'Alí. This good friend picked up the body in his arms and carried it out of the square to the Aghel Khatib cemetery. There he dug a grave, carefully placed his friend's body into it and covered it over with soil.[11]

❋ ❋ ❋

In an old abandoned house outside of town, the women and children of Shaykh Muḥammad Ḥusayn's family couldn't fall asleep. They heard voices of people outside in the night looking for Bahá'ís. Mashhadí Ḥasan, their guide, came in and told them that people were looking for Bahá'í males over twelve and that two Bahá'í men had been martyred earlier that day. The old house would not provide sufficient protection for them, he said, and he would return at dawn to bring them to homes in town where they would be safe. Then he went back out into the night.

Wide awake, the women and children huddled in the abandoned old house, waiting for dawn.[12]

Graves of Martyrs of 1909 Upheaval

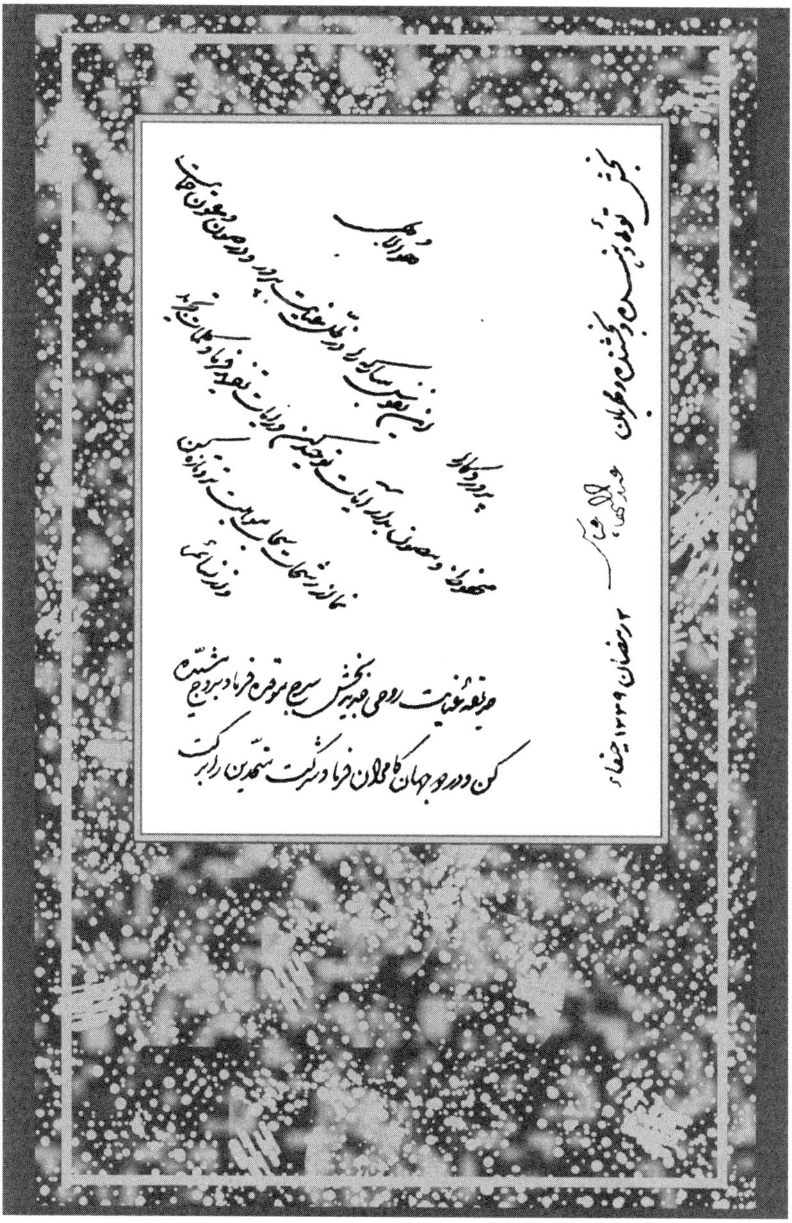

'Abdu'l-Bahá to Shaykh Muḥammad Ḥusayn

20

THE TEMPLE SACRIFICE

With these words, Thornton Chase, the first American Bahá'í, opened the first nationwide Bahá'í convention, on March 22nd, 1909, in Chicago, Illinois, over nine-thousand six-hundred kilometers and many worlds away from the town of Nayríz in the Persian heartland: "This is a Bahá'í Assembly; that means much. 'Abdu'l-Bahá has written that 'when one enters a meeting he should array himself in clean garments and purify himself. This signifies that all personal desires or ambitions should vanish. Although opinions may differ, they should be like ripples on the waving sea and be lost in the ocean of love. We should put ourselves actively under the guidance of the Spirit of God, and as there is but one Spirit of God, every action in its completion should be unanimous; there should never be a minority in a Bahá'í Convention.'"[1]

With violence descending on the Bahá'ís of Nayríz, the American delegates consulted on raising up the first House of Worship in the

Western world. Bahá'í representatives of thirty-six communities from all over the United States had come together for the Bahá'í Temple Convention. To open the meeting, Corinne True, a believer from Chicago who had been actively involved in the Temple effort, read this passage from a letter written by 'Abdu'l-Bahá to the Convention explaining the importance of building a House of Worship, a *Mashriqu'l-Azkár*:

> In the cycle of His Holiness the Christ, a long time elapsed before the fame of praise and sanctification became world-wide; nevertheless, consider how at length it encircled the globe. But the glorious radiance, like the shining twilight, of this Sun of the horizons, in the very inception of its dawn, was widespread; therefore, consider what great results will soon be forthcoming and what wondrous signs shall appear. Now is the commencement of organization, hence every affair concerning the Kingdom of God is of paramount importance.
>
> Among the most important affairs is the founding of the Mashriqu'l-Azkár, although weak minds may not grasp its importance; nay, perchance, they imagine this to be a Temple like others temples. They may say to themselves: "Every nation has a hundred thousand gigantic temples; what result have they yielded that now this one Mashriqu'l-Azkár (is said) to cause the manifestation of signs and prove a source of lights?" But they are ignorant of the fact that the founding of this Mashriqu'l-Azkár is to be the inception of the organization of the Kingdom. Therefore it is important and is an expression of the upraising of the Evident Standard, which is waving in the center of that continent, and the results and effects of which will become manifest in the hearts

> and spirits. No soul will be aware of this mature wisdom save after trial . . .
>
> . . . Moreover the accessories of the Mashriqu'l-Azkár are numerous. Among them are the School for Orphans, the great College for the Higher Arts, hospital, Home for the Cripple and Hospice. The doors of these places are to be opened to all sects—no differentiations. When these accessories are completed, and by God's help and aid the departments fully systematized, it will be proved that the Mashriqu'l-Azkár is to human society a great bounty and a great blessing.
>
> . . . This organization of the Mashriqu'l-Azkár will be a sample for the coming centuries and will hold the station of the mother, and thus later in other cities many Mashriqu'l-Azkár will be its offspring."[2]

The delegates were then officially seated from cities all over the United States—New York to Walla Walla, Washington; Racine, Wisconsin, to Denver; and Washington, DC to Los Angeles.

The morning session ended with the following resolution: "RESOLVED, That this Convention do confirm and select this site, situate in the Village of Wilmette, Cook County, Illinois, reported to us, and that we proceed to acquire, by purchase, this property as the site of the Mashriqu'l-Azkár."[3]

❋ ❋ ❋

While the delegates consulted in Chicago, in Nayríz, the twelve-year-old Muḥammad Shafí' walked through the streets of the Chinár-Súkhtih quarter wearing a chádur as a protective disguise. He held the hand of his second cousin. The boy had spent a sleepless night with the rest of his family in an old abandoned stone house outside of town. At dawn, Mírzá Muḥammad Sho'a, a Muslim relative whose cousin was on friendly terms with Shaykh Dhakaríyyá, had arrived to take them safely into town. Shafí' would be staying with his mother, Núríján, and his siblings, while the others would stay at his home. The boy Shafí''s father was far away in the Holy Land.[4]

As the two walked past the Great Mosque, Muḥammad Shafí' caught sight of the charred corpse hanging upside down from the tree. Beneath it were the stones that had been thrown at it. The cousin could feel Muḥammad Shafí''s hand begin to shake, and he immediately pulled Shafí' away from the frightening scene. When they reached the cousin's house, Shafí' fell ill from the shock of what he had just seen. Now he had to be put in a safe hiding place, so he hid under the saddlebags in the family storeroom. The other women refugees stayed in another room. He had to remain in that small space during the daytime and could only come out briefly at night.[5]

The hunt for Bahá'ís through the streets of Nayríz and the mountains intensified.

Soldiers went house-to-house extorting money from frightened Bahá'ís; the Shaykh also used cunning and threats of violence to have properties signed over to him.[6]

Out in the foothills of the mountains south of Nayríz, five Bahá'í men had tried to hide with Muḥammad Ismá'íl in his orchard. His father had lost his life in the conflict of 1853, after which he and his mother had been taken captive.* With him in the orchard were his sons, 'Alí

* They hid in another orchard known as 'baghe razi,' about twelve kilometers outside Nayríz (Rouhani v. 2, 97) in the foothills of the mountains to the south. Over forty owners had property there. There were several water sources, springs, and

and Rahmán; his brother, Muḥammad Ibráhim; and Ibráhim's sons-in-law, Mehdí and Asadu'lláh. Several Nayrízís, greedy for the reward money being offered and knowing where they were hiding, brought a few of the Shaykh's men to the orchard. The seven men were tied up and beaten as they marched toward town.[7]

They arrived battered and bloody at the public square in the bazaar. The Shaykh demanded that each one of them recant.[8]

Muḥammad Ismaí'íl faced his persecutor with a joyful expression and declared his faith. He was immediately taken away to be killed.[9]

Mullá 'Alí, his son, was to be married in two days, but when the Shaykh called him forward and demanded to know about his faith, he asserted his belief in Bahá'u'lláh. He was put to death while his brother Rahmán had to watch.[10]

Muḥammad Ibráhim was brought forward, and he affirmed his faith, looking forward to his martyrdom as the greatest offering he could give to God. He had been taken captive as a boy with his mother and brother in 1853, experienced the martyrdom of his father, and now joined him, his brother, and his nephew in martyrdom.[11]

Asadu'lláh, Ibráhim's son in law, had just gotten married and was looking forward to living a long life and raising a family. When confronted with the demand to recant, though, he gave his life willingly and eagerly for the Faith. He had no children; the only trace he left in this world was the example of his sacrifice.[12]

'Alí Akbar, the nephew of Muḥammad Ismá'íl, loved to write poetry, especially about 'Abdu'l-Bahá, whom he had met in the Holy Land a few years earlier. He would chant verses and express his desire to be a

---

the qanat. At the start of the 1853 conflict, many Bahá'ís hid in a 'baghe razi,' but in that case, it was the one outside the town (from a conversation with Shoja'ádin Sardári 5/10).

sacrifice. Standing before the Shaykh and refusing to recant, his desire was fulfilled.

Mehdí stood in front of the Shaykh and followed in the footsteps of his brethren. He was violently struck down.[13] His father, Mullá Ḥusayn, had been hiding from the Shaykh's men because his Muslim friends wanted to protect him. But when he heard that his son, Mehdí, had been captured, he ran out to find him. He was stopped by two soldiers, and he begged them to take him to his son. They agreed, for a price. So Mullá Ḥusayn took them to his house and paid them. He was then led to the public square in the bazaar where the soldiers were given rewards by the Shaykh for bringing a Bahá'í alive to him. When Mullá Ḥusayn saw his son Mehdí's bloody corpse lying on the ground, he begged the Shaykh to die with him. The Shaykh had Mullá Ḥusayn shot.[14]

After these six Bahá'ís had been killed, it was Rahmán's turn, and he was brought forward. He also courageously declared his faith. Suddenly, a Muslim man ran up to the Shaykh asking that Mullá 'Alí be freed because he was to marry his daughter in two days—but it was too late, 'Alí had already been killed by the Shaykh's men. To placate the Muslim man, Rahmán, 'Alí's brother, was spared and later released.[15]

Two more Bahá'ís, Jináb Amru'lláh and Jináb Ustád Atau'lláh, who were hiding in the mountains, were turned in by local Nayrízís looking for a reward. After a savage beating, the young Amru'lláh was thrown on the ground in front of the Shaykh. He whispered his wish for martyrdom. He was shot, and his body was dumped in a pit. His Muslim wife's family rescued it later and buried it properly, but his son was never raised as a Bahá'í. Atau'lláh appeared before the Shaykh after he had been whipped by his captors and stoned by local people, able to stand only long enough to testify to his faith. He was shot in the public square.[16]

South of the bazaar, in the streets of the <u>Ch</u>inár-Sú<u>kh</u>tih quarter, a few men eager for the reward money and to show their loyalty to the <u>Sh</u>ay<u>kh</u> pointed out the home of an elderly blind Bahá'í, Mullá 'Abdu'l Majíd, whose wonderful storytelling and good humor had been enjoyed for years by his neighbors. He sat pondering about the fear gripping his neighborhood when, suddenly, he was startled by the feeling of the hands of the <u>Sh</u>ay<u>kh</u>'s men grabbing him and pulling him outside. One blow after another came down on him. He fell into the dirt. He was then yanked up and dragged through the streets whose sounds and smell he knew so well from years of doing business in them.

Soon, he felt himself pushed forward forcefully and then heard himself denounced as a Bahá'í. A loud voice demanded that he recant. He remained silent. An order was given. He heard the clicks of rifles being cocked, the commander's shout, and then loud cracks and booms.[17]

❀ ❀ ❀

The water of the Mediterranean sparkled in the bay of Haifa on this clear spring day. In view of it, 'Abdu'l-Bahá walked with three Bahá'ís from Nayríz—Mírzá 'Abdu'l-Ḥusayn, Mírzá Aḥmad Vaḥídí, and Mírzá Fazlu'lláh, who were on pilgrimage in Haifa.

As they followed 'Abdu'l-Bahá, Mírzá Aḥmad Vaḥídí felt gratitude for the great privilege he was experiencing.

He remembered how he had become a believer. Many years before, he used to mock a simple cobbler, Karbalá'í Ḥusayn, for being a Bahá'í. The cobbler reminded him of an Islámic oral tradition, which stated that if a believer heard of someone claiming to be the Promised Qá'im, that believer should investigate the claim no matter what the effort. Instead of engaging in a conversation, the cobbler pointed out, Vaḥídí was simply cursing him like the unbelievers in the time of Muḥammad. Confronted with this challenge, Vaḥídí went to see a respected Muslim cleric and asked him about the hadíth. The cleric dismissed his question, saying that such issues were for the clergy to consider, and asked Vaḥídí why he would even consider going to a simple man like Karbalá'í Ḥusayn regarding such important questions. The arrogance of the cleric and the emptiness of his words caused Vaḥídí's eyes to open. He returned to Karbalá'í Ḥusayn, humbled himself, and declared himself a believer.[18]

The day before, Mírzá Aḥmad Vaḥídí and the other two Nayrízís had ridden with 'Abdu'l-Bahá in his carriage after the interment of the sacred remains of the Báb. Now the three men found themselves again in 'Abdu'l-Bahá's powerful presence. Mírzá Aḥmad Vaḥídí wondered about this.

Then 'Abdu'l-Bahá's expression turned somber as he looked out over the calm water and blue skies. He told them that there was a great storm and that they must return to Nayríz immediately . . .[19]

❁ ❁ ❁

In the dark of that night in Nayríz, two Muslim farm workers made their way quietly past the Great Mosque toward the charred remains of their employer, Mullá Muḥammad 'Alí, whose lands they had worked. Once they had reached the tree, they leaned over the ashes of the burnt-out fire and picked out their master's bones. One man held the sack cloth, and the other placed the bones in it. Then they quickly left the scene and walked to the Aghel Khatib cemetery, where they laid the remains in a pit and covered them with soil.[20]

21

THE THIRD DAY

This plea to God from a prayer by 'Abdu'l-Bahá opened the morning session of the second day of the first national Bahá'í convention in the United States on March 23rd, 1909: ". . . O our Lord! We are weak and Thou art the Mighty, the Powerful! We are mortals and Thou art the great life-giving Spirit! We are needy and Thou art the Powerful and Sustainer. O our Lord! Turn our faces unto Thy divine face; feed us from Thy heavenly table by Thy godly grace; help us through the hosts of Thy supreme angels and confirm us by the holy ones of the Kingdom of Abhá . . ."[1]

Then came the reading of a tablet from 'Abdu'l-Bahá specifically for this convention:

> . . . when the people find a person who is in word the sign of oneness, in behavior the essence of abstraction, and in deed the reality of sanctification, they may cry out, "This is a Bahá'í!"

> Should we become as such, the manifest light will shine in our brow . . .
>
> O My Lord! Make them Thy refulgent dawns which shine and gleam upon the Temple of Unity, so that they may be resuscitated from the tombs of negligence, unfurl the standard of virtue and chant the verses of self-abnegation and renunciation. While hastening towards the altar of sacrifice . . .[2]

Then the constitution for the new nationwide governing body, written by a committee of the delegates, was read:

> Article I: We acknowledge God as the Source and Preserver of our Unity, revealed to us through the Manifestation of His Glory in Bahá'o'llah and declared by the beloved Servant of God and man, 'Abdu'l-Bahá.
>
> Article II: The name of this Unity shall be Bahá'í Temple Unity.
>
> Article III: The object of this Unity shall be to aquire a site for and erect and maintain thereon a Bahá'í Temple or Meshrek-el-Azkar, with service accessory buildings, at Chicago, Ill., in accordance with the declared wishes of 'Abdu'l-Bahá . . .[3]

❋ ❋ ❋

That same morning in Nayríz, Núríján, the daughter of Muḥammad Shafí', was going hurriedly to her Muslim nephew's home to seek protection. Her husband, Mullá 'Abdu'l-Ḥusayn, was in the Holy Land and could not help them. Many of her relatives had fled to the caves at

Tang-i Láy-i Ḥiná. In the coming days, all the properties of her husband would be stolen, and she and her family would be left destitute.[4]

In the mountains south of Nayríz, Muḥammad 'Alí and Ibráhim hid in their Muslim friend Muḥammad's orchard. Their family had known persecution for as long as either could remember. Their father, Darvish, was killed during the conflict of 1853, and they were raised by Ḥájí Qasím, their relative. They grew into committed Bahá'ís and started a small trading business. Ibráhim married Fáṭimih and began a family. Now the two brothers were being forced to hide. Ibráhim and his son, Muḥammad Ḥusayn Mubraem Ain, hid in a tile factory on March 22nd; he told his son that he would eventually be martyred. Fáṭimih, anxious about the house-by-house searches taking place in the Bahá'í neighborhood, encouraged them to leave town. Muḥammad 'Alí, now sixty-three, was not able to make the trek into the mountains, so he went to hide with his son, Ṭahmásb, in Vaḥíd's old house, a more secure location, with another Bahá'í, Ustád 'Alí Sabbá<u>gh</u>.

The two brothers parted ways, never to see each other again in this life.

Ibráhim took a little food and walked south, but he had only enough food for one night, so the next day, he made his way back. As they approached town, a Muslim friend, Muḥammad, told him of the capture and killing of Bahá'ís and the burning of their homes. He warned Ibráhim not to go into town but to hide in his orchard. Ibráhim gave his friend some money for food, and Muḥammad set off. On the road, though, Muḥammad was stopped by some of the <u>Sh</u>ay<u>kh</u>'s men, who demanded to know if he knew the whereabouts of any Bahá'ís. They spoke menacingly to him and threatened him with death. Knowing full well that the <u>Sh</u>ay<u>kh</u>'s men were capable of great violence, Muḥammad told them that there was a Bahá'í in his orchard.[5]

Ibráhim was captured and taken into town. Standing before the Shaykh, he refused to recant, and the Shaykh ordered his execution. Ibráhim did not die immediately from being shot, so he was struck with a violent blow of a sword.[6]

On the second floor of Vaḥíd's house, Ustád 'Alí and Muḥammad 'Alí with his young son, Tahmásb, hid from the Shaykh's terror. Ustád had moved to Nayríz from Sírján with his brother Ḥasan in 1901 and then had become a devoted Bahá'í. When the Shaykh invaded Nayríz and the persecution began, he told his friend Mullá Darvish that he was willing to be martyred with the very sword he then held in his hand. When the Shaykh's men came through the streets of Chinár-Súkhtih, the three went to hide in Vaḥíd's old house near the Great Mosque. The women in the house put their fellow Bahá'ís on the second floor. Some local toughs, though, who knew the whereabouts of the three Bahá'ís, guided the Shaykh's men to this house. Soon, Ustád, Muḥammad 'Alí, and Ṭahmásb were captured.

On the way to the Shaykh, ten-year-old Ṭahmásb chanted Qur'ánic verses, and Muḥammad 'Alí and Ustád were shouted at and stoned by Nayrízís and the Shaykh's men. Muḥammad 'Alí appeared before the Shaykh badly bloodied. He was struck by a sword, a blow which practically severed his arm, but he retained his dignity and his faith at the moment of his martyrdom. His body was thrown into a ditch and covered with dirt.[7]

Ustád refused to recant and was offered his life in return for a bribe. Ustád agreed, and a few soldiers took him to his house to get the money. However, the soldiers had been told by the Shaykh to kill Ustád after he had given them his money.

Once inside his home, Ustád whispered to his wife while the Shaykh's men waited impatiently in another room. She had to hide their money, Ustád said, so that she and their family would have some for the future.

They said their good-byes. When he came out of the house without the bribe, the angry men took him in back of the Great Mosque next to a place called Bagh Kassabi—the "butcher's garden"—and shot him.[8]

❋ ❋ ❋

The first National Bahá'í Convention of the United States continued all afternoon in the home of Mrs. Corinne True of Chicago, Illinois. The members selected to serve on the Executive Board for the Temple—the first Bahá'í national organized body in the United States—were announced: Mr. Arthur Agnew and Mrs. Corinne True of Chicago; Mr. Bernard M. Jacobsen of Kenosha; Mr. Albert H. Hall of Minneapolis; Mrs. Anna L. Parmerton of Cincinnati; Mr. Mountfort Mills of New York; Mr. Charles Mason Remey of Washington, DC; Mr. William H. Hoar of New Jersey; and Mrs. Helen S. Goodall of Oakland.

At the close of the convention, all stood and repeated the Greatest Name, "Alláh'u'Abhá," in unison, then stood together in silent prayer.

They left each other that afternoon in a spirit of perfect unity.[9]

❋ ❋ ❋

That night, a brave Muslim woman quietly made her way to the site where her son-in-law Ibráhim's martyrdom had taken place. She picked up the upper and lower parts of his body with the help of Muslim relatives and removed them to the Gabrestane Sangar where she could bury them. Under cover of that same night, Taliati'e, the Bahá'í daughter of Muḥammad 'Alí, carried her father's body away with the help of her Muslim friends. They washed his corpse and lovingly buried it.[10]

22

FLIGHT TO SARVISTÁN

Outside the caves of Tang-i Láy-i Ḥiná, Shaykh Muḥammad Ḥusayn's extended family and other refugees had split into two in the pre-dawn darkness of New Year's Day. The women and children returned to town under the protection of Muslim friends. The men went southwest to Iṣṭahbánát.

Nearing Iṣṭahbánát, they saw their brethren emerging from the mountains in the grey early dawn. A Bahá'í was stationed at the fork in the road and told them to go to the nearby village of Runíz. The land around Runíz was owned by the Afnán family—the relatives of the Báb—so the town would be safer for Bahá'ís. When Mír Muḥammad-Ḥasan, the overseer of these lands, saw this large group of beleaguered fellow Bahá'ís—now in the dozens—he welcomed them immediately and offered them rest and food.* For two days and nights, he took care

* The sources cite the number in this group from a low of sixty (Rouhani, *Lam'átul-Anvár*) to a high of one hundred (Faizi, *Nayríz Mushkbiz*).

of them. But soon word arrived from a strongman* in the nearby town of Fasá that the S͟hayk͟h had ordered him to come and take the Bahá'ís captive. Knowing the brutality of this strongman, Mihr Muḥammad-Ḥasan recommended that the Bahá'ís go to the town of Sarvistán where there were other Bahá'ís who would help them and who were on friendly terms with their Muslim neighbors. There they would be out of the S͟hayk͟h's reach. One man was sent in advance to inform the Bahá'ís in Sarvistán that the large group was coming.¹**

The men gathered together at dawn for their westward trek. This time they would not follow the road but would go due west through the K͟harman-Kúh mountains.² The sun rose as the men clambered up the steep slope, rocks tumbling under their feet.

Among them was Mírzá Jináb-i-Muḥammad Ḥusayn, a gifted singer, who must have thought of his wife Maryam K͟hánum and their children, and the happy times he had spent giving children's classes to Bahá'ís and Muslims, sharing with them his knowledge of the Qur'án and the poetry of Háfiz and Sa'dí.† Little did he know that his father-in-law, Mullá Majíd, would be martyred in a few days.³ His younger brother, Mírzá Shukru'lláh, walked near him. In the coming

---

* Qaytas K͟hán (Afnán, *The genesis of the Babi and Baha'i Faiths in Shiraz and Fars*, 213; Faizi, *Nayríz Mushkbiz*, 146).

** Afnán (*The genesis of the Babi and Baha'i Faiths in Shiraz and Fars*, 214) states that "an Arab" arrived in Sarvistán prior to the large group of Bahá'ís.

† One of their sons was Mírzá Kouchak Gostaran, an active Bahá'í who went to live in Tihrán after his father's death. There he married 'Alíe Rafi'i, the daughter of Mírzá Muḥammad Rafi'i. They had four children: Farzaneh, Íraj, Hooshang, and one other whose name Ahdieh does not remember. Íraj and Hooshang married and had children who became Bahá'ís. Hooshang immigrated with his family. Mírzá Muḥammad Rafi'i had the following children: Núríján, Jahán Sultán, Fáṭimih Sultán, Zivar, Behjat K͟hánum, Hoboor K͟hánum, and 'Alí'e Rafi'i (Ahdieh, *Nayrízi-Shurangiz*, 149).

days, all of Shukru'lláh's property would be destroyed.* They were both sons of Mírzá Ibráhim Mo'alem, who tutored the children of wealthy Muslims, keeping his belief in Bahá'u'lláh hidden so that he could continue to assist the Bahá'ís. He imparted his deep spiritual convictions to his children and calligraphied the sacred writings for others.** His mother-in-law, deeply disturbed by her son-in-law and especially by her daughter's faith, poisoned the food she cooked for them. Knowing this, the couple did not touch the food, confusing the mother-in-law, who saw them alive the next day. To end this, the couple invited her to stay while they fed the chickens the food she had brought them. They watched the chickens dying, and the mother-in-law ran out of the house in shame.

The wind lashed the rocky mountain face up which the Bahá'í refugees struggled. The temperature steadily dropped, and they came into gulleys still covered with ice. By mid-morning, their guide had to admit that he was lost.[4] The men soldiered on. They praised God with their voices, and this sustained their courage.

Exhausted by midday, they stopped. They gathered up twigs and started a fire, melted snow over a piece of cloth, made bread by mixing in the small amount of flour they had left and hungrily ate their tiny rations.

With just enough energy, they continued. The guide found his way as daylight ebbed. They saw the lights of the village of 'Alí-Abád. They longed to enter into a warm house, to rest their injured feet, to eat a

* Ibid., 154. His only son, Aḥmad, would die young at the age of twenty.

** The couple had four children: Mírzá Jináb-i-Muḥammad Ḥusayn, Mírzá Muḥammad, Mírzá Báqir (also known as Mírzá Áqá and also a well-respected calligrapher), and Mírzá Shokro'lláh.

hot meal. But knowing the inhabitants might attack them, they moved on in the cold darkness.

In the depth of night, they lost their way again. They built a fire to ward off the cold that swirled around them. Karbalá'í Muḥammad Ṣalih felt the warmth of the flames. In the temporary rest this warmth gave him, he thought of the sacrifices made by his family. His mother Fáṭimih had become a believer immediately when Vaḥíd had proclaimed the Message of the Báb. He and his mother had been prisoners in Shíráz after the fall of Fort Kh̲ájih. He could see the faces of the many family members who had perished, and he remembered the desperate conditions in which they had lived for years after their return to Nayríz. Now he had been forced to leave his wife, Zohreh, and young son Amru'lláh. But he may have also felt the power and majesty of Bahá'u'lláh, Whom he had met in Baghdád, and the greatness of the Cause for which his family had given so much—and he was consoled.[5]

As dawn broke, they forced themselves to their feet. After this rest, they felt the full physical pain of their abused feet, strained muscles, and lack of food. Silently, they moved forward. To keep moving, they picked leaves and wild bracken to eat.

With less than three kilometers to go, some of the men could go no further and collapsed where they stood. Two of the younger men, who had more strength, hurried on to Sarvistán to get help.

After some time, groups of people appeared, coming toward them with mules and carriages. The people were carrying supplies. These were the Bahá'ís of Sarvistán.

The Sarvistán Bahá'í community had been blessed for weeks with the presence of Tarázu'lláh Samandarí and Mírzá 'Alí Akbar Rafsinjání, two Bahá'í teachers who had uplifted and opened the souls and hearts of the people with their teaching. The Sarvistán Bahá'ís had received the news of the events in Runíz from a messenger and had prepared provisions. Hearing of the presence of their fellow Bahá'ís on the outskirts of their town, they came to rescue them. The Sarvistánis offered them bread and other foods. After the punishing ordeal, the food revived the starving men. With helping hands, the refugees could stand up and climb onto the mules and into the carriages.

They were welcomed in town by the local Bahá'ís and their Muslim relatives and neighbors, who were shocked by their condition and astonished at their courage.[6]

❋ ❋ ❋

In the years before 1909, Muslims and Bahá'ís had lived harmoniously in Chinár Sháhi, a neighborhood just north of Chinár-Súkhtih, where a one-storey home donated by the Peymani family functioned as the Bahá'í center of Nayríz. It was close to the canal that divided these neighborhoods from the bazaar district. Approaching it, one walked through a garden with apple and orange trees and arrived at a brick structure with a large lobby serving as its main front room. The Bahá'í Feasts—during which the Bahá'ís would pray, discuss community matters, and have fellowship—were held in this lobby. On Friday nights, youth classes took place.

A visitor would certainly have met the humorous and kindly caretaker of the center, Áqá 'Abbás, and his wife, Khayru'll Nasa from Sarvistán.* Once, after attending a Nineteen-Day Feast in a believer's house, 'Abbás had signed in as "'Abdu'l-Bahá." In another instance,

* He married twice. His first wife and he had no children. The woman here is his second wife (Rouhani, *Lam'átul-Anvár,* v. 2, 67). He was the son of Muḥammad Sharíf (Faizi, *Nayríz Mushkbiz,* 151).

he had heard that a temporary resident at the center secretly smoked opium, so 'Abbás had ground up all the charcoal. When the opium smoker reached for the charcoal to light his pipe, it all crumbled. But his good-natured humor was forgotten by the local Muslims during this New Year season who burst into the center and dragged Áqá 'Abbás down the street to his martyrdom.[7]

In another part of town, a shoemaker and son of a shoemaker, Mírzá Akbar, was singing out loud some of the sacred verses of Bahá'u'lláh, much to the consternation of the Shaykh's men, who were hitting and pushing him down the street, with the drops of his own blood leaving a trail between them. He had fled Nayríz with others but then had decided to turn back. Upon his return, he had been captured.* The Shaykh's men were concerned that he might be just a lunatic instead of a Bahá'í. Akbar had come back from persecution once before when he and his siblings and his mother had been taken captive to Shíráz after the conflict of 1853. They had been released from Bibi Dukhtaran and survived for months in Shíráz where Akbar had to endure the death of each of his siblings. Back in Nayríz, he grew up and became a shoemaker like his father, Mírzá Ismá'íl, and a devoted believer. Now he had made the journey willingly back to his hometown, this time to his own martyrdom. Arriving in front of the Shaykh, who asked him about his faith, he smiled and said, "Bahá'í." The Shaykh hoped such a humorous person might give a bribe in return for his life, but Akbar refused, testifying that he had come back for this great privilege and would not turn away from it now.[8]

* The man who captured him was Mashhadí Shamsa, a man acting as a spy for the Shaykh (Rouhani, *Lam'átul-Anvár,* v. 2, 142; Faizi, *Nayríz Mushkbiz,* 161).

❋ ❋ ❋

In Sarvistán, the large group of Bahá'í refugees were finally able to lie down and close their eyes—they were out of danger now.

But out in the wilderness, another group of twelve Bahá'í refugees were still trying to get to safety. The group included Jináb Kh̲ájih Muḥammad,* who had been taken captive to Sh̲íráz with his mother in the violence of 1853. Back then, when they returned to Nayríz, they found their house ransacked, their belongings taken, and their orchards destroyed. Kh̲ájih's talent was recognized by Shafí', the leading Bahá'í in Nayríz, who appointed him head of a district. Now Kh̲ájih Muḥammad was again a refugee on the run with his two sons, Jináb Mírzá Muḥammad Báqir Paymani** and Jináb Mírzá Fazlu'lláh Paymani.[9] Back in Nayríz, their house was being destroyed.

Carrying whatever clothes and food they could, they struggled over the difficult and wild terrain. A group of Arab tribesmen rode toward them. The tribesmen dismounted, raised their swords and clubs and struck the refugees, then grabbed all their belongings. In that remote area, there was no one to help them. As their assailants rode away, the men had to help each other stand and move forward.

They straggled into Sarvistán, bloodied and barely standing. Sarvistánís were horrified at the sight and rushed to help them.

---

* He was the son of Karbalá'í Báqir (Ahdieh, *Nayrízi-Shurangiz,* 158).

** He lived to be eighty years old and served on the Spiritual Assembly of Nayríz. He and his wife had eight children: Bibi Beghum, Manúch̲ihr, Bah'o'din, Massoud, Sháhabudin, Nazamu'din, Jalaliyyeh, and Kahan, the mother of Pari Kh̲ánum Vakilzadeh (Ahdieh, *Nayrízi-Shurangiz,* 168).

23

THE PASSING OF 'ABDU'L-BAHÁ

The violence unleashed by Siyyid 'Abdu'l Ḥusayn Larí and Shaykh Dhakaríyyá plagued the entire province of Fárs. People cried out for help. These pleas were heard in Shíráz by the newly appointed governor who sent the military commander with a large contingent of soldiers out to restore order in the provincial towns.[1]

Word spread among the people of the province that they were coming.

Arriving in Sarvistán, the military commander heard the Bahá'ís tell of properties being taken, orchards being cut down, homes being ransacked and burned, innocent men being pummelled, dragged down streets and shot, corpses being thrown into ditches . . .

By the time the troops arrived in Nayríz, the Shaykh was long gone. He had evaded their punishment.[2] The soldiers kicked out the men he had left in charge, and now the city was safe again. The Bahá'ís began their return.

They found their material lives in ruins.

Shaykh Muḥammad Ḥusayn's orchards—all of his fruit trees, which had been the source of so much bounty—were nothing but charred stumps and cinders. Arriving at the plot of land where his home had stood, he saw nothing but dirt. It was completely demolished—even its stones and bricks had been removed.[3]

Mírzá 'Abdu'l Ḥusayn returned from several months away in the presence of 'Abdul-Bahá in the Holy Land, anxious to know the fate of his family. His wife Núríján and his children, he discovered, were destitute. All of their properties had been expropriated and their belongings stolen. Núríján had been offered many bags of corn from fellow Bahá'ís in Shíráz but had asked that they be given to the poor. She had not wanted to dishonor her husband by accepting aid.[4]

The Bahá'ís were resilient. They returned and rebuilt, and the community came back to life.

Homes rose up, businesses began, orchards and gardens grew, friendships with Muslim neighbors were renewed, and souls were strengthened in the knowledge that they had survived and had been steadfast in their faith.

One year later, the Shaykh's brother* attacked Nayríz from the north with the intention of destroying the Bahá'í community, but this time, the Muslims and Bahá'ís banded together and beat him back within three days.[5]

❋ ❋ ❋

Even though her last remaining son had died the night before—Tuesday, April 30th, 1912—Corinne True made her way through the

* Shaykh 'Abdu'l-Ḥasan Kúhistání (Hisámí, *History of the Faith in Nayríz*, 247).

streets of Wilmette this Wednesday morning, determined to witness 'Abdu'l-Bahá lay the cornerstone of the Bahá'í House of Worship, to which she had completely dedicated herself for many years. A large white tent had been set up. Standing under it, 'Abdu'l-Bahá spoke:

> The power which has gathered you here today notwithstanding the cold and windy weather is indeed mighty and wonderful. It is the power of God, the divine favour of Bahá'u'lláh which has drawn you together. We praise God that through His constraining love human souls are assembled and associated in this way.
>
> Thousands of Mashriqu'l-Azkars, dawning-points of praise and mentionings of God for all the religionists will be built in the Orient and Occident, but this being the first one erected in the Occident has great importance. In the future there will be many here and elsewhere; in Asia, Europe, even in Africa, New Zealand and Australia; but this edifice in Chicago is of special significance . . .[6]

The cornerstone of the edifice had been brought by Nettie Tobin, a seamstress of very limited means who wanted to give something for the Temple, by hand on two street cars, then dragged on the ground, carried on someone's back, then wheeled in a cart, then finally carried and deposited at the Temple site. 'Abdu'l-Bahá broke the hard ground by swinging an axe over his head—the trowel he had been handed was not strong enough—and beckoned individual Bahá'ís to step forward and, on behalf of Bahá'ís from the East and West, turn over the earth.[7]

The Bahá'í Mother Temple of the West, for which Corinne and many other Bahá'ís were laboring, was blessed by 'Abdu'l-Bahá. It was "already built."

❋ ❋ ❋

The Kingdom of Persia was in chaos. The sickly Qájár dynasty tottered. The central government had lost control of much of the country, and local tribal leaders were increasingly the only authority in their own region. The Bahá'í community of Nayríz became a good target, as Nayríz was a rich agricultural center with a few wealthy families.

Shaykh Dhakaríyyá's family attempted once again to take over Nayríz in 1913. This time, it was another brother[8] of the Shaykh's who destroyed fields and demanded large payments of money. He claimed to be representing the Qá'im, and his mission was to eradicate the Bahá'ís. The Nayrízís united against this threat.

Soon after that, a bandit,[9] claiming to act on behalf of Shaykh Dhakaríyyá and to be the representative of the Qá'im, attacked Nayríz with his men. Again, the cooperation of Bahá'ís and Muslims protected the town.

Worse than the bandits during this period was the lack of rainfall and the attack of locusts. The combination devastated the crops and brought on hunger and then famine. Many people struggled just to stay alive each day. Mírzá 'Abdu'l-Ḥusayn opened his storehouses to feed those who were in greatest need, helping his townspeople, Bahá'í and Muslim alike, to survive.[10]

In 1916, after having endured a lifetime of persecution, Mírzá 'Abdu'l-Ḥusayn, grandson of the great follower of Vaḥíd, Siyyid Jaf'ar Yazdí, passed away. At the time of his death, he was still being tormented, this time by having to pay a fine imposed by the authorities for the entire value of what he had been able to build up in assets since his return to Nayríz after the killings of 1909. As mentioned previously, he had been with 'Abdu'l-Bahá in the Holy Land and returned to find his wife and family destitute. His wife Núríján patiently endured these and many other hardships. Well-educated by her father, Mullá Muḥammad Shafí', she knew how to read and write and had spent much of her life educating children and using her writing skills to copy tablets for the Bahá'ís. She had been much sought after as a bride and had chosen her husband. Her bereavement at his passing was deepened by these unjust burdens.[11]

It was during these years—between 1909 and 1921—that the buildup of the Bahá'í community of Nayríz reached its fruition in the election of its first Spiritual Assembly, an institution ordained by Bahá'u'lláh to guide the affairs of the Bahá'ís in each locality. Among its first members were Shaykh Muḥammad Ḥusayn, who served as its secretary; Jináb Mírzá Muḥammad Báqir Paymani and Mírzá Fazlu'lláh Paymani, sons of Jináb Kháj ih Muḥammad; Khájih Muḥammad; and Karbalá'í Muḥammad-Ṣálih. Mrs. Nurat Míssáqí would be the first woman elected to the Assembly. Soon this Assembly became very influential in Nayríz with Muslims seeking its advice, referring to it as the "body of nine."[12]

❁ ❁ ❁

Ghámar Sultán and her children—two had died early—had fled their hometown of Iṣṭahbánát when her husband, Karbalá'í Ḥusayn, had been taken away; he had actively been teaching the Faith in secret, and he and a mujtahid whom he had taught made a proclamation about the Faith in the mosque resulting in violent reaction. His fabric shop—the family's livelihood—was ransacked. Ghámar Sultán's family told her that she should leave him, as the Faith was the cause of her misfortune. One day she received a message that her husband was being held in Nayríz, and a caravan, driven by a Bahá'í, could take her and her children there. Once she arrived in Nayríz, she was reunited with her husband. He began selling fabric and used his donkey to sell goods in the street. Though he began to lose his sight due to earlier beatings, he managed to teach his children, including his daughter Ṭubá, how to read and write. Living through repeated persecutions and deprivations, he withheld some of his share of the food to give more to his children. After he died, Ghámar Sultán had five daughters and one son to feed but no means of support; she could neither read nor write. She sold the items she had. When these were all gone, she washed the clothes of wealthier Nayrízís. She was cursed by a wealthy woman, who told her it was her Faith that had brought her misfortune. That night, having nothing to feed the children, she put them to bed. There was a knock on the door. The Bahá'í caravan driver who had brought her to Nayríz gave her a parcel with tea, sugar, and five tumans. With this she could buy food to feed her children. With gratitude she accepted the caravan driver's offer to bring them to the town of Bandar 'Abbás, where they could find support and shelter. Her greatest joy in the coming years was to make a pilgrimage to the Holy Land and spend a month in the presence of 'Abdu'l-Bahá. She wept in his presence, and seeing his face erased the sorrow of her suffering.[13]

Khájih Muḥammad, who as a boy was taken captive with his mother after the 1853 conflict in which his father had been killed, had gone from poverty to owning a cotton trading business and had become head of one of Nayríz's neighborhoods. He had used the wealth he had built to help the Bahá'ís of Nayríz in their need and opened his home for all Bahá'í activities. In 1921, he found himself blessed to be in the presence of 'Abdu'l-Bahá in the Holy Land.

In September of that year, 'Abdu'l-Bahá had a dream:

> I seemed to be standing within a Great mosque . . . in the place of the Ímám himself. I became aware that a large number of people were flocking into the Mosque; more and yet more crowded in, taking their places in rows behind me, until there was a vast multitude. As I stood I raised loudly the "Call to Prayer." Suddenly the thought came to me to go forth from the Mosque.
>
> When I found myself outside I said within myself, "For what reason have I come forth, not having led the prayer? But it matters not; now that I have uttered the Call to Prayer, the vast multitude will of themselves chant the prayer . . ."[14]

A few weeks later, he had a dream of Bahá'u'lláh, Who said to him, "Destroy this room!" When he related this dream to a couple, they wanted it to mean that he would come stay in their home and leave the room in the garden in which he was sleeping. However, unbeknownst to them, the "room" in 'Abdu'l-Bahá's dream symbolized his body.[15]

In early November, he spoke to an old believer:

> I am so fatigued! The hour is come when I must leave everything and take my flight. I am too weary to walk. It was during the closing days of the Blessed Beauty [Bahá'u'lláh], when I was engaged in gathering together His papers, which were strewn over the sofa in His writing chamber at Bahji that He turned to me and said, "It is of no use to gather them, I must leave them and flee away."
>
> I also have finished my work, I can do nothing more, therefore must I leave it and take my departure.[16]

In the middle of the night of November 28, 1921, 'Abdu'l-Bahá ascended; in the words of Shoghi Effendi and Lady Blomfield, the "'heart that had so powerfully throbbed with wondrous love for the children of God was now stilled. His glorious spirit had passed from the life of the earth, from the persecutions of the enemies of righteousness, from the storm and stress of well nigh eighty years of indefatigable toil for the good of others.'"[17]

Under a cloudless sky, clerics, officials, Bahá'ís, and people from all religions praised him, and the poor and common people who had lived under his shelter cried out, "O God! My God! Our Father has left us, our Father has left us!"[18]

Though grief-stricken, Bahá'ís would not be left fatherless. 'Abdu'l-Bahá had written a Will and Testament in which he chose his gifted grandson to be the Guardian of the Faith, the light who would now guide Bahá'ís everywhere: Shoghi Effendi.

24

EXODUS

News of 'Abdu'l-Bahá's passing flew from the Holy Land into the mansion of the governor of Fárs in Shíráz, who gave it to a messenger who rushed to Nayríz. The messenger told a Bahá'í teacher who ran out immediately to find the members of the Spiritual Assembly who had gathered at a marriage feast.[1] The teacher burst in. He brought them over to a quiet corner of the roof and unburdened himself of the terrible news. Stunned, the members of the Assembly silenced the musicians and sent everyone away.

A week later, the Assembly received the telegram from 'Abdu'l-Bahá's sister, Bahíyyih Khánum, confirming what they had been told. When the rest of the Bahá'ís were informed, they grieved mightily for the loss of their Master and wondered aloud who would be their shepherd now. Another message from Bahíyyih Khánum informed them that a Will and Testament existed and encouraged them to study Bahá'u'lláh's Tablet of the Holy Mariner.

Some Bahá'ís wondered if Bahíyyih Khánum might be his successor, but it was felt that speculation was undignified and that, instead, they would study, pray, and wait. Soon they received the news that Shoghi Effendi had been appointed head of the Faith in 'Abdu'l-Bahá's *Will and Testament.* One elderly Nayrízi believer had told them of a memory of his in which this had been foreseen: "I am illiterate but 'Abdu'l-Bahá's successor cannot be anyone but the child I saw in the cradle. He captivated my heart then. That child is Shoghi Effendi, and it cannot be anyone but him. In his childhood he so enraptured my heart that I called one of my sons Shoghi. When I wrote to 'Abdu'l-Bahá about it, he did not allow it and bestowed upon him another name."[2]

❋ ❋ ❋

By this time, the Bahá'í community of Nayríz had become strong. It had good relations with the governor—who many said was secretly a Bahá'í—a mature Spiritual Assembly, and financial stability. Now, they undertook an enormous new effort. They started two schools, one for boys and one for girls.

The Mansúrí schools were run by Mr. Rouhani and Mr. Hesamí. Mr. Mosleh was in charge of the boys' branch, and Mrs. Nuṣrat Míssáqí and Mrs. Bahíyyih Khánum Mostaghim were responsible for the girls' branch. Each school opened with about forty students in four or five classes. They were assisted by the participation of knowledgeable traveling teachers, such as Mírzá Munir Nabílzádih. Soon the head of education in Nayríz recognized the schools as the town's best and the Qavámu'l Mulk, the major tribal leader residing in Shíráz, confirmed this by donating money to them on one of his visits.[3]

Mírzá Munir Nabílzádih also helped in the protection of the Bahá'ís of Nayríz. During his 1922 visit, a thug came down from the mountains and organized a mob in the bazaar to attack the Bahá'í district. Nabílzádih rallied the Bahá'ís to stand up to these aggressors. The governor of Nayríz, sympathetic to the Bahá'ís, also met with prominent citizens and reminded them of the courage of the Bahá'í resistance in all the previous persecutions, and he encouraged them to remain calm. In this way, Bahá'ís and local officials worked together to maintain peace.[4]

❋ ❋ ❋

There had always been floods in Nayríz, but the flood of the winter of 1924 would long be remembered. For one week, torrential rains came down. The centuries-old dam gave way. Three quarters of the town, house after house, sank into the rising waters. Belongings floated away, and valuables were hopelessly damaged, among them Kh̲ávar Sultán's treasured tablets from Bahá'u'lláh. People fled to higher ground with whatever they could carry, homeless all—Bahá'ís, Muslims, Jews . . .[5]

A plea went to the Bahá'í Assembly of Sh̲íráz, which sent it to the Assembly of Ṭihrán, which informed Shoghi Effendi. He made an appeal to the Bahá'ís of the world, who responded with great generosity. Once the waters had receded, this outpouring of funds allowed the rebuilding to begin. The Bahá'í Assembly used these funds for many civic purposes, such as building a public bath and a dam, which were very much appreciated by their neighbors. They also bought land for a cemetery and a Bahá'í Center, and would later buy part of Fort Kh̲ájih and repair Vaḥíd's room as a memorial to the events of 1850.[6]

The elderly Karbalá'í Muḥammad-Ṣálih, who had been taken prisoner with his mother to Sh̲íráz in 1853, and enjoyed recounting the courage and bravery of the Nayríz Bahá'ís of the past, walked the ground around Fort Kh̲ájih and located the area where the bodies of the Bábís killed in 1850 had been dumped. The Spiritual Assembly of Nayríz, on which he also served, commissioned the building of a small shrine on the blessed spot. Karbalá'í Muḥammad-Ṣálih also went up into the mountains and, remembering that dramatic afternoon when 'Alí Sardár had been killed, located his grave so that the prayers of posterity in remembrance of his sacrifice could be offered on that spot.[7]

❋ ❋ ❋

The dying Qájár dynasty was declared dead by the Parliament of Persia in 1925. Riḍá Sháh became ruler—the first king of the new Pahlavi dynasty.[8] Nayríz enjoyed a peaceful period.

The end of the old dynasty caused turmoil in the countryside, which eventually brought intermittent persecution to Nayríz. In 1928, and again in 1929, clerics organized mobs that roamed the Bahá'í neighborhood, attacked Bahá'í homes, and demanded large sums of money from the Bahá'ís. The mobs broke up only when threatened with force by government soldiers.[9]

Throughout Fárs province, the large tribes took control in the absence of any strong central government in Ṭihrán. The Shaykh who headed the Kúhistání tribe wanted to take control of Nayríz and other towns in its region.[10] Most Bahá'ís knew that this Shaykh was the nephew of the one who had murdered eighteen of them in 1909, so many of them fled to the mountains. The Shaykh's forces defeated those of the government, and when he entered Nayríz, he ordered that the houses of all the Bahá'ís be destroyed unless they paid a large sum of money. A list of names of local Bahá'ís and how much they would have to pay was drawn up. The sum of 1500 rials, a great deal of money, was written next to the name *Shaykh Muḥammad Ḥusayn.* One of the wealthier members of the community, Mírzá Aḥmad Vaḥídí, immediately intervened. Since everyone was at the mercy of the Shaykh, Mírzá Aḥmad Vaḥídí went directly to him and offered his life and money in exchange for the safety of others. The Shaykh accepted that he collect the payments from the Bahá'ís. In this way, Vaḥídí protected the properties of the Bahá'ís from being destroyed, though some damage was done to them, and, thanks to his connections in Shiraz, his soldiers were finally sent to drive the Shaykh out.

❋ ❋ ❋

In 1930, it became the law in Iran for people to have identification cards with last names. Traditionally, people had a series of identifiers instead of last names, such as the town from which they came and honorific titles, if any. The person in Nayríz assigned to give out last names was a Bahá'í. He named his fellow Bahá'ís after spiritual qualities often related to the Covenant because they had been so obedient to the authority of 'Abdu'l-Bahá and Shoghi Effendi during the great periods of transition in the history of the Faith. He gave out names such as Sabet (Steadfastness), Míssáqí (Covenant), Bahin Aein (One who discovers the Faith), Peymani (everlasting promise), Rouhani (spiritual one), Ahdieh (helper of the Covenant), and Sháhidpour (child of martyr).

One believer who had faithfully served and suffered through the entire history of the Nayríz community was Kh́ájih Muḥammad. So respected was he by the local authorities that they made him the head of one of Nayríz's districts. In 1933, he passed away.[11]

❋ ❋ ❋

By the late 1930s, dramatic, large-scale persecution of the Bahá'ís of Nayríz was over.

Now began decades of constant low-level harassment which, like seasonal plagues, would make life almost unbearable for the Bahá'ís of Nayríz and greatly weaken their community.

As World War II raged and communication between Bahá'ís around the world was cut off, a mullá began many years of preaching against the Bahá'ís.[12] He did not, though, advocate killing the Bahá'ís. He knew this would lead to his removal by authorities.

Instead, he incited hatred for Bahá'ís in his Muslim faithful every Friday from his pulpit in the mosque. He pushed his trusting listeners to leave their Bahá'í spouses, to boycott Bahá'í businesses, to dissolve their partnerships with them, and to harass Bahá'í children on their way to school. He demanded that 'Alí Akbar Rouhani's orchard near town be sold to him. When Rouhani refused, every tree in his orchard was cut down, and the water cut off. The local policemen were too intimidated by the hate-filled mullá to put a stop to this.

A siyyid influenced by this mullá roamed the mountainside with some of his henchmen looking for Bahá'ís laboring unprotected on their properties so they could kidnap them and extort money from their families. The police didn't try to capture him because he had the permission of the mullá. One day, while 'Abdu'l-Samí Shahídpúr was in his orchards with his nephew, the siyyid came up with his men and forced the two up the mountain, where they beat 'Abdu'l Samí with a chain and his nephew with a club. The siyyid demanded that 'Abdu'l Samí give him his hunting rifle, but 'Abdu'l Samí protested that he had no such weapon. He was held there and beaten over the course of two days. This only stopped when the siyyid received a small Qur'án from 'Abdu'l Samí's mother with one thousand tumans, a very large sum, and a note in which she wrote that she trusted the authority of the Qur'án even if the siyyid did not. 'Abdu'l Samí and his nephew were released. When a doctor came to see 'Abdu'l Samí in his home, his shirt and his bloody wounds had dried together. The wounds took six months to heal, but deep scars remained the rest of his life.[13]

This same siyyid also kidnapped Shaykh Bahá'í in 1947, took him up into the mountains, and beat him severely. Shaykh Bahá'í had arranged a debate between the mullá, who had been stirring up this hatred against Bahá'ís, and Mr. Tarázu'lláh Samandarí, a well-known Bahá'í teacher. The governor—knowing that the mullá was up to something—had the debate cancelled to protect Mr. Samandarí. The mullá instructed the siyyid to punish Shaykh Bahá'í for this embarrassment. In addition, Shaykh Bahá'í was the corresponding secretary for the Bahá'í Assembly and had written many letters to Shíráz and Ṭihrán about the situation in Nayríz. Fortunately, an influential man and a cousin of Shaykh Bahá'í, 'Abdu'l Ḥusayn Shu'á'y, rescued him. As a bloodied Shaykh Bahá'í was being helped away, the siyyid yelled out to him: "Go back and keep writing those letters about me and you will be punished again!" Shaykh Bahá'í answered back, "Inshalláh" ('God willing') and "I will continue!" Back in town, young Bahá'ís came to his house with weapons to protect him and ward off further attacks. As a result of this trauma and all the suffering brought on his family—the mullá even rebuilt a mosque next to his house—the Ahdieh family soon left for Ábádan.[14]

The siyyid and his men even attacked an older woman in the mountains, broke her legs, and stole her produce and her donkey. Eventually she was rescued. One day, as she lay in her bed recovering, she saw her donkey outside her door with blood on it. She later discovered why. At the government's request, a land supervisor from the region, Mr. Faraj, had sent a messenger to the siyyid to negotiate with him and get him to stop his attacks. The siyyid shot the messenger and, in retaliation, Mr. Faraj shot and killed the siyyid. His corpse was loaded on the donkey, taken into town, and hung in public for all to see.[15]

The mullá who had inspired this siyyid sent his verbal attacks like swarms of locusts against the Bahá'ís. He spoke out against public baths being used by Bahá'ís, doctors treating them, merchants selling food to them, schools accepting them as students, their marriages being recognized (thereby making their children illegitimate), or the dead being buried in public cemeteries. He encouraged the destruction of Bahá'í grave sites, of their harvest, of their livestock . . .[16]

Women and girls also got swept up in this rising tide.

Ustád Habíbu'lláh Memar's wife opposed her husband's conversion and devout observance of the teachings of the Bahá'í Faith. Because of the mullá's destructive influence, her thoughts were infected with his hatred. The Bahá'í Assembly encouraged Ustád to show greater love for his wife to try to change her heart, but her heart only hardened. She decided to kill him. To carry this out, she got the help of her brother, mother, a relative, and their servant.* One day in 1942, while Ustád was out, the plotters hid in one of the rooms of the house.[17] When Ustád returned, lay down, and went to sleep, they set upon him and strangled him. They dragged the blade of a knife over his skin to see if he was really dead or just unconscious. He bled but didn't wake. Still, they grabbed a pickax and struck him in the head with it. As they were killing him, his two young daughters woke up, came out, and were frightened, but Ustád's wife ordered them back to bed. The wife's mother wanted to kill the two girls to keep them quiet, but their mother convinced her that the two children hadn't understood what was going on. The killers didn't know where to hide the evidence, so they took the bloody mattress and sheets, rope and pickax and put

* The relative was Muḥammad, the son of Mas͟hhadí Aṣg͟har. The servant's name was K͟horam (Ahdieh, 192).

them in one room. Then they carried the body out and dumped it into a dry well.

They spread the word the next day that Ustád had gone missing. They wondered aloud if he had been at a Bahá'í meeting so as to cast suspicion on the Bahá'ís. The brother asked around about Ustád's whereabouts. The mother-in-law wrote pleas for help to the police. But the Assembly did not believe these shows of concern. Two Bahá'ís, 'Alí 'Askar Khán Mansúrí and 'Abdu'l-Ḥusayn Vaḥídí, went to the authorities and told them of the wife's previous behavior. Everyone now searched for Ustád, and his corpse was found at the bottom of the dry well. The police went to the victim's house and found the evidence. The wife was taken in, and she confessed and gave up the names of the other killers who, in turn, confessed but pointed their fingers back at the wife. A police captain, Mr. Samandarí, who happened to be a Bahá'í, came to Nayríz to supervise the case. The killers were sent to prison in the town of Fasá. The mother-in-law died there while the wife, brother, and servant were released two years later and returned to Nayríz. The wife married the servant so she would have a protector and lived on in poverty. The servant died shortly after, and the wife followed soon of an illness.

A young Bahá'í woman, Eshraghieh, suffered greatly as a result of the incitement to hatred for Bahá'ís caused by the mullá's sermons. As a young girl, she had walked to school while being insulted and pelted with stones by other children. Her books and lunch were snatched. Being shy and sensitive, she could not continue her schooling under these conditions, and her family left Nayríz. She returned as the reluctant young wife of a Muslim man. Her husband's family, under the influence of the hate-filled mullá, tried to force her to his mosque to recant. She resisted but did her best to serve the family loyally by cleaning clothes, preparing meals, fetching water, and taking care of the animals. In return, she was prevented from praying, fasting, or visiting other Bahá'ís. She was often reminded that she was unclean because she was a Bahá'í. After fifteen years of this, she became ill with tuberculosis and an ulcer but was not given any treatment. As her days grew shorter, she went for the last period of her short life to be with her sister in <u>Sh</u>íráz, where she passed away at the age of forty. Her body was buried in the Bahá'í cemetery in <u>Sh</u>íráz.

In the dead of a night in 1946, a frightened seven-year-old Jahántáb Sardári watched as many strange and masked men entered her home. She knew something was very wrong. Several men struck down her beloved father, Háfiz Sardári, with the butt of their rifles; her pregnant mother, Legha, was crying, begging not to be hurt. Unbeknownst to the little girl, the men, some local, had been organized by a gang leader from the village of Ij; dozens of his men were in town and had surrounded their house to loot it. Her family was known to be wealthier than others in the area. They were the first home to have a private bath in the <u>Ch</u>inár-Sú<u>kh</u>tih district; the home also had a woodburning system under the bath house floor that could warm the water and the floor. Now, this large group of strange men went throughout her house. They ate all of her family's food, took what they could not consume on the spot, and found the hiding place where the family valuables were kept—they had been tipped off by someone in the neighborhood. Mules waited outside the door for the robbers to load them up with everything of any value in the home, including little Jahántáb's clothes. Once the robbers had left, her father reported the robbery to the police. Two years later, the gang leader from Ij was arrested. By then, Jahántáb's father had built up his wealth and forgave the man.[18]

❋ ❋ ❋

In 1949, with communication reestablished after the end of World War II, instructions regarding the eighteen martyrs of 1909 arrived in Nayríz. Shoghi Effendi wished their bodies to be transferred to the Bahá'í cemetery and buried with the honor due their sacrifice. The Bahá'í Assembly of Nayríz asked Mírzá Aḥmad Vaḥídí to supervise this delicate task. He selected two trustworthy Bahá'ís, Haqgu and Míssáqí, to carry it out. They made up eighteen white bags. Three of the bodies had been buried in the bazaar and fifteen in the Bahá'í district. At night, each grave was carefully opened, each set of remains carefully lifted out and respectfully placed in a bag. On each bag they wrote the identity of the body. In a pocket of the jacket worn by one of the martyrs, there were watermelon seeds. Such seeds, when roasted, were a delicacy eaten on festive occasions—he must have been killed near his wedding day. As soon as the seeds were touched, they turned to powder.* By the moonlight of several nights, eighteen white bags moved from various locations into the ground of the Bahá'í cemetery. When all was done, the community gathered in the Sháhidpour family's home to pray using 'Abdu'l-Bahá's Tablet of Visitation for the eighteen martyrs, called the place of burial a "Hallowed Spot."[19]

❋ ❋ ❋

To help inspire and strengthen the Bahá'ís, Bahá'í teachers such as Mr. 'Alí-Akbar Furútan, Mr. Tarázu'lláh Samandarí, and Mr. Muḥammad 'Alí Faizi came to Nayríz. The Zarghan family and others did

* A piece of this young man's clothing was sent to the Bahá'í World Center and placed in the Archives. It can now be seen during pilgrimage (from a private conversation with Dr. Ṭáhirih Ahdieh, September, 2010).

much to help the Bahá'í community survive and prosper economically through investment in the development of factories. Shoghi Effendi encouraged these families to move to Nayríz and support the community.

But the current against the Bahá'ís was strong and growing stronger . . .

In 1956, a cleric broadcast nationally over Ṭihrán radio messages of hatred toward Bahá'ís. He claimed to be speaking on behalf of the government. This set off a wave of persecution and vandalism. Among the many acts of violence carried out throughout the country, the House of the Báb in Shíráz was ransacked; cemeteries were dug up, including the one in Nayríz; and the Bahá'í Center in Ṭíhran was destroyed and its caretaker killed.

Nayrízís, inflamed by these broadcasts, threatened to burn down the Shahídpúr family home, and they piled up wood for fire behind the house. During a visit with Mírzá Aḥmad Vaḥídí, Mr. Shahídpúr abruptly cut short his visit to return and defend his family. As he passed the mosque bordering the bazaar and Bahá'í district, a mob of men with butcher knives attacked him and lacerated his forehead. Blood poured down his face onto his clothes. The enraged men beat him while shouting that they would bring him to the mullá's house—he who was the driving force behind such attacks—and force him to recant. Through the pain and blood, Mr. Shahídpúr responded that he came from a family of martyrs and would gladly give up his life before going before that mullá. This enraged the mob further, and it dragged him toward a public fountain to clean him up before bringing him to the mullá, saying all Bahá'ís were unclean. The police, hearing that things were getting out of control in the street, rushed out and broke up the mob by promising it that they would punish Mr. Shahídpúr themselves. Once inside the safety of the police station, Mr. Shahídpúr wrote a letter to the Bahá'í National Assembly of Iran telling them what had happened to him. Drops of his blood dripped onto the page.[20]

The husband of Khánum Humáyún, who ran a daycare center for children of all backgrounds, had opened a company that made thread. Some thugs, motivated by the cleric on the radio, entered his small factory and stabbed him repeatedly. Badly injured, the victim forgave his assailants and offered them cloth with which to wash the blood from their hands.[21]

Bahá'í businesses began to close under the renewed harassment, forcing families to leave the town. Some left for Arabia and the Gulf states, where they prospered financially. Over time, the wealthier families left Nayríz for Shíráz; eventually, even the poorer ones were forced to leave as well, though they lacked sufficient means to do so. The ability of the community to resist the persecutions was diminished by disagreements among the Bahá'í families, who were under enormous pressure. The Bahá'í community of Nayríz was eroding.

Núríján, who with her children had been made destitute in the persecution of 1909, passed away in 1968 at eighty-nine years of age.[22]

Páríján, who had lived through seeing her father's corpse desecrated in the violence of 1909, died in 1970 at the age of eighty-seven.[23]

'Abdu'l-Bahá had written to her words that might well describe the Bahá'í community of Nayríz—he acknowledged the degree of her suffering while telling her she must be grateful for having been singled out for suffering in the path of the Blessed Beauty.[24]

In 1979, clerics overthrew the King of Persia and became the new rulers of the country. Any men in authority who had sometimes protected the Bahá'ís were now gone. The Shí'ah clergy that had caused the killing of the Bábís, the execution of the Báb, and the exile of Bahá'u'lláh and His family, finally took control of Iran.

Destruction of the Bahá'í community became the official policy of the new government. Now there was no protection anywhere.

Mrs. Shaybání, who had moved to Nayríz with her daughter Shokuh from 'Iráq to help the Bahá'í community, walked through the streets of Nayríz, trying not to draw attention to herself. When they were on pilgrimage in the Holy Land in 1957, they had been encouraged to move to Nayríz to serve the Bahá'í community. Though they had been raised in much bigger and more developed cities, they had accepted life in this small agricultural town, wearing the chádur in public and suffering public insults and the stoning of their home.* On Muslim holy days, local people would light items and throw them into their garden. One day, as Mrs. Shaybání walked in the street, a group of women surrounded her and began beating her with their shoes. In the corner of her eye, the elderly victim could see a man across the street—an ironmonger—reach for a metal bar, get up, and start to come over as if he were going to join in the beating. Then a passer-by broke up the attackers and shamed them for having picked on a defenseless woman. He told Mrs. Shaybání to go home immediately, but despite this kind of mistreatment, Mrs. Shaybání and her daughter continued to educate Bahá'ís and seekers about the Faith. Mrs. Shaybání passed away after the revolution of 1979 in Shíráz. Her daughter, Shokuh, wished to stay in Nayríz, but the Bahá'ís knew it was too dangerous and came to take her to Shíráz.[25]

In the years following the revolution, gasoline was poured on both the home where children's classes were held and on the Bahá'í center, then set on fire. Bahá'í homes were ransacked and torched, and the Bahá'í cemeteries were covered over with concrete and buildings.[26]

---

* They lived on a Bahá'í property owned by Mr. Masoud Ímámí (from a private conversation with Mrs. Nura [Shahídpúr] Jamer, September, 2010 CE).

The revolution gave free reign to mullás who encouraged violence, and, no longer able to resist, one Bahá'í family at a time was forced to leave Nayríz.

❋ ❋ ❋

Near the derelict, old Fort Khájih, a young woman puts a note on a branch of the old tree with a wish written on it that she would find a good husband. She spends a quiet moment with herself, though in the background, the din of cars and trucks can be heard. Nayrízís come to this tree to seek favors because a great Siyyid had done wonders and been killed near here. But she doesn't know who he was or what had happened, only that he was holy. She has never heard the Message. She is of a new generation. She does not yet know that this Message has spread out from Iran to the whole world.

Meanwhile, her elderly father makes his way into the Great Mosque to offer his prayers. Leaving his shoes in the entrance, he kneels, lifts his hands, and turns his palms up to the heavens. His words mingle with those from across the centuries given by the old Zoroastrian priest and generations of mullás. His gaze floating inward, he prays, unaware that the voice of Vaḥíd had once echoed against these very walls announcing the New Day of God, unaware of all that had been or, one day, could be.

Appendix A

LIST OF MARTYRS OF THE NAYRÍZ CONFLICT OF 1853 AS LISTED IN SHAFÍ'S MANUSCRIPT

Zaynál, the brother of the above-mentioned Karím; Karbalá'í Yúsuf Najjár, the carpenter, the son of Mashhadí Muḥammad; Khájih Zaynu'l-'Ábidín, son of Khájíh Ghaní; Mashhadí Báqir Ṣabbágh; Mashhadí 'Askar, the son of Mashhadí Báqir; Mullá Muḥammad-Taqí and his brother, Mullá 'Alí-Naqí, the sons of Ákhúnd Mullá 'Abdu'l-Ḥusayn; Mullá 'Alí, Mullá Ḥasan, Mu'man, and Mullá Aḥmad, the sons of Ákhúnd Mullá Músá; Muḥammad Kuchack, the son of Mashhadí Rajab; Mashhadí Mírzá Muḥammad; Mullá Darvísh; Zaynu'l-'Abidín, the son of Mullá Muḥammad; Zaynu'l-'Abidín, son of Ustád Muḥammad; Mashhadí 'Alí, the son of Najf; Karbalá'í Báqir and his son Mullá Muḥammad; Mashhádí Taqí-i-Baqal, the son of 'Abid; Mírzá Aḥmad, the son of Mullá Sádiq, uncles of 'Alí Sardár; Ákhúnd Mullá Aḥmad, the son of Muḥsin; Ákhúnd Mullá 'Alíy-i-Katib, the son of Mullá 'Abdu'llah; Muḥammad 'Abdu'l-Karím; Mírzá 'Alí; Mullá Sádiq;

LIST OF MARTYRS OF THE NAYRÍZ CONFLICT OF 1853 AS LISTED IN SHAFÍ‘’S MANUSCRIPT

Asadu’lláh, the son of Mírzá ‘Alí; Mírzá Yúsuf, the son of Mírzá Akbar; ‘Abid-i Yár-Kash; Malik, the son of Mullá ‘Alí Báqir; Abú-Ṭalíb, the son of Mírzá Aḥmad; Muḥammad, known as Yíkih; Mírzá Ḥasan and his son; Ḥasan, son of Ya‘qúb; Mullá Ḥusayn and ‘Abid, sons of Mullá Barkhudár; Barkhudár, son of Mullá Ḥusayn; Lu¬fu’lláh Shumal; Karbalá’í Muḥammad; Karbalá’í Shamu’d-Dín, who was martyred in Nayríz by Áqá Riḍáy-i Áqa ‘Alí Naqí; Asadu’lláh Mírzá Mihdí; Aḥmad Ḥájí Abú’l-Qásim; Muḥammad Mullá Musá; Ḥusayn, the son of Rajab; Ḥasan Mírzá, one of the bravest; Karbalá’í Ḥusayn, the son of Ḥájí; Karbalá’í Ismá’íl Mashhadí ‘Ábidín; Mírzá Bábá; Mírzá Aḥmad; the sons of Kháјih Ḥasan; Ḥájí, the son of Karbalá’í Báqir, and his son, ‘Askar; Muḥammad-‘Alí; Shaykh Ḥasan; Ḥusayn-‘Alí, the son of Mírzá Áqa; ‘Alí, the son of Karbalá’í Báqir; Mashhadí ‘Alí, the son of Sulaymán; Ḥasan, the son of Mashhadí Muḥammad; Muḥammad-‘Alí and his son Kázim; Mullá Ḥájí Muḥammad; Ḥájí Shaykh ‘Abd-‘Alí; Áqá Shaykh Muḥammad, and his son Ḥusayn; Hádí Khayri, who was martyred in Shíráz (details forthcoming); Ḥusayn Mashhadí Ismá‘íl; ‘Abdu’lláh Karbalá’í Akbar; Muḥammad-Sádiq Ḥusayn; Khájih Burhán; ‘Askar, the son of ‘Alí; Sádiq; Mírzá Ḥusayn; Mírzá Akbar; Ḥusayn, the son of Zamán; Muḥammad, the son of Akbar Farzí; Mullá Sháh-‘Alí; Khájíh Ismá’íl; Khájih ‘Alí Karam; Ustád ‘Askar; Karbalá’í Ḥasan; Mashhadí Sifr; Muḥammad, the son of Mullá ‘Alí; Sharrif Karbalá’í Rajab; Muḥammad-‘Alí Naw-Rúz; Akbar Muḥammad-Qásim; Ustád Ja‘far; Muḥammad-‘Alí Ḥájí ‘Alí-Sháh; Aḥmad, the son of ‘Isá; ‘Abid Mashhadí Muḥsin; Ghulám-Riḍá Yazdí; Khájih Ustád Nabí; Muḥammad, the son of Riḍá; Mullá ‘Alí-Muḥammad, the son of Mullá Áqá Bábá; Taqí, the son of Sifr; Siyyid Ḥusayn; Siyyid Nazar, son of Mullá ‘Alí Naqí; son of ‘Alí Murád; ‘Abdu’llah ‘Alí; Akbar, his son; Ḥájí Muḥammad Mullá ‘Ashúrá; Ḥájí Naqí; Karbalá’í ‘Askar-i Bírq-Dar, the flag-bearer; Rahím Ustád ‘Alí-Naqí; ‘Alí the son of

LIST OF MARTYRS OF THE NAYRÍZ CONFLICT OF 1853 AS LISTED IN SHAFÍ'’S MANUSCRIPT

Mashhadí Aḥmad; ‘Alí and Ḥusayn, the sons of Qásim-Sifr; Mu’min Ustád Aḥmad; Muḥammad, the son of Báqir; Ḥusayn Ustád Aḥmad; Shamsu’ḍ-Dín, son of ‘Askar; Muḥammad, the son of Karbalá’í Naqí; Akbar Muḥammad-Sháh; Muḥammad Karbalá’í Maḥmúd; Mullá Ḥusayn ‘Abdu’lláh; Karbalá’í Qurbán; Sha‘bán, the son of ‘Ábidín; ‘Abdu’lláh, the son of Mullá Muḥammad; Mírzá Shikar ‘Alí, the son of Mullá ‘Ashúrá; Kabalá’í Báqir; Ustád Taqí, whose slayer was Mírzá Shikar Rajab; Muḥammad-‘Alí; Sádiq and ‘Abidín, the sons of Karbalá’í Ismá’íl Hamamí, Mullá ‘Ábidín; Mírzá Muḥammad-Ḥusayn; Mírzá Taqí, martyred on his way to Ṭihrán; Taqí and Karam, the sons of ‘Alí; son of Ustád Taqí; Mashhadí Muḥammad-‘Alí, the son of Naw-Rúz; Abú-T’álib, son of Zaynu’l-‘Ábidín; ‘Abdu’lláh, the son of ‘Askar; another Abú-Tálib; Mashhadí Mírzá Ḥusayn, surnamed Quṭbá; Mírzá Ḥusayn; Mírzá Musá; Mírzá Aḥmad; Mírzá Zaynu’l-Abidín, who was Mashhadí Mírzá Ḥusayn’s nephew; Mírzá Muhsin Áqá Nasru’lláh; Karbalá’í Muḥammad-Ja‘far, son in law of Ḥájí Muḥammad-Taqí Ayyúb; Mullá Akbar, the brother of Karbalá’í Ja‘far; Karbalá’í Hádí; Mírzá Mihdí; Ḥasan Ḥaydar Bayk; ‘Alí-Murád, the brother of Jináb Vaḥíd’s murderer; Murád Lurr; Karbalá’í Sádiq, the son of Mashhadí Rajab; Ḥusayn, the brother of Karbalá’í Riḍá; Ḥasan and ‘Alí, the sons of Mullá Qásim; Mullá ‘Ashúrá; Ḥasan-‘Alí, the son of Nurí, and his mother, Safr Karbalá’í Zamán; Ḥasan Mashhadí Safr; ‘Askar, the son of ‘Alí; Mullá Abú’l-Qásim; and Ḥusayn, the son of Ustád ‘Alí.

Appendix B

ABOUT OUR SOURCES

Vaḥíd, and the events of 1850, have been covered in other important sources, such as *The Dawn-Breakers*, an early account of the birth of the Bábí and Bahá'í Faiths; and *God Passes By*, written by Shoghi Effendi, regarded by Bahá'ís as having special authority due to the high station of its author. We have included additional information from other sources, such as an account of Vaḥíd's arrival written by hand on the wall of a local mosque, translated by Rabbani.

The mountain battles of 1853 are told using the following sources:

The memoirs of Mullá Muḥammad Shafí': Shafí' was an eyewitness to the 1850 and 1853 conflicts—he was a young boy at the time—and he survived the conflicts and went on to become one of the main educators of the Bahá'í community of Nayríz. The translation used is by Hussein Ahdieh; there is a somewhat different translation in the work of Ahang Rabbani. In this memoir, some of the events may be out of order, as the memoir was written many years after the events in question. As Shafí' was young and could not be in multiple places, he could not possibly have seen all of the things he writes about—he must have heard them as part of an oral retelling of events among the Bahá'ís. Great effort was made to put events in a correct chronological order. To do this, we used dates given in more precise sources, such as the reports written by the British agent in Shíráz, collected in the work of Moojan Momen, as benchmarks. When there were no dates given for events, we tagged groups of individuals to see where that exact same group occurred in various sources and to which event they were linked. We then tried to establish the chronological placement of that event. Using methods such as these, we were able to establish a reasonably accurate, though by no means certain, chronology.

We also used these established sources, currently available only in Persian:

1. Mirzá Asadu'lláh Fádil-i Mázindarání: An eminent Baha'í historian who wrote a nine-volume history of the Faith, *Zuhúr al-Haqq*, based on extensive research that included personal interviews and primary sources. One feature of his approach was to compile stories of the early Bábí and Bahá'ís, providing an invaluable source of information, as well as providing the perspective of the people from that time. For this book, volumes 1–4 were consulted.
2. Muḥammad-'Alí Faizi: distinguished historian who wrote several major works, including one on the life of the Báb and another on the life of 'Abdu'l-Bahá. His history of Nayríz, *Nayríz Mushkbiz*, was written based on his firsthand interviews with survivors of all three conflicts.
3. Mírzá Muḥammad Shafi' Rouhani: A native of Nayríz and an accomplished teacher of the Faith, his history of the Faith in Nayríz, *Lam'átul-Anvár*, was based on many stories and materials that he collected locally. After he retired from his work as

a businessman, he was encouraged by Mr. Álí Nakhjavaní to write down this history.

We also benefited greatly from Ahang Rabbani's extensive and current work, *The Bábís of Nayríz: History and Documents, Witnesses to Bábí and Bahá'í History*, as a source for information on the lives and backgrounds of individuals from 1850 to 1900. This source was also valuable in helping guide us to relevant sections of other sources and in establishing a chronology.

The persecution of 1909 is recounted using Faizi, Rouhani, and a new source—the unpublished memoirs of Shaykh Bahá'í Ahdieh. Ahdieh was for many years the secretary of the Spiritual Assembly of the Bahá'ís of Nayríz, and he had access to many primary source materials. He lived in the aftermath of the persecutions of 1909 and knew intimately all of the families who suffered during these persecutions. After he moved to the United States, he committed his memories to paper. He passed away in his sleep, the same evening he had signed his notes.

There are many other primary and secondary sources that helped us develop this narrative as well as bring that period to life, and these are listed in the bibliography.

Notes

1 / The Town of Nayríz

1. From a private conversation with Hussein Ahdieh, December, 2010 CE.
2. Ibid.
3. Túrán Mírhádí, "Education viii. nursery schools and kindergartens," *Encyclopaedia Iranica,* accessed December 20, 2010, http://www.iranica.com/articles/education-viii-nursery-schools-and-kindergartens.
4. Jalíl Dústkáh and Eqbál Yagmá'í, "Education iii. the traditional elementary school," *Encyclopaedia Iranica,* accessed December 20, 2010, http://www.iranica.com/articles/education-iii.
5. From a private conversation with Hussein Ahdieh, December, 2010 CE.
6. Husang 'Alam, "Henna," *Encyclopaedia Iranica,* accessed December 20, 2010, http://www.iranica.com/articles/henna; from a private conversation with Hussein Ahdieh, December, 2010 CE; Massoume Price, "Iranian Marriage Ceremony, Its History & Symbolism," Iran Chamber Society, accessed December 21, 2010, http://www.iranchamber.com/culture/articles/iranian_marriage_ceremony.php.
7. Bibi Fáṭimih Estarabadi, unpublished manuscript, 42–43, 47 (on the subject of the obedience of the wife), 121, 184 (on the subject of the dowry), 150–51 (on the subject of beatings by drunken husbands).
8. Shireen Mahdavi, "Qajars: the Qajar-period household," *Encyclopaedia Iranica,* accessed December 20, 2010, http://www.iranica.com/articles/qajars-period-household.
9. From a private conversation with Hussein Ahdieh, December, 2010 CE.

10. These are the memories of Bahman Jazabi, son of Mrs. Jahántáb (Jazabi) Sardári, of his grandfather's work habits. Bahman would go along with him as a young boy. Though this was many years later than the manuscript, the work routines did not change much for local farmers.
11. W. M. Floor, "Asnáf," *Encyclopaedia Iranica*, accessed December 20, 2010, http://www.iranica.com/articles/asnaf-guilds.
12. Estarabadi, unpublished manuscript, 121, 170, 174 (on the subject of sex with prostitutes and with boys), 155 (on the subject of gambling).
13. From a private conversation with Hussein Ahdieh, December, 2010 CE.
14. Nancy H. Dupree, "Etiquette," *Encyclopaedia Iranica*, accessed December 20, 2010, http://www.iranica.com/articles/etiquette; Willem Floor, "Gift giving," *Encyclopaedia Iranica,* accessed December 20, 2010, http://www.iranica.com/articles/gift-giving-v.
15. A. Shapur Shahbazi, "Nowruz ii. In the Islamic Period," *Encyclopaedia Iranica*, accessed December 20, 2010, http://www.iranica.com/articles/nowruz-ii.
16. From a private conversation with Hussein Ahdieh, December, 2010 CE.
17. Donaldson, *The Wild Rue, a study of Muhammadan Magic and Folklore in Iran*, 194–200; Mahmoud Omidsalar, "Divination," *Encyclopaedia Iranica*, accessed December 20, 2010, http://www.iranica.com/articles/divination.
18. Ibid., 102–5; C. 15.
19. Ibid., 66.
20. Ibid., C. 3.
21. Ibid., 16–20.
23. Donaldson, *The Wild Rue*, 40–41.
24. Dr. Siamak Tavangar, "Iran Dried figs," accessed December 20, 2010 CE, http://www.iranfig.com/Driedfigs.htm; from private conversations with Mrs. Jahántáb (Jazabi) Sardári and Maziar Jazabi, January 2010 CE.
25. From private conversations with Mrs. Jahántáb (Jazabi) Sardári and Maziar Jazabi, January 2010 CE.

2 / The Báb

1. Balyuzi, H. M., *Khadíjih Bagum: The Wife of the Báb*, 2; Afnán, Mírzá Habib'u'lláh, *The Báb in Shíráz*, 11.
2. Afnán, *The Báb in Shíráz*, 12, 16; Nabíl-i-A'ẓam, *The Dawn-Breakers*, 51–52, 75.
3. Afnán, *The Báb in Shíráz*, 20; Balyuzi, *The Báb*, 40–41; Balyuzi, *Khadíjih Bagum: The Wife of the Báb*, 2; Nabíl-i-A'ẓam, *The Dawn-Breakers*, 53.
4. The Báb, *Selections from the Writings of the Báb*, 7:12:1; Nabíl-i-A'ẓam, *The Dawn-Breakers*, 21.
5. Balyuzi, *Khadíjih Bagum: The Wife of the Báb*, 3.

6. Afnán, *The Báb in Shíráz*, 29; Balyuzi, *Khadíjih Bagum*, 5; Afnán, A. Q. Afnán private communication, 29; Balyuzi, *The Báb in Shíráz*, 29.
7. Rabbani, *The Bábís of Nayríz: History and Documents*, c.1, 24, f. 43.
8. Balyuzi, *Khadíjih Bagum*, 5–6.
9. Ibid., 7.
10. Nabíl-i-A'ẓam, *The Dawn-Breakers*, 53.
11. Balyuzi, *Khadíjih Bagum*, 9–10.
12. Ibid., 13. These are not scriptural words from the writings of the Báb but the words remembered decades later by Khadíjih Bagum when recalling these days.
13. Ibid., 7–9.
14. The information in this section is from chapter 3, "The Declaration of the Báb," of Nabíl-i-A'ẓam, *The Dawn-Breakers*.
15. These words are the recollections of Mullá Ḥusayn about this interview found in Nabíl-i-A'ẓam, *The Dawn-Breakers*, 57–65. They convey the gist of their conversation and are not meant to be a verbatim transcript, though some words may be the exact ones.
16. The Báb gave the following chronology of His travels (Ishráq-Khávarí, Kitáb Muhádirát, 729–31). Also see Balyuzi, *Khadíjih Bagum*, 15:
    1). Left Shíráz 10 September 1844 / Arrived Búshihr 19 September 1844.
    2). Left the port 2 October 1844 / Reached Mecca 12 December 1844.
    3). Hajj Completed 24 December 1844 / Left Mecca 7 January 1845.
    4). Arrived Medina 16 January 1845 / Left Medina 12 February 1845.
    5). Arrived Jiddah 24 February 1845 / Embarked on Ship 27 February 1845.
    6). Sailed for Iran 4 March 1845.
17. Balyuzi, *The Báb*, 69–71.
18. Balyuzi, *Khadíjih Bagum*, 2.
19. Nabíl-i-A'ẓam, *The Dawn-Breakers*, 99.
20. Balyuzi, *The Báb*, 89.
21. Browne, *A Traveller's Narrative*, Vol. 2., 7; Hájí Mírzá Muḥammad-Sádiq Mu'allim, quoted in Afnan, *The Bab in Shiraz,* 59; Nabíl-i-A'ẓam, *The Dawn-Breakers*, 108. Nabíl-i-A'ẓam's states in *The Dawn-Breakers* that the Báb spoke these words: ""The condemnation of God be upon him who regards me either as a representative of the Ímám or the gate thereof." In *A Traveller's Narrative* (v.2, p.7), 'Abdu'l-Bahá states that, ". . . afterwards it became known and evident that his meaning was the Gate-hood [*Babiyyat*] of another city." Our version has put together the versions of 'Abdu'l-Bahá, Hájí Mírzá Muḥammad-Sádiq Mu'allim, and Nabíl-i-A'ẓam, in the hope that this gives the most complete idea of what the Báb proclaimed that day and why it touched off an angry, if puzzled, reac-

tion from those listening. It seems that the Báb made His proclamation in such a way that its deeper meaning could be understood but also could be easily missed.

22. Browne, *A Traveller's Narrative*, Vol. 2, 7.
23. Balyuzi, *The Báb*, 99. According to Khadíjih's recollections years later this happened prior to the appearance of the Báb at the mosque and was the cause of it (Balyuzi, *Khadíjih Bagum: The Wife of the Báb*, 19–20).
24. Balyuzi, *Khadíjih Bagum: The Wife of the Báb*, 20–21.

3 / Vaḥid

1. Mázandarání, *Amr Va Khalq*, v. 2, 87.
2. Nicolas, *Seyyed Ali Mohammed dit le Bab*, 189, f. 56. The order was the Ni'matullahi tariqa (Amanat, *Pivot of the Universe,* 456 n. 10); Ávárih, 'Abdu'l-Ḥusayn, *Kawakibu'd-Durriyih*, v. 1, 52; Nicolas, *Seyyed Ali Mohammed dit le Bab*, 189, f. 56.
3. Rabbani, *Nayriz : The First Century,* "Appendix 2: The family of Vaḥíd Dárábí" 33, n. 6, 1–3.
4. Ahdieh, *Nayrízi-Shurangiz*, 13.
5. Mirza Abu'l Faz'l and Siyyid Mehdi Gulpaygani, quoted in Rabbani, *Nayriz: The First Century*, 77–78.
6. Mázandarání, *Amr Va Khalq*, v. 3, 465; Rouhani, *Lam'átul-Anvár*, v. 1, 43; Nabíl-i-A'ẓam, *The Dawn-Breakers*, 124.
7. Mázandarání, *Amr Va Khalq*, v. 3, 466; Nabíl-i-A'ẓam, *The Dawn-Breakers*, 124–25.
8. The Holy Qur'án, Súrih 108, quoted in Nabíl-i-A'ẓam, *The Dawn-Breakers*, 125.
9. Nicolas, *Seyyed Ali Mohammed dit le Bab*, 234; Nabíl-i-A'ẓam, *The Dawn-Breakers*, 125–26.
10. The Báb, quoted in Shoghi Effendi, *The World Order of Bahá'u'lláh*, 62–63.

4 / Separate Ways

1. Nicolas, *Seyyed Ali Mohammed dit le Bab*, 235.
2. Rabbani, *The Bábís of Nayríz: History and Documents*, c. 2, 4.
3. Nabíl-i-A'ẓam, *The Dawn-Breakers*, 127; Rabbani, *The Bábís of Nayríz: History and Documents*, appendix 2, 3; Rabbani, *The Bábís of Nayríz: History and Documents*, 4; Ávárih, *Kawakibu'd-Durriyih*, v. 1, 57.
4. Balyuzi, *Khadíjih Bagum*, 16–17; Nabíl-i-A'ẓam, *The Dawn-Breakers*, 141, 142–43; 'Abdu'l-Bahá, *A Traveller's Narrative*, v. 2, 11.
5. Balyuzi, *Khadíjih Bagum*, 18.

6. The Báb, in *Bahá'í Prayers*, 226.
7. Balyuzi, *Khadíjih Bagum*, 21.
8. Nabíl-i-A'ẓam, *The Dawn-Breakers*, 144–45.
9. Amanat, *Resurrection and Renewal*, 257; Nicolas, *Seyyed Ali Mohammed dit le Bab*, 93; Nabíl-i-A'ẓam, *The Dawn-Breakers*, 149–53.
10. Nicolas, *Seyyed Ali Mohammed dit le Bab*, f. 3, 223; Nabíl-i-A'ẓam, *The Dawn-Breakers*, 151–53.
11. Nabíl-i-A'ẓam, *The Dawn-Breakers*, 163–64.
12. Nicolas, *Seyyed Ali Mohammed dit le Bab*, 257, f. 3.
13. Rabbani, *The Bábís of Nayríz: History and Documents*, c. 2, 13, 16.
14. Nabíl-i-A'ẓam, *The Dawn-Breakers*, 181–82.
15. Ibid., 222–23.
16. The Báb, quoted in Nabíl-i-A'ẓam, *The Dawn-Breakers*, 315–16.
17. Nabíl-i-A'ẓam, *The Dawn-Breakers*, 229–32.
18. Balyuzi, *The Báb*, 147.
19. Dr. Cormick, quoted in Browne, *Materials for the study of the Bábí religion*, quoted in Balyuzi, *The Báb*, 146–47.
20. Balyuzi, *The Báb*, 140; Amanat, 'Abbás, *Pivot of the Universe: Nasir al-Din Sháh Qájár and the Iranian Monarchy, 1831–1896*, 150; Nabíl-i-A'ẓam, *The Dawn-Breakers*, 232.
21. Nabíl-i-A'ẓam, *The Dawn-Breakers*; Rabbani, *The Bábís of Nayríz: History and Documents*, 343; c. 20.
22. The Báb, quoted in Faizi, *The Life of the Báb*, 37; Rabbani, *The Bábís of Nayríz: History and Documents*, c. 2, 21.

5 / Vaḥíd Nears Nayríz

1. Nabíl-i-A'ẓam, *The Dawn-Breakers*, 350. The sources do not agree on which children were taken to Nayríz and which were left in Yazd, and the authors could not resolve this.
2. Ibid., 351.
3. Nicolas, *Seyyed Ali Mohammed dit le Bab*, 392, and Fasá'í, *Fárs Námih-yi Násií*, quoted in Rabbani, *The Bábís of Nayríz: History and Documents*, c. 8, 12; Nabíl-i-A'ẓam, *The Dawn-Breakers*, 351–52; Bahá'í Ahdieh, *Nayrízi-Shurangiz*, v. 1, 53.
4. Faizi, *Hadrat-i-Nuqtay-i Úlá: The Life of the Báb*, 53; from a private conversation with Hussein Ahdieh, June, 2010.
5. Faizi, *Hadrat-i-Nuqtay-i Úlá: The Life of the Báb*, 197.
6. Mullá Muḥammad Shafi' Nayrízí, *Narrative of Mulla Muḥammad Shafi' Nayrízí*, 1; Bahá'í Ahdieh, *Nayrízi-Shurangiz*, 19; Faizi, *Hadrat-i-Nuqtay-i Úlá, The Life of the Báb*, 52; Bahá'í Ahdieh, *Nayrízi-Shurangiz*, v. 1, 55; Nabíl-i-A'ẓam, *The Dawn-Breakers*, 352; Mázandarání, *Zuhúr al-Haqq*, v. 2, 409.

7. Nabíl-i-A'ẓam, *The Dawn-Breakers*, 352–53.
8. Mullá Ḥasan's sister was married to Zaynu'l-'Ábidín K͟hán's brother, possibly the one who was assassinated (from a conversation with Mrs. S͟hahídpúr, March, 2010/166 BE).
9. Bahá'í Ahdieh, *Nayrízí-Shurangiz*, v. 1, 260.
10. Ibid., 20.
11. Ibid., v. 1, 260.
12. Ibid., v. 1, 53; Nabíl-i-A'ẓam, *The Dawn-Breakers*, 353; Shafí', *Narrative of Mulla Muhammad Shafí' Nayrízí*, 2.

6 / The Great Announcement and the Heroic Stand at Fort K͟hájih

1. Afnán, *The genesis of the Babi and Baha'i Faiths in S͟hiráz and Fars*, 51. Ḥájí Mírzá Jání Ká͟shání, quoted in Rabbani, *The Bábís of Nayríz: History and Documents*, c. 6, 8. Mázandarání, *Zuhúr al-Haqq*, v. 2, 410. It is unclear when exactly these messages were exchanged—whether Vaḥíd was on his way to Nayríz, or if he had already entered.
2. According to Mulla Muḥammad Shafí', *Narrative of Mulla Muhammad Shafí' Nayízí* (2), and Mázandarání, *Zuhúr al-Haqq, Volumes 1–4* (v. 2, 409), he had two armed men on either side of the pulpit to protect him. Nabíl-i-A'ẓam, *The Dawn-Breakers* (353) does not have this detail. According to Rouhani, *Lam'átul-Anvár* (v. 1, 57–58), Vaḥíd told the congregants on the first day that he had a great message for them and that he would give it when more people were gathered at the mosque. He said this again the second day. On the third day a large crowd had gathered and he spoke of the Báb and His Revelation. Shafí', *Narrative of Mullá Muḥammad Shafí'* (3), states that Vaḥíd spoke to crowds on ten consecutive days and that the crowds grew. Sources put the size of the crowd from at least 1,000 (Nabíl-i-A'ẓam, *The Dawn-Breakers*, 353) all the way up to 2,500 (Faizi, *Nayríz Mushkbiz*, 54).
3. A non-Bábí source, Siyyid Ibráhím, wrote his memories of Vaḥíd in Nayríz on the wall of the Jami' Saghir mosque in the Bázár quarter. He characterizes Vaḥíd's motives and actions as rebellion: "Upon arrival, he (Vaḥíd) went directly to the Masjid Jami' Kabír, in the Chinár-Súkhtih quarter, where his followers had gathered from all corners, preparing for battle. The congregation numbered nine hundred men armed with guns and swords and he ascended the pulpit with his saber ready. He spoke to the assembled people and prepared them for combat, and in that quarter raised the standard of revolt." This wasn't the call raised by Vaḥíd, and he gathered a fighting force only when the Bábís were threatened by the authorities. Nabíl-i-A'ẓam, *The Dawn-Breakers* (354) states that he was there for a "few" days. Nicolas, *Seyyed Ali Mohammed dit le Bab* (395), states that he spoke for ten consecutive days.

4. Afnán, *The genesis of the Babi and Baha'i Faiths in Shíráz and Fars*, 51–52; Nabíl-i-A'ẓam, *The Dawn-Breakers*, 353–54.
5. Mázandarání, Zuhúr al-Haqq, (v. 2, 410) and Hamadání, quoted in Rabbani, *The Bábís of Nayríz: History and Documents* c. 9, 12; Nabíl-i-A'ẓam, *The Dawn-Breakers*, 354 and Shafí', *Narrative of Mulla Muhammad Shafi' Nayrízí*, 3.
6. Nabíl-i-A'ẓam, *The Dawn-Breakers*, 354; Shafí', *Narrative of Mulla Muhammad Shafi' Nayrízí*, 3.
7. Guy Murchie, "Nayríz—Scene of Vahid's Heroism," *Bahá'í News* 6 (1965).
8. Nabíl-i-A'ẓam, *The Dawn-Breakers*, 355.
9. Ahdieh, *Nayrízi-Shurangiz*, 20; Nicolas, *Seyyed Ali Mohammed dit le Bab*, 396; Nabíl-i-A'ẓam, *The Dawn-Breakers*, 355.
10. Mázandarání, *Zuhúr al-Haqq*, v. 2, 412; Nabíl-i-A'ẓam, *The Dawn-Breakers*, 355–56.
11. Shafí', *Narrative of Mulla Muhammad Shafi' Nayrízí*, 4; Faizi, *Nayríz Mushkbiz*, 60.
12. Afnán, *The genesis of the Babi and Baha'i Faiths in Shíráz and Fars*, 55.
13. Nicolas, *Seyyed Ali Mohammed dit le Bab*, 397; Nabíl-i-A'ẓam, *The Dawn-Breakers*, 356.
14. Rouhani, *Lam'átul-Anvár*, v. 1, 66; Nabíl-i-A'ẓam, *The Dawn-Breakers*, 356; Shafí', *Narrative of Mullá Muḥammad Shafí'*, 4.
15. Faizi, *Nayríz Mushkbiz*, 79; Rouhani, *Lam'átul-Anvár* (v. 1, 131); Shafí', *Narrative of Mullá Muḥammad Shafí'*, 5; http://bahai-library.com/provisionals/surih.sabr.html.
16. Rabbani, *The Bábís of Nayríz*, c. 10, 19.
17. Shafí', *Narrative of Mullá Muḥammad Shafí'* (5). Shafí' states that the "first seventy" were allowed into the fort—those from Iṣṭahbánát and the bazaar who had come with him when he first entered Nayríz.
18. Nabíl-i-A'ẓam, *The Dawn-Breakers*, 357. There are several other versions of this story. Shafí', *Narrative of Mullá Muḥammad Shafí'* (6), and Nicolas, *Seyyed Ali Mohammed dit le Bab* (400–401), state that Vaḥíd told him to accept the truth of the Báb and when Mullá Báqir refused, he was executed. Faizi, *Nayríz Mushkbiz* (61), gives a completely different account in which Mullá Báqir is released only to be picked up by soldiers who, after seeing him leave the Bábí compound, thought he was a traitor and killed him. The authors have chosen to include the *The Dawn-Breakers* version because of the importance given to this source.
19. Nabíl-i-A'ẓam, *The Dawn-Breakers*, 358. For a brief biography of Shaykh Abú Turáb, the Ímám Jámi' of Shíráz, go to http://www.Nayríz.org.
20. Afnán, *The genesis of the Babi and Baha'i Faiths in Shíráz and Fars*, 53.
21. Unnamed British agent, quoted in Momen, *The Bábí and Bahá'í Religions*, 109–10.
22. Nicolas, *Seyyed Ali Mohammed dit le Bab*, 401.

7 / Massacre of the Faithful

1. Nicolas, *Seyyed Ali Mohammed dit le Bab*, 401; Shafí', *Narrative of Mulla Muhammad Shafi' Nayrízí*, 7.
2. Nabíl-i-A'ẓam, *The Dawn-Breakers*, 358.
3. Shafí', *Narrative of Mulla Muhammad Shafi' Nayrízí*, 7; Nicolas, *Seyyed Ali Mohammed dit le Bab*, 402.
4. Nabíl-i-A'ẓam, *The Dawn-Breakers*, 359–60.
5. Nabíl-i-A'ẓam, *The Dawn-Breakers*, 360, lists the following deceased: Ghulám-Riḍáy-i-Yazdí (not the commander, another one); his brother, 'Alí, son of Khayru'lláh; Khájih Ḥusayn-i-Qannád, son of Khájih Ghaní; Aṣghar, son of Mullá Mihdí; Karbilá'í 'Abdu'l-Karím; Ḥusayn, son of Mashhadí Muhammad; Zaynu'l-'Ábidín, son of Mashhadí Báqir-i-Sabbágh; Mullá Ja'far-i-Mudhahhib; 'Abdu'lláh, son of Mullá Músá; Muhammad, son of Mashhadí Rajab-i-Ḥaddád; Karbilá'í Ḥasan, son of Karbilá'í Shamsu'ḍ-Dín-i-Malikí-Dúz; Karbilá'í Mírzá Muhammad-i-Zári'; Karbilá'í Báqir-i-Kafsh-Dúz; Mírzá Aḥmad, son of Mírzá Ḥusayn-i-Káshí-Sáz; Mullá Ḥasan, son of Mullá 'Abdu'lláh; Mashhadí Ḥájí Muhammad; Abú-Ṭálib, son of Mír Aḥmad-i-Nukhud-Biríz; Akbar, son of Muhammad-i-'Áshúr; Taqíy-i-Yazdí; Mullá 'Alí, son of Mullá Ja'far; Karbilá'í Mírzá Ḥusayn; Ḥusayn Khán, son of Sharíf; Karbilá'í Qurbán; Khájih Kázim, son of Khájih 'Alí; Áqá, son of Ḥájí 'Alí; Mírzá Nawrá, son of Mírzá Mu'íná. Nicolas, *Seyyed Ali Mohammed dit le Bab,* 402, states that according to the "Fárs-Nameh" there were three hundred soldiers and one hundred and fifty Bábís killed. He also numbers the Bábí deaths at around sixty.
6. Vaḥíd, quoted in Rabbani, *The Bábís of Nayríz: History and Documents, Witnesses to Bábí and Bahá'í history vol. 2,* Appendix 2, 17–18; Rouhani*, Lam'átul-Anvár,* v. 1, 100.
7. Nabíl-i-A'ẓam, *The Dawn-Breakers*, 361–62.
8. From a provisional translation of the "Tablet of Job" by Khazeh Fananapazir, 21 April, 1997. http://bahai-library.org/provisionals/surih.sabr.html.
9. Nabíl-i-A'ẓam, *The Dawn-Breakers*, 362; Ahdieh, *Nayrízi-Shurangiz,* 29.
10. Rouhani*, Lam'átul-Anvár,* v. 1, 79, n. 1.
11. Ávárih, *Kawakibu'd-Durriyih,* 208.
12. Rouhani, *Lam'átul-Anvár,* v. 1, 79, n. 1; Ahdieh, *Nayrízi-Shurangiz,* 31; *The Holy Qur'án*, Súrih of Toubeh, Verse 32.
13. Nabíl-i-A'ẓam, *The Dawn-Breakers*, 362–63.
14. Faizi, *Nayríz Mushkbiz,* 65; Nabíl-i-A'ẓam, *The Dawn-Breakers*, 363.
15. Afnán, *The genesis of the Babi and Baha'i Faiths in Shiraz and Fars,* 54; Hamadání, quoted in Rabbani, *The Bábís of Nayríz: History and Documents, Witnesses to Bábí and Bahá'í history,* vol. *2,* c. 9, 15; Siyyid Ibráhim, quoted in Rabbani, *The Bábís of Nayríz: History and Documents, Witnesses to Bábí and Bahá'í history,*

vol. 2, c. 7, 6; Ḥájí Mírzá Jání, quoted in Rabbani, *The Bábís of Nayríz: History and Documents, Witnesses to Bábí and Bahá'í history, vol. 2,* c. 6, 11; Faizi, *Nayríz Mushkbiz,* 62–63, 65.

16. Nabíl-i-A'ẓam, *The Dawn-Breakers,* 364; Shafí', *Narrative of Mulla Muhammad Shafi' Nayrízí,* 9; Rouhani, *Lam'átul-Anvár,* v. 1, 313; Ahdieh, *Nayrízi-Shurangiz,* 33.
17. Nicolas, *Seyyed Ali Mohammed dit le Bab,* 404; Shafí', *Narrative of Mulla Muhammad Shafi' Nayrízí,* 10. Afnán, Hamadání, or Jání don't mention this second note.
18. Nabíl-i-A'ẓam, *The Dawn-Breakers,* 364; Shafí', *Narrative of Mulla Muhammad Shafi' Nayrízí,* 10.
19. Nabíl-i-A'ẓam, *The Dawn-Breakers,* 364; Rouhani, *Lam'átul-Anvár,* v. 1, 86, n. 1; Ahdieh, *Nayrízi-Shurangiz,* 34. According to Rouhani, four hundred were killed there. Nabíl-i-A'ẓam, *The Dawn-Breakers* (364), describes the casualties there as "a few" and that many who were wounded got to town and to the Great Mosque. Shafí', *Narrative of Mulla Muhammad Shafi' Nayrízí,* 10, states that "many of them" were killed by the soldiers before reaching the mosque.
20. Nabíl-i-A'ẓam, *The Dawn-Breakers,* 364; Shafí', *Narrative of Mulla Muhammad Shafi' Nayrízí,* 10.
21. Nabíl-i-A'ẓam, *The Dawn-Breakers,* 364–65; Shafí', *Narrative of Mulla Muhammad Shafi' Nayrízí,* 10. One Bábí was able to climb up a minaret and shoot the defender, who then fell to the ground, though he lived to persecute the Bábís another day.
22. Nabíl-i-A'ẓam, *The Dawn-Breakers,* 365; Shafí', *Narrative of Mulla Muhammad Shafi' Nayrízí,* 10; Faizi, *Nayríz Mushkbiz,* 61; Rouhani, *Lam'átul-Anvár,* v. 1, 87.
23. Nabíl-i-A'ẓam, *The Dawn-Breakers,* 365. Nicolas, *Seyyed Ali Mohammed dit le Bab,* 424, lists the following men also having stepped forward to kill Vaḥíd in addition to the one mentioned in this narrative: Ṣafar, whose brother Sha'bán had been killed in the conflict; and Áqá Khán, the son of 'Alí-Aṣghar Khán, the brother of Zaynu'l-'Ábidín Khán, who was also killed. This incident gives weight to *The Dawn-Breakers'* account of Báqir's death, since his brother volunteered to attack Vaḥíd based on Báqir's having been killed.
24. Shoghi Effendi, *God Passes By,* 43; Nabíl-i-A'ẓam, *The Dawn-Breakers,* 365; Rouhani, *Lam'átul-Anvár,* v. 1 89; Faizi, *Nayríz Mushkbiz,* 70; Taherzadeh, *Revelation of Bahá'u'lláh,* v. 1, 365; Rouhani, *Lam'átul-Anvár,* v. 1, c. 7; Nicolas, *Seyyed Ali Mohammed dit le Bab,* 406; Ahdieh, *Nayrízi-Shurangiz,* 36.
25. Shafí', *Narrative of Mulla Muhammad Shafi' Nayrízí,* 11; Shoghi Effendi, *God Passes By,* 43; Faizi, *Nayríz Mushkbiz,* 7; Ahdieh, *Nayrízi-Shurangiz,* 36; Nabíl-i-A'ẓam, *The Dawn-Breakers,* 366; Rouhani, *Lam'átul-Anvár,* v. 1, 90. Much of the information in the three previous paragraphs is taken from Rouhani.

26. Rouhani, *Lam'átul-Anvár,* v. 1, 90; Faizi, *Nayríz Mushkbiz,* 70–71, n.1, 199–200; Ahdieh, *Nayrízi-Shurangiz,* 37.
27. Nabíl-i-A'ẓam, *The Dawn-Breakers,* 366. These same words had been spoken by the Ímám Ḥusayn on the plains of Karbilá prior to his martyrdom. It is not sure from the sources when exactly they were spoken, so the authors have taken some liberty here.
28. Ahdieh, *Nayrízi-Shurangiz,* 42.

8 / Punishment

1. Momen, *The Bábí and Bahá'í Religions, 1844–1944,* 110–11.
2. 'Abdu'l-Bahá, *A Traveler's Narrative,* 258, n. H; Áqá Mírzá Áqá Afnán, quoted in Rabbani, *The Bábís of Nayríz: History and Documents,* c. 10, 4.
3. Mázandarání, *Zuhúr al-Haqq,* v. 4, 31–32; Rouhani, *Lam'átul-Anvár,* v. 1, 52; Momen, *The Bábí and Bahá'í Religions,* 1844–1944, 110–11.
4. Nicolas, *Seyyed Ali Mohammed dit le Bab,* 407; Mázandarání, *Zuhúr al-Haqq,* v. 2, 423.
5. Quoted in Afnán, *The genesis of the Bábí and Bahá'í Faiths in Shíráz and Fárs,* 56–57.
6. Browne, *Materials for the study of the Bábí religion,* 317; Mázandarání, *Zuhúr al-Haqq,* v. 2, 423.
7. Browne, *Materials for the study of the Bábí religion,* 317; Ahdieh, *Nayrízi-Shurangiz,* 48.
8. Munírih Khánum, (cited as "Khándán Afnán," 165), quoted in Rabbani, *The Bábís of Nayríz: History and Documents,* c.10, 32, endnote 12.
9. Afnán, *The genesis of the Babi and Baha'i Faiths in Shiraz and Fars,* 57, states that there were twelve who attempted to reach the Sháh with a petition and that all but one was apprehended in Isfahán; Nicolas, *Seyyed Ali Mohammed dit le Bab* , 409.
10. Mázandarání, *Zuhúr al-Haqq,* v. 4, 22, n.1.
11. Rabbani, *The Bábís of Nayríz: History and Documents, Witnesses to Bábí and Bahá'í history,* v. 2, c. 10, 2; Mírzá Mahmúd, quoted in Momen, *The Bábís of Nayríz: History and Documents, Witnesses to Bábí and Bahá'í history,* 111.
12. Nicolas, *Seyyed Ali Mohammed dit le Bab,* 408; Taherzadeh, *Revelation of Bahá'u'lláh,* v. 1, 140.
13. Mázandarání, *Zuhúr al-Haqq,* v. 3, 293–94; Shafí', *Narrative of Mulla Muhammad Shafí' Nayrízí,* 11.
14. Taherzadeh, *Revelation of Bahá'u'lláh,* v. 1, 138; Ahdieh, *Nayrízi-Shurangiz,* 107; Nabíl-i-A'ẓam, *The Dawn-Breakers,* 367; Shafí', *Narrative of Mulla Muhammad Shafí' Nayrízí,* 11.
15. Habib Taherzadeh, quoted in Taherzadeh, *Revelation of Bahá'u'lláh,* v. 1, 139–42.

16. Rouhani, *Lam'átul-Anvár,* v. 1, 146; Rabbani, *The Bábís of Nayríz: History and Documents, Witnesses to Bábí and Bahá'í history,* c. 10, 13.
17. Shafí', *Narrative of Mulla Muhammad Shafi' Nayrízí,* 11; Faizi, *Nayríz Mushkbiz,* 78; Ahdieh, *Nayrízi-Shurangiz,* 51.
18. Málmírí, *Khátirát-i-Málamírí,* 27–31.
19. Nicolas, *Seyyed Ali Mohammed dit le Bab,* 408–9; Shafí', *Narrative of Mulla Muhammad Shafi' Nayrízí,* 11; Rabbani, *The Bábís of Nayríz: History and Documents, Witnesses to Bábí and Bahá'í history,* c. 10, 23.
20. Málmírí, *Khátirát-i-Málamírí,* 25–26.
21. Faizi, *Nayríz Mushkbiz,* 79. These Bábís included Shaykh 'Abdu'l-'Alí, Mullá 'Abdu'l-Ḥusayn, Khájih Quṭbá, Mírzá Muḥammad Ḥusayn, Mírzá 'Alí Sardár, Khájih Muḥammad Ḥusayn, Zaynu'l-'Ábidín Khán Iṣṭahbánátí, Ibráhim, son of Sálih, Siyyid Ḥusayn and Siyyid Ḥasan, sons of Ḥájí Siyyid Aḥmad, Mullá Ḥasan, son of Karbalá'í Qásim, Shaykh Muḥammad-Ismá'íl, son of Mullá Muḥammad Báqir, Mullá 'Alí Akbar, son of Mullá Muḥammad Iṣṭahbánátí, Shaykh Yúsuf, Luṭf-'Alí Qa'id, Mírzá Muḥammad, son of Mírzá Muḥammad 'Abid, the Iṣṭahbánátí Bábís.
22. Rouhani, *Lam'átul-Anvár,* v. 1, 158; Faizi, *Nayríz Mushkbiz,* 72.

9 / Attempt on the Life of the King of Persia

1. Nabíl-i-A'ẓam, *The Dawn-Breakers,* 440.
2. Ibid, 439.
3. Amanat, *Resurrection and Renewal,* 205
4. *Waqáyi' Ittifáqiyyah,* #81, published on Thursday, 3 Dhi'l-Qa'dih 1268 AH, quoted in Rabbani, *The Bábís of Nayríz: History and Documents,* c. 10, 20.
5. *Waqáyi' Ittifáqiyyah,* #82, quoted in Rabbani, *The Bábís of Nayríz: History and Documents,* c. 10, 20. A brief biography of Mullá Muḥammad Nayrízí is available at http://www.Nayríz.org.
6. Nabíl-i-A'ẓam, *The Dawn-Breakers,* 443.
7. Ibid., 443–44, footnote.
8. Amanat, *Resurrection and Renewal,* 205.
9. Nabíl-i-A'ẓam, *The Dawn-Breakers,* 445.
10. Esselmont, *Bahá'u'lláh and the New Era,* 60.
11. Nabíl-i-A'ẓam, *The Dawn-Breakers,* 446, f. 1.

10 / Upheaval in Nayríz

1. Mirzá Qábil Ábádi'í, quoted in Rabbani, *The Bábís of Nayríz: History and Documents, Witnesses to Bábí and Bahá'í history vol. 2,* c. 13, 2; Rabbani, *The Bábís of Nayríz: History and Documents, Witnesses to Bábí and Bahá'í history vol. 2,* c. 11, 3.

2. Shafí', *Narrative of Mulla Muhammad Shafi' Nayrízí,* 12; Rouhani, *Lam'átul-Anvár,* v. 1, 173–79; Ábádi'í, quoted and translated in Rabbani, *The Bábís of Nayríz: History and Documents, Witnesses to Bábí and Bahá'í history vol. 2,* c. 13, 2; Shafí', *Narrative of Mulla Muhammad Shafi' Nayrízí,* 12.
3. Rouhani, *Lam'átul-Anvár,* v. 1, 269.
4. Rabbani, *The Bábís of Nayríz: History and Documents, Witnesses to Bábí and Bahá'í history vol. 2,* c. 10, 26; Nabíl-i-A'ẓam, *The Dawn-Breakers,* 471.
5. Rouhani, *Lam'átul-Anvár,* v. 1, 173–79.
6. Ibid., v. 1, 177; Mehrabkhani, *Disciple at Dawn,* 162; Rouhani, *Lam'átul-Anvár,* v. 1, 170–72; Shafí', *Narrative of Mulla Muhammad Shafi' Nayrízí,* 14.
7. Ahdieh, *Nayrízi-Shurangiz,* 114.
8. Shafí', *Narrative of Mulla Muhammad Shafi' Nayrízí,* 14.
9. Momen, *The Bábí and Bahá'í Religions, 1844–1944,* 515; Mázandarání, *Zuhúr al-Haqq,* v. 4, 26; Shafí', *Narrative of Mulla Muhammad Shafi' Nayrízí,* 15.
10. Mázandarání, *Zuhúr al-Haqq,* v. 4, 28.
11. Nabíl-i-A'ẓam, *The Dawn-Breakers,* 471.
12. Shafí', *Narrative of Mulla Muhammad Shafi' Nayrízí,* 15.
13. Ibid., 15.
14. Faizi, *Nayríz Mushkbiz,* 106.
15. Shafí', *Narrative of Mulla Muhammad Shafi' Nayrízí,* 16; Ma'ani, *Against Incredible Odds,* 229.
16. Shafí', *Narrative of Mulla Muhammad Shafi' Nayrízí,* 16; Rouhani, *Lam'átul-Anvár,* v. 1, 176; Faizi, *Nayríz Mushkbiz,* 102–3.
17. Momen, *The Bábí and Bahá'í Religions, 1844–1944,* 147–148, footnotes.
18. Shafí', *Narrative of Mulla Muhammad Shafi' Nayrízí,* 16.
19. Ibid., 16.

11 / Battle in the Vineyard

1. Shafí', *Narrative of Mulla Muhammad Shafi' Nayrízí,* 16–17; Ahdieh, *Nayrízi-Shurangiz,* 114.
2. Shafí', *Narrative of Mulla Muhammad Shafi' Nayrízí,* 17.
3. Nicolas, *Seyyed Ali Mohammed dit le Bab,* 413.
4. Shafí', *Narrative of Mulla Muhammad Shafi' Nayrízí,* 17.
5. Nicolas, *Seyyed Ali Mohammed dit le Bab,* 413; Shafí', *Narrative of Mulla Muhammad Shafi' Nayízí,* 17.
6. Shafí', *Narrative of Mulla Muhammad Shafi' Nayrízí,* (17), describes the orchards in the foothills of the mountains south of town as being "half a fársang away" in Bídlang. A fársang is a measurement equaling 3.5 miles or 5.6 kilometers. Rouhani, *Lam'átul-Anvár* (180), gives the name of 'Bid-Bikhubih' for this area;

Ma'ani, *Against Incredible Odds,* (229), calls it *Bídbukhúyih.* Nayrízí, *"The Account of Siyyid Ibrahim concerning Nayriz," Translations of Shaykhi, Bábí and Bahá'í Texts, vol. 4, no. 5* (3), calls it 'Bid Najviyyih.' Local sources contacted by the authors place Bídlang at around 6 km from Nayríz, though one stated it was 12 km. While the area with a water source south of Nayríz known as 'Bid Bukhun' is a more logical destination, because it is on the way to the paths up the mountain where the Bábís eventually go, the authors have no conclusive evidence as to which of these areas the Bábís went to. As a result, the authors have put *Bid Bukhun* since it is the most reasonable location given the series of events.

7. Shafí', *Narrative of Mulla Muhammad Shafi' Nayrízí* (22), and Ahdieh, *Nayrízi-Shurangiz* (115), put the number of area villagers involved at this point at two thousand.
8. From the October report of Mírzá Faḍlu'lláh, the British agent in Shíráz (Momen, The *Bábí and Bahá'í Religions, 1844–1944,* 148).
9. According to Shafí', *Narrative of Mulla Muhammad Shafi' Nayrízí* (18), Mírzá Na'ím arrives "after several days."
10. Ahdieh, *Nayrízi-Shurangiz,* 116. Nayrízí, *"The Account of Siyyid Ibrahim concerning Nayriz," Translations of Shaykhi, Bábí and Bahá'í Texts, vol. 4, no. 5,* 3. Ma'ani, *Against Incredible Odds* (229), spells this place *Darb-i-Shigift.*
11. Shafí', *Narrative of Mulla Muhammad Shafi' Nayrízí* (18), notes that these gunmen from the villages of Iṣṭahbánát and 'Aynálú arrive "twenty days later." The Sharíf of Nayríz is Mírzá Yúsif.

12 / The Bloody Mountain: Darb-i-Shikáft and Bálá-Taram

1. The three who were killed were Ismá'íl Khájih Aḥmadí, custodian of the Khájih Aḥmad Shrine near Nayríz, Sha'ban, the son of Abidin, and Muḥammad, son of Mullá Ḥusayn. Two who were shot and died later were Mullá Ḥusayn, son of Mullá 'Alí Muḥammad, and a son of Áqá Bábá. The Bábí who counterattacked successfully was Taqí, son of Safr (Nicolas, *Seyyed Ali Mohammed dit le Bab,* 415).
2. Nicolas, *Seyyed Ali Mohammed dit le Bab,* 416. In Nicolas's version, the men are thrown off the mountain cliff. In Rabbani, *The Bábís of Nayríz: History and Documents, Witnesses to Bábí and Bahá'í history vol. 2* (c. 11, 15), they are beheaded "on the spot."
3. Rabbani, *The Bábís of Nayríz: History and Documents, Witnesses to Bábí and Bahá'í history vol. 2,* c. 11, 16.
4. Mázandaraní, *Zuhúr al-Haqq,* v. 4, 35.
5. Rabbani, *The Bábís of Nayríz: History and Documents, Witnesses to Bábí and Bahá'í history vol. 2,* c. 11, 16.

6. Shafí', *Narrative of Mulla Muhammad Shafi' Nayrízí,* 20.
7. This Bábí was Siyyid Ḥusayn. According to Nicolas, *Seyyed Ali Mohammed dit le Bab,* (416), he was in the group at the Darb-i-Shikáft pass. According to Rabbani, *The Bábís of Nayríz: History and Documents, Witnesses to Bábí and Bahá'í history vol. 2,* (c. 11, 17), he was coming from the "Ásbúrán" heights. (Mázandarání, *Zuhúr al-Haqq,* v. 4, 35-36).
8. Shafí', *Narrative of Mulla Muhammad Shafi' Nayrízí,* 20; Nayrízí, *"The Account of Siyyid Ibrahim concerning Nayriz,"* 4.
9. Nicolas, *Seyyed Ali Mohammed dit le Bab,* 417.
10. Report by Mírzá Faḍlu'lláh dated November 14th (Momen, *The Bábí and Bahá'í Religions, 1844–1944, Some contemporary Western accounts,* 148-49).
11. Rouhani, *Lam'átul-Anvár,* v. 1, 182–83, 72; Mázandarání, *Zuhúr al-Haqq,* v. 4, 32.
12. Rouhani, *Lam'átul-Anvár,* v. 1, 183. Nayrízí, *"The Account of Siyyid Ibrahim concerning Nayriz",* 4; Shafí', *Narrative of Mulla Muhammad Shafi' Nayrízí,* 19.
13. Rouhani, *Lam'átul-Anvár,* v. 1, 182–83.
14. Shafí', *Narrative of Mulla Muhammad Shafi' Nayrízí,* 20–21. Rouhani, *Lam'átul-Anvár,* v. 1, 183.
15. Rouhani, *Lam'átul-Anvár,* v. 1, 181, 183; Nicolas, *Seyyed Ali Mohammed dit le Bab,* 417; Mázandarání, *Zuhúr al-Haqq,* v. 4, 36–37; Nicolas, *Seyyed Ali Mohammed dit le Bab,* 417; Shafí', *Narrative of Mulla Muhammad Shafi' Nayrízí,* 21.
16. Shafí', *Narrative of Mulla Muhammad Shafi' Nayrízí,* 21; Mázandarání, *Zuhúr al-Haqq,* v. 4, 36; Rouhani, *Lam'átul-Anvár,* v. 1, 184.
17. Report of Mírzá Faḍlu'lláh dated November 14th, 1853 (Momen, *The Bábí and Bahá'í Religions, 1844–1944, Some contemporary Western accounts,* 149).

13 / Death of the Commander

1. One tuman was worth two dollars in the mid-nineteenth century (Ruhe, *Robe of Light: The Persian Years of the Supreme Prophet Baha'u'llah 1817–1853,* 80). Mírzá Na'ím paid 5,500 tumans, or 11,000 dollars. Using the Consumer Price Index as a means of comparing worth, this would be $250,000 in today's money (Lawrence H. Officer, Samuel H. Williamson, Measuring Worth, 2010, University of Illinois at Chicago, viewed: November 4th, 2009, http://www.measuringworth.com).
2. Rabbani, *The Bábís of Nayríz: History and Documents, Witnesses to Bábí and Bahá'í history vol. 2,* f. 46, p. 46, c. 11. Momen, *The Bábí and Bahá'í Religions, 1844–1944,* 149; Shafí', *Narrative of Mulla Muhammad Shafi' Nayrízí,* 21; Nicolas, *Seyyed Ali Mohammed dit le Bab,* 418.
3. Shafí', *Narrative of Mulla Muhammad Shafi' Nayrízí,* 21. Mírzá Na'ím brought the sharpshooters to a place called Bayd-Khánih, also known as *Bid Najviyyih*

(from a personal map made by Shoja'ádin Sardári). The field near the Darb-i-Shikáft passage was called *'Áqá-Miry*. The information regarding the paths from the spring comes from a conversation with Jahántáb (Jazabi) Sardári and a map drawn by her brother, Shoja'ádin Sardári.

4. Shafí', *Narrative of Mulla Muhammad Shafí' Nayrízí*, 21–22.
5. Nicolas, *Seyyed Ali Mohammed dit le Bab*, 418. Shafí', *Narrative of Mulla Muhammad Shafí' Nayrízí*, 22.
6. The account given here of the death of 'Alí Sardár is a composite one based on Shafí' and Ḥájí Muhammad Nayrízí's memories and several secondary sources. It includes details the authors believe most likely happened given the circumstances and situation and events to come.
7. Rouhani, *Lam'átul-Anvár*, v. 1, 186–87.
8. Shafí', *Narrative of Mulla Muhammad Shafí' Nayrízí*, 22; Nicolas, *Seyyed Ali Mohammed dit le Bab*, 418.
9. Rouhani, *Lam'átul-Anvár*, v. 1, 186–87; Nicolas, *Seyyed Ali Mohammed dit le Bab*, 418–19.
10. Shafí', *Narrative of Mulla Muhammad Shafí' Nayrízí*, 22. Faizi, *Nayríz Mushkbiz*, 112. Nicolas, *Seyyed Ali Mohammed dit le Bab*, 419. In the Rouhani, *Lam'átul-Anvár* (187), and the Nayrízí, *"The Account of Siyyid Ibrahim concerning Nayriz,"* in *Translations of Shaykhi, Bábí and Bahá'í Texts* (5) versions, Sardár is not killed by the bullets but severely injured, and he manages to return to the fortification where he dies.
11. His name was Siyyid 'Alí, son of Karbalá'í Báqir, and his brother's name was Táju'd-Dín (Shafí', *Narrative of Mulla Muhammad Shafí' Nayrízí,* 22).
12. Willem Floor, "Gift giving," *Encyclopaedia Iranica*, December 15, 2001, Columbia University, New York City, December 20, 2010, http://www.iranica.com/articles/gift-giving-v.
13. Nayrízí, quoted in Rabbani, *The Bábís of Nayríz: History and Documents, Witnesses to Bábí and Bahá'í history vol. 2*, c. 12, 5.
14. Shafí', *Narrative of Mulla Muhammad Shafí' Nayrízí*, 23.
15. Mázandarání, *Zuhúr al-Haqq*, v. 4, 41; Ruhe, *Robe of Light: The Persian Years of the Supreme Prophet Baha'u'llah 1817–1853*, 100, 2nd footnote; Shafí', *Narrative of Mulla Muhammad Shafí' Nayrízí*, 24.
16. Shafí', *Narrative of Mulla Muhammad Shafí' Nayrízí*, 23.
17. From a private conversation with Mrs. Jahántáb (Sardári) Jazabi, December, 2009. In the Shafí' manuscript, the name of this location is Ásbúrán.
18. Shafí', *Narrative of Mulla Muhammad Shafí' Nayrízí*, 23–24. Nicolas, *Seyyed Ali Mohammed dit le Bab*, 420.
19. Shafí', *Narrative of Mulla Muhammad Shafí' Nayrízí*, 24.
20. Ibid., 24; Nicolas, *Seyyed Ali Mohammed dit le Bab*, 420.

21. Shafí', *Narrative of Mulla Muhammad Shafi' Nayrízí,* 24.
22. To get to the village of Cháhr-Bulúk, one must take the road going south from the large town of Sírján, which is northeast of Nayríz, to the village of Pahnove (from a conversation with Shoja'ádin Sardári, May, 2010).
23. Shafi', *Narrative of Mulla Muhammad Shafi' Nayrízí,* 25.
24. Ibid., 25.
25. Shafi', *Narrative of Mulla Muhammad Shafi' Nayrízí,* 25–26. The Bábí who went to speak to the attackers was named Mullá 'Alí. Shafí' gives the distance between the soldiers and the Bábí fortification as "a quarter of a fársang" which is about 1.2 kilometers. This makes other details in this part of his narrative, such as the soldiers shooting at the Bábís, difficult to gauge since rifles could not reach that distance. There is no exact number for the men killed in the mountain battles and beheaded immediately after. The general number of men given as participating in these battles is four hundred (Shafí', *Narrative of Mulla Muhammad Shafi' Nayrízí,* 18; Nayrízí, *"The Account of Siyyid Ibrahim concerning Nayriz," Translations of Shaykhi, Bábí and Bahá'í Texts,* 5). The number of men killed based on the number of severed heads or if a specific number is given ranges from a low of 180 (Shafí', *Narrative of Mulla Muhammad Shafi' Nayrízí,* 28; Mázandarání, *Zuhúr al-Haqq,* v. 4, 50) to a high of 400 (Ábádi'í, quoted in Rabbani, *The Bábís of Nayríz: History and Documents, Witnesses to Bábí and Bahá'í history vol. 2,* c. 13, 4). Shoghi Effendi, *God Passes By* (165) and Rouhani, *Lam'átul-Anvár* (190) give the number 200.

15 / The Long Road into Captivity

1. Faizi, *Nayríz Mushkbiz,* 198.
2. Mázandarání, *Zuhúr al-Haqq,* v. 4, 50–54.
3. Shafí', *Narrative of Mulla Muhammad Shafi' Nayrízí,* 31.
4. Rouhani, *Lam'átul-Anvár,* v. 1, 192; Ahdieh, *Nayrízi-Shurangiz,* 55.
5. The authors conjecture that this was the reason, as no other reason is given for this selection process, and because once in Shíráz, the Bábí women were taken by soldiers and other officials—so they must have been physically healthy.
6. Rouhani, *Lam'átul-Anvár,* v. 1, 297. The boy's name was Mírzá Ja'far. He was given the surname *Mírzá Jalal* by Bahá'u'lláh, whom he later met and from whom he received several tablets.
7. The various sources state different numbers of male prisoners, but all state that there were three hundred women taken captive. The number of children is not specified anywhere. Rabbani, *The Bábís of Nayríz: History and Documents, Witnesses to Bábí and Bahá'í history vol. 2* (c. 11, 51, f. 73), states that there were "several hundred" children, but no source is given for this number. All the sources

mention the presence of children, but no estimates are given. Shafí' and Nayrízí, both eyewitnesses to these events, were themselves children at the time. There are different numbers given for the male prisoners as well as their identities. Shafí' has eighty going with Luṭf 'Alí Khán, and sixty captured later in Nayríz by Mírzá Na'ím, but he gives no number of how many went to Shíráz. Mázandarání, *Zuhúr al-Haqq* (v. 4, 52), states that there were eighty male prisoners, plus the Bábís who had escaped and were not "well-known" individuals. Rabbani, *The Bábís of Nayríz: History and Documents, Witnesses to Bábí and Bahá'í history vol. 2* (c. 11, 51, f. 73), states that there were two hundred male captives in all, though he states that "several hundred more believers" were rounded up in a sweep of the Chinár-Súkhtih quarter. Rouhani, *Lam'átul-Anvár* (v. 2, 458), states that two hundred male prisoners, mostly elderly and ill, were sent. The sources leave many questions to be answered—for example, some sources state that all men over twenty were beheaded, but if this is the case, who were the men who were marched to Shíráz? A safe estimate for total prisoners, given all the sources and information, would be between four hundred and fifty and five hundred, men and women, with an unknown number of children.

8. From the narrative of Mirzá Qábil Ábádi'í, quoted in Rabbani, *The Bábís of Nayríz: History and Documents, Witnesses to Bábí and Bahá'í history vol. 2*, c. 13, 4.
9. He would have been the older half-brother of Khávar Sultán. He was Fáṭimih's son by her first marriage (Hussein Ahdieh, "Biography of Khávar Sultán," http://www.Nayríz.org).
10. Mullá Muḥammad-Alí Qábid (Shafí', *Narrative of Mulla Muhammad Shafi' Nayrízí*, 33).
11. Mírzá Muḥammad 'Abid (Shafí', *Narrative of Mulla Muhammad Shafi' Nayrízí*, 32).
12. Cartwright-Jones, *The Patterns of Persian Henna*, 43–44.
13. Shafí', *Narrative of Mulla Muhammad Shafi' Nayrízí* (33). Mirzá Qábil Ábádi'í (Ábádi'í, quoted in Rabbani, *The Bábís of Nayríz: History and Documents, Witnesses to Bábí and Bahá'í history vol. 2*, c. 13, 5), states the procession avoided the bázár and went by a side path because it evoked too much sympathy from the people.
14. Mázandarání, *Zuhúr al-Haqq*, v. 4, 54; Shafi', *Narrative of Mulla Muhammad Shafi' Nayrízí*, 33. According to Rouhani, *Lam'átul-Anvár* (v. 1, 197), the heads were kept at the caravanserai and the women were kept next to a soldiers' barracks, but on this same page he has the version given here. The Shafi' version seems more likely and is corroborated by Mázandarání, *Zuhúr al-Haqq* (v. 4, 54).
15. Mázandarání, *Zuhúr al-Haqq*, v. 4, 55.
16. Ibid., 54–55.

17. Shafí', *Narrative of Mulla Muhammad Shafi' Nayrízí,* 34. Faizi, *Nayríz Mushkbiz,* 115. Rouhani, *Lam'átul-Anvár,* 117. The men were Ḥájí, the son of Aṣghar, Alí Garmsiri; Ḥusayn, the son of Hádí Khayrí; Sádiq, the son of Sálih; Muḥammad, the son of Mohsin. It is not clear from the Shafí' manuscript how the first two were killed. It states only that they were taken out to the public square and killed.
18. Mázandarání, *Zuhúr al-Haqq,* v. 4, 55. Rouhani, *Lam'átul-Anvár,* v. 1, 196. The tribal leader was Ḥájí 'Qavámu'l-Mulk. He was the appointed head of the Khamseh federation of five tribes, sometimes called the "Bahárlú" or "Arab" tribes (Martin, *The Qájár Pact,* 52). This confederation had been put together by the central government as a way to counterbalance the large nomadic Qashqá'í tribe which, in the mid-19th century, could put 120,000 men into the field (Abrahamian, *Iran between two revolutions,* 45–46).
19. Mázandarání, *Zuhúr al-Haqq,* v. 4, 55.
20. Ibid.
21. Momen, *Bábí and Bahá'í religions,* 150–51. The source cited here is the report of the British agent in Shíráz who, earlier in the same report, states that back in Nayríz, three hundred women had 'been "violently compelled to become their (the soldiers) wives".
22. Balyuzi, *Khadíjih Bagum,* 30; Rouhani, *Lam'átul-Anvár,* v. 1, 276; Rabbani, *The Bábís of Nayríz: History and Documents, Witnesses to Bábí and Bahá'í history vol. 2,* c. 15, 11; Ma'ani, *Against Incredible Odds,* 8.
23. Rabbani, *The Bábís of Nayríz: History and Documents, Witnesses to Bábí and Bahá'í history vol. 2,* c. 11, 37. The number 73 is consistent in the sources. If we follow the Shafí' manuscript and put the number of captives from the two groups of male prisoners together, we get 140. Two died on the way, 60 were released in Shíráz, and 5 were killed in Shíráz, reaching a total of 67, which leaves 73 to be transported to Ṭihrán. Mázandarání, *Zuhúr al-Haqq* (v. 4, 56), states that there were 140 male prisoners in Shíráz, some who had languished there since 1850, and that 67 men died in Shíráz and were beheaded, leaving 73 to be taken to Ṭihrán.
24. Rouhani, *Lam'átul-Anvár,* v. 1, 193.
25. Ábádi'í (Ábádi'í, quoted in Rabbani, *The Bábís of Nayríz: History and Documents, Witnesses to Bábí and Bahá'í history vol. 2* (c. 13, 5)).
26. Provisional translation by Ṭahiríh Ahdieh, Nabíl Hanna, Abir Majíd, Rosann Velnich available at http://www.nayriz.org.
27. Shafí', *Narrative of Mulla Muhammad Shafi' Nayrízí* (34–35), lists these people as having perished on the road: "Mullá 'Abdu'l-Ḥusayn died in Sídán; his head was cut off and added to others. 'Alí Karbalá'í Zamán and Akbar Karbalá'í Muhammad died in Ábádih; Ḥasan, the son of 'Abú'l-Vaḥíd, and Mullá 'Alí-Akbar, the brother of Jináb Amír, died in Isfahán. Karbalá'í Báqir, the son of

Muḥammad, and his brother Ḥasan; Dhu'l-Faqár Karbalá'í Taqí, the son of Farqi, and his son 'Alí; 'Alí Khán; Mullá Karím Ákhúnd; Akbar Ra'ís; Ghulám-'Alí Pír-Muḥammad, and Taqí and Muḥammad 'Alí, the sons of Muḥammad Jamál, all died on the way."

28. Shafí', *Narrative of Mulla Muhammad Shafi' Nayrízí* (35), remembers the following names: "One of them was Karbalá'í 'Alí-Yár who died in Darōl Salam and was buried in Tall-i-Hamrá. Two others were Ustád 'Innáyát and Ibráhim, the son of Sharif, who are still alíve. Also Áqá Siyyid Ḥusayn and Ustád 'Alí, the son of Mashhadí Ṣafar, returned home . . . Karbalá'í Zaynu'l-'Ábidín stayed in Tihrán and died after a while."

16 / The Transformation of the Bábís into Bahá'ís

1. According to Mázandaránî, *Zuhúr al-Haqq* (v. 4, 57–59), men are released in the summer of 1857.
2. Faizi, *Nayríz Mushkbiz*, 130.
3. Her husband is the son of Mashhadi Ismá'íl. They have a son, Mírzá 'Alí, and two daughters (Rouhani, *Lam'átul-Anvár,* v. 1, 275).
4. Hajji Mírzá Aḥmad Káshání (Rouhani, *Lam'átul-Anvár,* v. 1, 276); Taherzadeh, *Revelation of Bahá'u'lláh,* v. 2, 137–38; Rouhani, *Lam'átul-Anvár,* v. 1, 276.
5. Rouhani, *Lam'átul-Anvár,* v. 1, 278.
6. Ahdieh, *Nayrízi-Shurangiz,* 158. Khájih Muḥammad and his two sons fled to Sarvistán during the persecution of 1909.
7. Ibid, 110. Their sons were Muḥammad-'Alí, Muḥammad-Ḥasan, Asadu'lláh; their daughters were Khávar and Munavvar.
8. Ahdieh, *Nayrízi-Shurangiz,* 134. Mírzá Akbar is martyred during the persecution of 1909. The other son is Mírzá Faḍlu'lláh. The second husband is Mírzá Muhsin.
9. Rouhani, *Lam'átul-Anvár,* v. 2, 69.
10. Ibid., v. 1, 255.
11. Ibid., v. 1, 278.
12. Faizi, *Nayríz Mushkbiz,* 131.
13. Rouhani, *Lam'átul-Anvár,* v. 1, 240.
14. Ibid, v. 1, 237, 239.
15. Shoghi Effendi, *God Passes By,* 121.
16. Faizi, *Nayríz Mushkbiz,* 131; Rabbani, *The Bábís of Nayríz: History and Documents, Witnesses to Bábí and Bahá'í history,* c. 15, 4.
17. Edward Granville Browne, *Materials for the study of the Bábí religion* (Cambridge, UK: Cambridge University Press, 1918) viewed at: http://www.archive.org/stream/materialsforstud00browuoft/materialsforstud00browuoft_djvu.txt.

18. Taliqani, quoted in Mázandarání, *Zuhúr al-Haqq,* 490–92, quoted and translated in Rabbani, "Efforts to preserve the remains of the Bab: Four historical accounts," 88.
19. Faizi, *Nayríz Mushkbiz,* 78–79; Rouhani, *Lam'átul-Anvár,* v. 1, 379.
20. Shoghi Effendi, *God Passes By,* 153.
21. Bahá'u'lláh, by Mázandarání, *Amr Va Khalq* 1:10–11, in Nader Saiedi, *Logos and Civilization* (Bethesda, MD: University of Maryland Press, 2000), 242.
22. 'Abdu'l-Bahá, passage from Esslemont, *Bahá'u'lláh and The New Era,* 170. Bahá'u'lláh was very concerned that a Bábí had carried out violence and resolved to help guide the community. It took a long time for Bahá'u'lláh to train Bábís to change their attitude and refrain from taking revenge. Later Mullá Muḥammad Shafí'—the source of information for the events of the second Nayríz upheaval—would read the Book of Laws to the Bahá'ís in a special large meeting and explain its contents.
23. Shoghi Effendi, *God Passes By,* 154.
24. Bahá'u'lláh, quoted in Taherzadeh, *Revelation of Bahá'u'lláh,* v. 1, 205.
25. Ahdieh, *Nayrízi-Shurangiz,* 62.
26. Bahá'u'lláh, in *Bahá'í Prayers,* 309.
27. Shoghi Effendi, *God Passes By,* 171–77.
28. Bahá'u'lláh, "Súriy-i-Haykal," *Summons of the Lord of Hosts,* ¶145.
29. Ahdieh, *Nayrízi-Shurangiz,* 159.
30. Taliqani, quoted in Mázandarání, *Zuhúr al-Haqq,* 490–92, quoted and translated in Rabbani, "Efforts to preserve the remains of the Bab: Four historical accounts," 88.
31. Rouhani, *Lam'átul-Anvár,* v. 1, 224; Rabbani, *The Bábís of Nayríz: History and Documents, Witnesses to Bábí and Bahá'í history,* c. 15, 9.
32. Rabbani, *The Bábís of Nayríz: History and Documents, Witnesses to Bábí and Bahá'í history,* 4–5; Ahdieh, *Nayrízi-Shurangiz,* 171. After his father's passing, Ḥáj Muḥammad marries the niece of 'Alí Sardár, from Sardár's sister's side. They have many children: Sakfina Kh́ánum, Farj'u'lláh, Habíb'u'lláh, Ghodrat'u'lláh, Faḍl'u'lláh, and Muḥammad *Qásim.* Ahdieh met Haj Muḥammad when Muḥammad was over one hundred years old.
33. Ahdieh, *Nayrízi-Shurangiz,* 166. The other children were Mírzá 'Abdu'l Ḥusayn, Núríeh, Shaykh Muḥammad Ḥusayn, Gawhar, Ṭubá, Jahán Sultan, and Fáṭimih. Rabbani (c. 15, 3) states that Khávar Sultán is the granddaughter of Shaykh Abú Turáb.
34. Ahdieh, *Nayrízi-Shurangiz,* 160. He had one child, a daughter, Saheb Jan, from his first wife, who was raised by his father's brother, Jináb Mírzá Muḥammad. After this brother moved to Tihrán, she was raised by Jináb Mírzá Shuqr'u'lláh. Saheb Jan married Shaykh Muḥammad Ḥusayn Ahdieh, the son of Shafí'. They

had many children: Ruha, Hobur, Afife, Eshragiye, Badí'e, Mahin Dokht, Shaykh Áqá, and Bahá'í. Hobur died at ten years old.

35. Rabbani, *The Bábís of Nayríz: History and Documents, Witnesses to Bábí and Bahá'í history,* c. 15, 13. The children are named: Amír Khán, Bibi Bagum, Khayru'n-Nisa, Fáṭimih Bagum, and Khánum Jan.
36. Ibid, 19–20. His three daughters are Mardiyyih, Samaddiyih, and Zahra.
37. Momen, *Bábí and Bahá'í religions,* 515.
38. 'Abdu'l-Bahá, *The Secret of Divine Civilization,* 4–5.
39. Rouhani, *Lam'átul-Anvár,* v. 1, 214. Provisional translation by Ṭahiríh Ahdieh, Nabíl Hanna, Abir Majíd, Rosann Velnich available at http://www.nayriz.org.
40. Faizi, *Nayríz Mushkbiz,* 162.
41. Richard Francis, "Aḥmad the recipient of the Arabic Tablet of Aḥmad," Bahá'í Library Online, 2003, viewed: January 30, 2011, http://bahai-library.com/?file=francis_ahmad_biography.
42. Ahang Rabbani, translator, "Translations of Shaykhi, Babi and Baha'i Texts," No. 9 (October, 1997), http://www.h-net.org, http://www.h-net.org/~bahai/trans/vol1/khadija/khadija2.htm.
43. The three children are Núrí Jan, Sughrá Bagum, and Mírzá 'Abdu'l Ḥusayn, http://www.nayriz.org.
44. Browne, *A Year Amongst the Persians,* 441.
45. Balyuzi, *Eminent Bahá'ís in the time of Bahá'u'lláh,* 28. His name is Faraju'lláh Khán.
46. Balyuzi, *The Báb,* 191–92.
47. Balyuzi, *Edward Granville Browne and the Bahá'í Faith,* 50.
48. Ibid., 56–57.
49. Shoghi Effendi, *God Passes By,* 222.
50. Ibid, 236–39.
51. Provisional translation by Ṭahiríh Ahdieh, Nabíl Hanna, Abir Majíd, Rosann Velnich of tablet #139 from 'Abdu'l-Bahá to Shafí', available at http://www.Nayríz.org.
52. Rouhani, *Lam'átul-Anvár,* v. 1, 219.
53. Amanat, *Pivot of the Universe,* 440.
54. Áqá Ḥusayn 'Alí, quoted in Rabbani, "Efforts to preserve the remains of the Bab: Four historical accounts," 93; Shoghi Effendi, *God Passes By,* 274.
55. Baha'u'llah, The Kitáb-i-Aqdas, ¶92–93.

17 / The Kingdom of Persia in Chaos

1. Mozaffar ad-Dín Sháh; various authors, "Mozaffar ad-Din Shah Qajar," January 12th, 2011, http://en.wikipedia.org/wiki/Mozaffar_ad-Din_Shah_Qajar.

2. Balyuzi, *E. G. Browne and the Bahá'í Faith*, c. 8; Geula, *Iranian Baha'is from Jewish Background*, 18.
3. Balyuzi, *'Abdu'l-Bahá*, 91.
4. Bahá'u'lláh, *Summons of the Lord of Hosts*, "Súriy-i-Haykal," ¶173.
5. Balyuzi, *'Abdu'l-Bahá*, 90; Sepehr Arya, "Bábís and Bahá'í role in the Constitutional Revolution," http://www.ohamzodai.com, September, 2006; Geula, 15.
6. 'Abdu'l-Bahá, *The Secret of Divine Civilization*, 14–15.
7. Mackey, *The Iranians: Persia, Islam and the Soul of a Nation*, 150–55.
8. Balyuzi, *'Abdu'l-Bahá*, 93.
9. Ibid., 94; class notes from lectures by Chehre Negar, 1960.
10. Afnán, *The Genesis of the Bábí and Bahá'í Faiths in Shíráz and Fárs*, 208–9.

18 / The Invasion of 1909

1. Afnán, *The Genesis of the Bábí and Bahá'í Faiths in Shíráz and Fárs*, 208; Ahdieh, 135. Afnán places the number of fighters at one thousand. Balyuzi (94) describes the men as "discontented."
2. Rouhani, v. 2, 40; Ahdieh, 127; Afnán, 209. Balyuzi (*E. G. Browne and the Bahá'í Faith*, 94) states that Shaykh Dhakaríyyá took advantage of the turmoil in the province to settle a personal dispute in Nayríz and that this is what brought him there. The attacks on the Bahá'ís of Nayríz that followed are blamed variously in these sources. Rouhani, *Lam'átul-Anvár* (40), and Afnán, *The genesis of the Babi and Baha'i Faiths in Shiraz and Fars* (209), state that the order to attack Bahá'ís came from Siyyid 'Abdu'l Ḥusayn Lárí. Ahdieh, *Nayrízi-Shurangiz* (127), has the local clergy of Nayríz as the ones who directed Shaykh Dhakaríyyá to attack, and Balyuzi, *Edward Granville Browne and the Bahá'í Faith* (94), in a similar vein, states that Shaykh Dhakaríyyá carried out the persecutions to atone for having let his men attack the local Muslims.
3. Afnán, *The genesis of the Babi and Baha'i Faiths in Shiraz and Fars*, 209. Afnán is the only source to mention such a note but it seems possible as a way for Shaykh Dhakaríyyá to let the Nayrízís know he was coming and the nature of his demands.
4. Balyuzi, *Edward Granville Browne and the Bahá'í Faith* (94), describes the conflict as "a feud with a local magnate." The authors have guessed that, given what happened next, the "local magnate" was the governor of Nayríz. No other sources mention this directly.
5. Rouhani, *Lam'átul-Anvár*, v. 2, 38.
6. Ahdieh, *Nayrízi-Shurangiz*, 127.
7. Ibid.
8. Ibid.; Rouhani, *Lam'átul-Anvár*, v. 2, 39. It is not clear from the sources why

some residents supported the Shaykh; the reason given in this paragraph is a conjecture by the authors.

9. Rouhani, *Lam'átul-Anvár,* v. 2, 39.
10. Faizi, *Nayríz Mushkbiz,* 164.
11. Afnán, *The genesis of the Babi and Baha'i Faiths in Shiraz and Fars,* 210. Afnán is the only one to state that the people at Sayf-Ábád supported the Shaykh. Rouhani, *Lam'átul-Anvár* (v. 2, 41), states that Shaykh Dhakaríyyá received an order, a "fatwa," that day from Siyyid 'Abdu'l Ḥusayn Lárí with instructions to attack the government forces and the Bahá'ís. Ahdieh does not mention this meeting at all and states that, at a later meeting with clerics, Shaykh Dhakaríyyá told them he had an order from Siyyid 'Abdu'l Ḥusayn Lárí. Afnán has Shaykh Dhakaríyyá sending his orders to the citizens in advance of his coming—the version found in the present rendition. The authors chose this version as the more likely scenario—that Shaykh Dhakaríyyá came to Nayríz with written orders in hand rather than receiving them once the attack had begun. Afnán, *The genesis of the Babi and Baha'i Faiths in Shiraz and Fars* (210), does not mention the chádur disguises of the men. The military commander's name was Muḥammad-Ḥasan Khán; he was also the Deputy-Governor of Nayríz.
12. Rouhani, *Lam'átul-Anvár,* v. 2, 41.
13. Ibid., v. 2, 44–45. Ahdieh, *Nayrízi-Shurangiz* (135), does not mention the governor fleeing; only Rouhani has the detail of the governor disguised in a chádur.
14. Afnán, *The genesis of the Babi and Baha'i Faiths in Shiraz and Fars* (210), writes that at this point, Shaykh Dhakaríyyá invited people from neighboring towns to come to Nayríz and join the plunder: "Overtaken by greed, the residents of those towns decided to proceed to Nayríz, knowing well that booty and spoils of pillage awaited them." None of the other sources verify this and given the short time frame—13 days—of Shaykh Dhakaríyyá's time in Nayríz, the authors thought this scenario was unlikely.
15. Rouhani, *Lam'átul-Anvár,* v. 2, 43; Ahdieh, *Nayrízi-Shurangiz,* 128.
16. Ibid. This version of the events is a combination of these two sources. Ahdieh attributes the cause of the attack on the Bahá'ís to the influence of the local clergy, but Rouhani emphasizes the fatwa from Siyyid 'Abdu'l Ḥusayn Lárí as the main cause.
17. Rouhani, *Lam'átul-Anvár,* v. 2, 43; Ahdieh, *Nayrízi-Shurangiz,* 136. Afnán, *The genesis of the Babi and Baha'i Faiths in Shiraz and Fars* (210), states that the announcement offered a free rifle, not tumans, for capturing a Bahá'í dead or alive. He mentions that the announcement included a reassurance to Muslims, but Ahdieh and Rouhani do not write this. It is clear from all accounts that relations had become much closer between Bahá'ís and Muslims prior to this new persecution. Ahdieh emphasizes the betrayal of Muslim neighbors, while Rouhani gives more information conveying the aid provided by Muslims.

18. Faizi, *Nayríz Mushkbiz,* 146; Rouhani, *Lam'átul-Anvár,* v. 2, 45; Ma'ani, *Against Incredible Odds,* 9; Afnán, *The genesis of the Babi and Baha'i Faiths in Shiraz and Fars,* 210–11; Ahdieh, *Nayrízi-Shurangiz,* 128; Rouhani, *Lam'átul-Anvár,* v. 2, 45.
19. Faizi, *Nayríz Mushkbiz,* 150; Rouhani, *Lam'átul-Anvár,* v. 2, 45; Ahdieh, *Nayrízi-Shurangiz,* 128, 131.
20. Rouhani, *Lam'átul-Anvár,* v. 2, 118; v. 2, 142; Ma'ani, *Against Incredible Odds,* 10. Rouhani's list includes additional people in this group—sisters, nieces, nephews, and brothers-in-law. Ma'ani's list doesn't include these but does include the grandmother.
21. Afnán, *The genesis of the Babi and Baha'i Faiths in Shiraz and Fars,* 210.
22. Rouhani, *Lam'átul-Anvár,* v. 2, 117.

19 / Suffering of the Faithful

1. Rouhani, *Lam'átul-Anvár,* v. 2, 117.
2. Ahdieh, *Nayrízi-Shurangiz,* 125. She was buried by the Bahá'ís in the Aghil Ahatib cemetery.
3. Ahdieh, *Nayrízi-Shurangiz,* 133.
4. Ibid., 133; Rouhani, *Lam'átul-Anvár,* v. 2, 123; Afnán, *The genesis of the Babi and Baha'i Faiths in Shiraz and Fars,* 211. Afnán indicates that the two were "working the farm fields of Bídlang," but given the context, it is more likely they were hiding from their persecutors.
5. Ahdieh, *Nayrízi-Shurangiz,* 133; Rouhani, *Lam'átul-Anvár,* v. 2, 123. The detail concerning the recitation of a verse appears only in Rouhani.
6. Ahdieh, *Nayrízi-Shurangiz,* 140–41, 133–34; Rouhani, *Lam'átul-Anvár,* v. 2, 55–59; Faizi, *Nayríz Mushkbiz,* 148–49. The last gruesome detail in the paragraph is found only in the Ahdieh account. Mullá Muḥammad 'Alí left behind three grown children: Páríján Shahídpúr, Muḥammad Báqir, and Fazlu'lláh. In the memories of Páríján, the bodies were gathered up after three days and buried. Her memories also include Mullá Ḥasan's body being strung up on a tree in the bázár in front of a mosque.
7. Faizi, *Nayríz Mushkbiz,* 166.
8. Rouhani, *Lam'átul-Anvár,* v. 2, 123.
9. Shoghi Effendi, *God Passes By,* 276.
10. Ibid., 276.
11. Rouhani, *Lam'átul-Anvár,* v. 2, 55; Faizi, *Nayríz Mushkbiz,* 149. In Rouhani, it is not clear where his body was left. Mullá Ḥasan was taken before Shaykh Dhakaríyyá and then shot. The Shaykh made his headquarters in the bázár. Mullá Muḥammad 'Alí, Mullá Ḥasan's father-in-law witnessed this killing and was then

killed as well, and his body was dragged through the streets. Ahdieh, *Nayrízi-Shurangiz* (140–41), differs from this only in adding that Mullá Muḥammad's body was dragged through the streets from the bázár district to the Chinár-Súkhtih district where it was hung from a mulberry tree and a fire set beneath it. Ma'ani, *Against Incredible Odds* (12), states that as a boy, Rouhani was told that Mullá Ḥasan was hung from a tree as well. In Rouhani, the man who comes to recover Mullá Ḥasan's body is his Muslim friend, Ḥájí Bághal, but in Faizi (149), the man who picks up the body is 'Alí, a Muslim friend who grew up with him.

12. Rouhani, *Lam'átul-Anvár,* v. 2, 120. Mashhadí Ḥusayn tells them, according to Rouhani, that Mullá Ḥasan and Mullá Muḥammad 'Alí had been captured the "day before." When the authors were constructing the timeline, they interpreted this as the days that had just passed.

20 / The Temple Sacrifice

1. Bahá'í Temple Unity. "Minutes of the 1909 National Convention." Mary Rabb papers, Bahá'í National Archives. United States of America.
2. Ibid.
3. Ibid.
4. Núríján had married Mírzá 'Abdu'l Ḥusayn, the grandson of Siyyid Jafar Yazdí (Rouhani, *Lam'átul-Anvár,* v. 2, 126).
5. Rouhani, *Lam'átul-Anvár,* v. 2, 129; Ma'ani, *Against Incredible Odds,* 13.
6. Afnán, *The genesis of the Babi and Baha'i Faiths in Shiraz and Fars,* 211. Afnán relates an account that three Bahá'í men were "cunningly compelled to turn over all their properties and possessions to him (i.e. the Shaykh) and then they were released." Shaykh Dhakaríyyá had announced that all Bahá'í men would be killed, and Afnán gives no names for the three Bahá'ís, nor does he cite any sources, nor the story verified in other sources. As a result, this anecdote is not included in the narrative.
7. Rouhani, *Lam'átul-Anvár,* v. 2, 97; Ahdieh, *Nayrízi-Shurangiz,* 131; Afnán, *The genesis of the Babi and Baha'i Faiths in Shiraz and Fars,* 211.
8. It is not clear from the sources in what order the men were martyred. Rouhani, *Lam'átul-Anvár* (v. 2, 69), writes that the first of the group to be killed was Muḥammad Ismá'íl. The rest of the order is devised by the authors.
9. Faizi, *Nayríz Mushkbiz,* 151; Ahdieh, *Nayrízi-Shurangiz,* 121; Rouhani, *Lam'átul-Anvár,* v. 2, 69. Muḥammad Ismá'íl was survived by two sons: 'Alí, who was martyred; and Rahmán; and two daughters, Khánum Taliatie and Khánum Marzieh. The first daughter was married to Asad'u'lláh, and the second daughter was married to Mehdí, son of Mullá Ḥusayn. Both husbands were martyred in this incident.

10. Ahdieh, *Nayrízi-Shurangiz,* 131; Rouhani, *Lam'átul-Anvár,* v. 2, 71.
11. Rouhani, *Lam'átul-Anvár,* v. 2, 99; Ahdieh, *Nayrízi-Shurangiz,* 131. Muḥammad Ibráhim was married and was survived by his children: Amru'lláh Madani, Amír Qayyumi, and Zahra Khánum Loghmanee.
12. Ahdieh, *Nayrízi-Shurangiz,* 132; Rouhani, *Lam'átul-Anvár,* v. 2, 77. Asad'u'lláh had recently married Khánum Taliatie, the daughter of Muḥammad Ismá'íl.
13. Rouhani, *Lam'átul-Anvár,* v. 2, 78; Ahdieh, *Nayrízi-Shurangiz,* 131.
14. Rouhani, *Lam'átul-Anvár,* v. 2, 101. Mullá Ḥusayn was married to Banu Sultan, sister of Muḥammad Ibráhim, and had other children: 'Abdu'lláh, Muḥammad Ḥasan, Khánum Zaynab, and Maryam (Ahdieh, *Nayrízi-Shurangiz,* 132).
15. In Rouhani's account (*Lam'átul-Anvár,* v. 2, 101), this story and that of the other six martyrdoms are somewhat inconsistent in their details. The men are said to have been brought to the public square. In some cases, it is stated that the Shaykh was the one interrogating them. But in the case of Rahmán, Rouhani states that the Shaykh wrote a note to his men to free 'Alí, indicating that he was not there at the interrogations and martyrdoms. But since the Bahá'í men were captured and taken into town as a group, and since they seem from the narrative to all have been martyred that day, the authors have put the Shaykh at the scene the entire time. Rouhani also mentions that Rahmán witnessed the killing of the other six. Rahmán passed away in 125 B.E. (1968–69 CE), And he was survived by two sons and two daughters. One son, Zaykr'u'lláh Loghmanee, married Ghodsieh Shu'á'i, the daughter of Mashhadí Darvish; they had nine children. The second son, Jalál Loghmanee, married Eshrat Qayumi; they had three children. One daughter, Jahán Loghmanee, married Yad'u'lláh Sufi; they had four children. The second daughter, Zivare Loghmanee, married Masi'u'lláh Masbohy, and they had six children (Rouhani, *Lam'átul-Anvár,* v. 2, 309–10; Ahdieh, *Nayrízi-Shurangiz,* 131).
16. The sources are lacking in details regarding these two martyrs, and there are some contradictions. Faizi, *Nayríz Mushkbiz* (160), states that Amr'u'lláh was arrested with Ata'u'lláh and killed on the second day, and he states that they were arrested in the mountains. However, he does not specify whether this occurred in the northern or southern mountains. Ahdieh, *Nayrízi-Shurangiz* (141), states that Ata'u'lláh was captured in the northern mountains, but he does not say where Amru'llah was captured. Rouhani (*Lam'átul-Anvár,* v. 2, 328–29) states that Ata'u'lláh was found in the southern mountains, but he does not indicate where Amr'u'lláh was captured. He does say that Amru'lláh was the last martyr and that Mírzá Akbar was killed on the "5th day," so Amr'u'lláh would have to have been martyred at least on that day. The authors have not specified in which mountains the two were found and have used the Faizi source for the date of their capture and martyrdom.

17. Ahdieh, *Nayrízi-Shurangiz,* 133; Faizi, *Nayríz Mushkbiz,* 150; Rouhani, *Lam'átul-Anvár,* v. 2, 66; Afnán, *The genesis of the Babi and Baha'i Faiths in Shiraz and Fars,* 212. This account is pieced together from details of these four sources. The significant difference is that Afnán states that Mullá 'Abdu'l Majíd's corpse was burned, whereas Rouhani states it was buried in a public cemetery and does not mention it being burned. According to Rouhani (*Lam'átul-Anvár,* v. 2, 64), 'Abdu'l-Majíd was married with two sons, who died without children. He also had three daughters. The first married Mírzá Fazlu'lláh; the second married Mírzá 'Alí Muḥammad; and the third, Maryam Jan, married Mírzá Muḥammad Ḥusayn. These last two were teachers by profession. As he was very handsome, he also worked as a Rawḍih-Khán, a reenactor of the tragedy of Ímám Ḥusayn at Karbilá. He escaped to Sarvistán during this period of persecution. He and his wife had one son and two daughters, who all became Bahá'ís.
18. Ahdieh, *Nayrízi-Shurangiz,* 163. He later met 'Abdu'l-Bahá. His business prospered, and he did much to support and protect the Bahá'ís. Shoghi Effendi asked him to move to Arabia, which he did. That government later forced him to leave Arabia and move back to Iran. He played an active role in protecting the Bahá'ís during the persecutions of Shaykh Javád (Ahdieh, *Nayrízi-Shurangiz,* 168).
19. Ma'ani, *Against Incredible Odds,* 13. Later, the families of these three men took the family names of *Rouhani* (Mírzá 'Abdu'l-Ḥusayn's descendants), *Vaḥídi* (Mírzá Aḥmad's descendants), and *'Ináyati* (Mírzá Faḍlu'lláh's descendants), respectively (Ma'ani, *Against Incredible Odds,* 262, n. 10).
20. Faizi, *Nayríz Mushkbiz,* 150. In Rouhani (*Lam'átul-Anvár,* v. 2, 302), there is only a farm worker. His name is Ḥasan Yazdí, and he takes Mullá Ḥasan's body to be buried in a place called *'Abbás Abbad.*

21 / The Third Day

1. Bahá'í Temple Unity minutes 1909. A new translation of this prayer can be found in *Bahá'í Prayers: A Selection of Prayers Revealed by Bahá'u'lláh, the Báb, and 'Abdu'l-Bahá* (Wilmette, IL: Bahá'í Publishing Trust, 1991), 268.
2. Ibid.
3. Ibid.
4. Rouhani, *Lam'átul-Anvár,* v. 2, 339.
5. Ibid., v. 2, 96.
6. Ibid., v. 2, 96. Ahdieh, *Nayrízi-Shurangiz,* 137.
7. 'Alí had four children. The first was Mullá Darvish Maghtoli, an active teacher of the Bahá'í Faith all his life. He had two children, Legha Khánum and Vaḥíd, both active in serving the Faith. The second was 'Abdu'l-Hamid Maghtoli, who remained a Bahá'í all his life and passed away in Tihrán. The third was Talatie

Khánum, who was very active in the Nayríz Bahá'í community, and the fourth was Rahmán Maghtoli, an active Bahá'í youth, who passed away at a young age. Ibráhim had one son, Muḥammad Ḥusayn Mobramaeen, whose children all became Bahá'ís (Ahdieh, *Nayrízi-Shurangiz,* 137).

8. Rouhani, *Lam'átul-Anvár,* v. 2, 104; Ahdieh, *Nayrízi-Shurangiz,* 143. The following details are found only in Rouhani: his wish to be martyred with a sword, taking refuge in Vaḥíd's house, the names of the men who reveal their location, and the location of Ustád's martyrdom. These details appear only in the Ahdieh source: the body dragged and set on fire, the city of origin of Ustád, and the statement that Ustád was the last martyr. Neither account explains what becomes of Muḥammad 'Alí, but the authors assume that he was martyred. There are differing accounts of soldiers going to Ustád's house to get money. Rouhani's account is given above; Ahdieh's account states that the soldiers "tortured" Ustád's wife in their home following Ustád's martyrdom.
9. Bahá'í Temple Unity minutes 1909.
10. Rouhani, *Lam'átul-Anvár,* v. 2, 104.

22 / Flight to Sarvistán

1. Rouhani, *Lam'átul-Anvár,* v. 2, 48; Afnán, *The genesis of the Babi and Baha'i Faiths in Shiraz and Fars,* 234, 213; Faizi, *Nayríz Mushkbiz,* 146.
2. Rouhani, *Lam'átul-Anvár,* v. 2, 48.
3. Ahdieh, *Nayrízi-Shurangiz,* 149.
4. Muḥammad Kalu (Faizi, *Nayríz Mushkbiz,* 147).
5. The story of Karbalá'í Muḥammad Saleh is taken from Ahdieh (*Nayrízi-Shurangiz,* 165–66). He lived to the age of ninety and was survived by two children: Ḥáj Amr'u'lláh and Fáṭimih Khánum. Ḥáj Amr'u'lláh suffered greatly under the persecutions of Shaykh Javad, but he was blessed to be able to visit 'Abdu'l-Bahá. He had several children: Ḥáj Saleh, Aḥmad Ruhu'lláh, Ṭúbá, Zahra, Shokat, and Bahá'dín, who died before the age of twenty. Fáṭimih, the daughter of Karbalá'í Muḥammad Saleh, also suffered in the persecutions of Shaykh Javád and served the Faith. She married Mírzá Akbar, and they had two children: Haj Áqá Mahmoud, and Zahra.
6. The account of this flight from Sarvistán is taken largely from Afnán (*The genesis of the Babi and Baha'i Faiths in Shiraz and Fars,* 212–15), Rouhani (*Lam'átul-Anvár,* v. 2, 298), and Faizi (*Nayríz Mushkbiz,* 146–47).
7. Ahdieh, *Nayrízi-Shurangiz,* 139; Rouhani, *Lam'átul-Anvár,* v. 2, 67; Faizi, *Nayríz Mushkbiz,* 151. There is no information about the date of this martyrdom; the authors are placing it here.
8. Ahdieh, *Nayrízi-Shurangiz,* 136; Rouhani, *Lam'átul-Anvár,* v. 2, 100–101; Faizi, *Nayríz Mushkbiz,* 160. Akbar left behind a son, Mírzá Ḥusayn Ala'i, who served

the Faith but left Nayríz during the next persecutions. He married Jahán Etehadi, the daughter of Mírzá 'Abdu'lláh. They had five daughters: Riḍván, Ṭúbá, Bahiyyih, Bushra, Olya—and four sons—'Alí Akbar, Bahá'í, Mouhebatu'lláh.

9. He was later a member of the Spiritual Assembly of Nayríz. He married Nosrat Khánum, and they had many children. Their daughters were Nehjat, Ruhangiz, Eshrat, Barolzaman, Mahin, Puran, Baharriyeh, and Esmat. Their sons were Cyrus and Soroosh (Ahdieh, *Nayrízi-Shurangiz,* 169).

23 / The Passing of 'Abdu'l-Bahá

1. Afnan, *The genesis of the Bábí and Bahá'í Faiths in Shíráz and Fárs*, 215. According to Muḥammad 'Alí, "Neireez," http://neyrizfars.blogfa.com, the new governor was Nuṣratu'd-Dawlih, the son of 'Qavámu'l-Mulk Shírází, the important tribal head in Shíráz. According to the same source, the soldiers marched on Fasá, Dáráb, Jahrum, Lorestan, Sarvistán, and Nayríz. According to Afnán (*The genesis of the Babi and Baha'i Faiths in Shiraz and Fars*, 215), they moved on Galih-Dar, Bastak, Lár, Dáráb, Iṣṭahbánát, Sar-Kúh, and Nayríz; the military commander was Mírzá Muḥammad-'Alí Khán.
2. Ibid., 216. Afnán states that the Shaykh went to Sar-Kúh. Muḥammad 'Alí (http://neyrizfars.blogfa.com) states that it was Navayegan. All the sources give two weeks as the length of the Shaykh's presence in Nayríz, but some sources state that he left Nayríz only when he heard that the governor's armies were approaching. The problem is the timeline: the Bahá'ís were in Sarvistán for forty days, according to the sources. That is almost six weeks, at which point they went with the army to Nayríz, a far longer period than two weeks.
3. Ahdieh, *Nayrízi-Shurangiz*, 81.
4. Rouhani, *Lam'átul-Anvár*, v. 2, 126.
5. This attack occurred in 1289 Hejri Shamsi, 1911 CE (Hisámí, *History of the Faith in Nayríz*, 248).
6. Balyuzi, *'Abdu'l-Bahá,* 186.
7. http://www.bahai.us/bahai-temple/history-and-architecture/cornerstone/; Bruce Whitmore, *The Dawning Place*, 64.
8. Shakh Kamál Kúhistání (Hisámí, *History of the Faith in Nayríz*, 249).
9. 'Alí Aṣghar Khán (Hisámí, *History of the Faith in Nayríz*, 252).
10. Ma'ani, *Against Incredible Odds*, 25–26.
11. Rouhani, *Lam'átul-Anvár*, v. 2, 126.
12. Those listed here are among the ones known to be the first group of Bahá'ís to serve on the Spiritual Assembly of Nayríz. Other early members were Siyyid Abúl Qásim (Misaghi family), Ḥájí Mírzá Aḥmad (Vaḥídi family), Mírzá 'Abdu'l Hussein (Rouhani and Misaghi families), Mírzá Aḥmad (Momtahen family),

Khájih 'Alí (Izadi family), Áqá Mírzá Bába (Eshraghi family), and Mrs. Rouha Dianat, daughter of Mírzá Aḥmad (Vaḥídi). (From a private conversation with Mrs. Rouha Zianat, September, 2010).

13. Interview with Ghámar Sultán, unpublished, in the possession of 'Abbás Eblaghie, her great-grandson. She most likely made her pilgrimage between the mid-1910s and 'Abdu'l-Bahá's passing; she passed away in her 90s.
14. Balyuzi, *'Abdu'l-Bahá*, 457.
15. Ibid., 458.
16. Ibid., 459.
17. Shoghi Effendi and Lady Bloomfield, quoted in Balyuzi, *'Abdu'l-Bahá*, 464.
18. Balyuzi, *'Abdu'l-Bahá*, 464–65.

24 / Exodus

1. The information for this section is taken from Ma'ani (*Against Incredible Odds*, 37–38).
2. Mashhadí Zaynu'l-'Abidín, quoted in Ma'ani, *Against Incredible Odds*, 38.
3. Hisámí, *History of the Faith in Nayríz*, 338.
4. Ibid., 259.
5. Muḥammad 'Alí, "Neireez," 2006–2007, http://neyrizfars.blogfa.com.
6. Hisámí, *History of the Faith in Nayríz*, 265; Ma'ani, *Against Incredible Odds*, 45–48.
7. Rabbani, *The Bábís of Nayríz: History and Documents, Witnesses to Bábí and Bahá'í history*, c. 15, 18.
8. No author given, "The Iranian history 1926 AD," 2009, November 3rd, 2010, http://www.fouman.com, viewed: December 2nd, 2010 http://www.fouman.com/history/Iranian_History_1926.html#BKM758.
9. The two clerics were Siyyid 'Aziz-i-Yazdí and Shaykh Muḥammad Yazdí (Hisámí, *History of the Faith in Nayríz*, 268).
10. Shaykh Javád (Hisámí, *History of the Faith in Nayríz*, 286; Ma'ani, *Against Incredible Odds*, 57).
11. Ahdieh, *Nayrízi-Shurangiz*, 167.
12. Siyyid Muḥíyu'd-Dín Falí (Hisámí, *History of the Faith in Nayríz*, 296).
13. From a conversation with Mrs. Nura (Shahídpúr) Jamer, August, 2010 CE.
14. Rouhani, *Lam'átul-Anvár*, v. 2, 379; Hisámí, *History of the Faith in Nayríz*, 296.
15. Rouhani, *Lam'átul-Anvár*, v. 2, 380.
16. Hisámí, *History of the Faith in Nayríz*, 296; Rouhani, *Lam'átul-Anvár*, v. 2, 374.
17. Rouhani, *Lam'átul-Anvár*, v. 2, 375; Ahdieh, *Nayrízi-Shurangiz*, 192.
18. From a private conversation with Mrs. Jahántáb (Jazzábi) Sardári, December, 2010.

19. From a provisional translation by Ṭáhirih Ahdieh, Nabíl Hanna, Abir Majíd, Rosann Velnich, available at http://www.nayriz.org.
20. From a private conversation with Mrs. Nura (Shahídpúr) Jamer, August, 2010 CE. The Shahídpúr home survived the incident. It remained in the family's name but was expropriated by the government to be used as housing for refugees from Ábádán during the Iran-'Iráq war.
21. From a conversation with Mrs. Nura (Shahídpúr) Jamer, August, 2010 CE.
22. Rouhani, *Morvareed*, 98.
23. Faizi, *Nayríz Mushkbiz,* 194.
24. Provisional translation by Ṭáhirih Ahdieh, Nabíl Hanna, Abir Majíd, Rosann Velnich available at http://www.nayriz.org.
25. These stories were told to the authors by Shokuh's daughter, Najla Baghdádi, who heard them while visiting Iran in the years just before the Revolution of 1979. They had to meet at their uncle's home in Tihrán because it was not safe for a Bahá'í visitor in Nayríz. After the Revolution, her only contact with her mother was by telephone. Shokuh, who had married a relative of Zia Baghdádi, passed away in 2008 CE, in Shíráz. Additional information also provided by Mrs. Nura (Shahídpúr) Jamer.
26. Hisámí, *History of the Faith in Nayríz,* 330.

Bibliography

Works of Bahá'u'lláh

Gleanings from the Writings of Bahá'u'lláh. Wilmette, IL: Bahá'í Publishing, 2005.

Provisional translation by Khazeh Fananapazir, "Tablet of Job" or "Surih of Patience," http://bahai-library.com/provisionals/surih.sabr.html, October 10th, 2009.

The Summons of the Lord of Hosts: Tablets of Bahá'u'lláh. Wilmette, IL: Bahá'í Publishing, 2006.

Writings of Bahá'u'lláh. New Delhi: Bahá'í Publishing Trust, 2006.

Works of the Báb

Selections from the Writings of the Báb. Compiled by the Research Department of the Universal House of Justice. Translated by Habib Taherzadeh et al. Wilmette, IL: Bahá'í Publishing Trust, 2006.

Works of 'Abdu'l-Bahá

A Traveller's Narrative Vol. 2. Translation by E. G. Browne. Cambridge, UK: Cambridge University Press, 1891.

Memorials of the Faithful. Wilmette, IL: Bahá'í Publishing Trust, 1997.

The Promulgation of Universal Peace: Talks Delivered by 'Abdu'l-Bahá during His Visit to the United States and Canada in 1912. Wilmette, IL: Bahá'í Publishing Trust, 2007.

The Secret of Divine Civilization. Wilmette, IL: Bahá'í Publishing, 2007.

Works of Shoghi Effendi

God Passes By. Revised ed. Seventh printing. Wilmette, IL: Bahá'í Publishing Trust, 1994.

The World Order of Bahá'u'lláh. Wilmette, IL: Bahá'í Publishing Trust, 1991.

Compilations

Bahá'u'lláh, the Báb, and 'Abdu'l-Bahá. *Bahá'í Prayers*. Wilmette, IL: Bahá'í Publishing Trust, 2002.

Other Works

'Abd al-Hamíd Ishráq Khávárí. *Núrayn-i Nayyirayn*. Tihrán, Iran: Bahá'í Publishing Trust, 1967.

———. *Má'idih Ásmání*. Nine volumes. Tihrán, Iran: Bahá'í Publishing Trust, 1971–1973.

———. *Má'idiy-i-Ásmání pt. II*. New Delhi, India: Bahá'í Publishing Trust, 1984.

Abrahamian, Ervand. *Iran between two revolutions*. Princeton, NJ: Princeton University Press, 1982.

Abu'l Fazi'l, Mírzá. Siyyid Mehdi Gulpaygani, and Kashfu'l-Ghata, quoted in Ahang Rabbani, *Nayriz: The First Century* (eBook Publications: March 2007 edition) c.1, p. 12.

Afnán, Abu'l Qasím. *'Ahd-i A'lá Zindigániy-Hadrat-Báb (The Bábi Dispensation: The life of the Báb)*. Oxford: One World, 2000.

Afnán, Mírzá Habíb'u'lláh. "The Bab in Shiraz," v. 16. *Witnesses to Babi and Baha'i history*. Translated by Ahang Rabbani. Ebook: Ahang Rabbani, 2008.

———. *The genesis of the Babi and Baha'i Faiths in Shiraz and Fars*. Translated by Ahang Rabbani. Boston, MA: Brill Publishing, 2008.

Ahdieh, Bahá'í. *Nayrízi-Shurangiz*. Unpublished memoirs.

'Alam, Husang. "Henna." *Encyclopaedia Iranica*. New York City: Columbia University, December 15, 2003. http://www.iranica.com/articles/henna.

'Alí, Muḥammad. *"Neireez."* 2006–2007. http://neyrizfars.blogfa.com.

Amanat, Abbas. *Pivot of the Universe: Nasir al-Din Sháh Qájár and the Iranian Monarchy, 1831–1896*. Berkeley and Los Angeles, CA: University of California Press, 1997.

———. *Resurrection and Renewal*. Ithaca, NY: Cornell University Press, 1989.

Arya, Sepehr. "Babis and Baha'i role in the Constitutional Revolution." September, 2006, http://www.ohamzodai.com/maghalat.html.

Avarih, 'Abdu'l-Husayn. *Kawakibu'd-Durriyih*. Cairo: Bahá'í Publishing Trust, 1914.

Bahá'í Temple Unity. *Minutes of the 1909 National Convention.* Wilmette, IL: Mary Rabb papers, Bahá'í National Archives.

Balyuzi, H. M. *'Abdu'l-Bahá.* Oxford, UK: George Ronald Press, 1971.

———. *The Báb: The Herald of the Day of Days.* Oxford, UK: George Ronald Press, 1975.

———. *Bahá'u'lláh: The King of Glory.* Oxford, UK: George Ronald Press, 1980.

———. *Edward Granville Browne and the Bahá'í Faith.* Oxford, UK: George Ronald Press, 1970.

———. *Eminent Bahá'ís in the time of Bahá'u'lláh.* Oxford, UK: George Ronald Press, 1985.

———. *Khadíjih Bagum, The Wife of the Báb.* Oxford, UK: George Ronald Press, 1985.

Binning, Robert B. M. *A journal of two years' travel in Persia, Ceylon, etc, Volume 1.* Adamant Media Corporation, June 26, 2001. Facsimile reprint of a 1857 edition by Wm. H. Allen and Co., London.

Browne, Edward Granville. *A Year Amongst the Persians: Impressions as to the life, character, and thought of the people of Persia.* Cambridge, UK: Cambridge University Press, 1927.

———. *Materials for the study of the Bábí religion.* Cambridge, UK: Cambridge University Press, 1918. Viewed at http://www.archive.org.

———. "The Bábís of Persian." *Journal of Royal Asiatic Society* (1889): 21.

———. "Some remarks on the Bábí Texts." Edited by Baron V. Rosen. *Journal of Royal Asiatic Society* (1892): 24.

Bushrú'í, Hasan Fuádi. *The History of the Bahá'í Faith in Khorásán 1844–1926.* Germany: Asre Jadid Publisher, 2007.

Chehrenegar, Nassrulláh. Lectures and notes, Shíráz summer school summer, 1960.

Donaldson, Bess Allen. *The Wild Rue: a study of Muhammadan Magic and Folklore in Iran.* London, UK: Luzac and Company, 1938.

Dupree, Nancy H. "Etiquette." *Encyclopaedia Iranica* (December 15, 1998): Columbia University, New York City.

Dústkáh, Jalíl, and Eqbál Yagmá'í. "Education iii. the traditional elementary school." *Encyclopaedia Iranica.* Columbia University, New York City: December 15, 1997. Accessed December 20, 2010. http://www.iranica.com/articles/education-iii.Edward Eastwick. *Journal of a Diplomate's Three Years' Residence in Persia v. 2.* Smith, Elder and Co.: January 1, 1864.

Esselmont, John. *Bahá'u'lláh and the New Era.* Wilmette, IL: Bahá'í Publishing, 2006.

Faizi, Muḥammad-'Alí. *Hadrat-i-Nuqtay-i Úlá: The Life of the Báb.* Tihrán, Iran: Bahá'í Publishing Trust, 1973.

———. *Nayríz Mushkbiz.* Tihrán, Iran: Bahá'í Publishing Trust, 129 BE/1349 AH.

———. *Nuqta-yi Úlá.* Tihrán, Iran: Bahá'í Publishing Trust, 1973.

Fasá'í, Hájí Mírzá Hasan. *Fárs Námih-yi Násií.* Two volumes. Tihrán, Iran: Bahá'í Publishing Trust 1894–1895.

Fátimih, Bibi. Manuscript. Chicago, IL: 1992.

Floor, Willem. "Asnáf." *Encyclopaedia Iranica*. New York City: Columbia University, December 15, 1987. Accessed December 20, 2010. http://www.iranica.com/articles/asnaf-guilds.

———. "Gift giving." *Encyclopaedia Iranica.* New York City: Columbia University, December 15, 2001. Accessed December 20, 2010. http://www.iranica.com/articles/gift-giving-v.

Francis, Richard. *"Ahmad the recipient of the Arabic Tablet of Ahmad."* Bahá'í Library Online, 2003. Accessed January 20, 2011. http://bahai-library.com/?file=francis_ahmad_biography.

Fu'ádí, Hasan. *The History of the Bahá'í Faith in Khorasan.* Germany, Darmstadt: Asr-e-Jadid, 2007.

Geula, Arsalan. *Iranian Baha'is from Jewish Background.* Independent Publisher, 2008.

Gobineau, Comte Joseph A. de. *Religions et philosophies dans l'Asie Centrale.* Paris: Ernest Leroux, 1900.

Hamadani, Siyyid Husayn. *The Tarikh-i-Jadid.* Translated by E. B. Browne, quoted in H. M. Balyuzi, *The Báb: The Herald of the Day of Days* (Oxford UK: George Ronald Press, 1975).

Hisámí, Habib'u'lláh. *History of the Faith in Nayríz.* Unpublished manuscript. Shiraz, Iran, 2007.

Hodgson, Marshall G. S. *The Venture of Islam Vol. 1.* Chicago IL: University of Chicago Press, 1977.

Husainí, Nusrat'u'lláh Muḥammad. *The Báb: His Life, His Writings and the disciples of the Báb's Dispensation.* Dundas, Ontario: Institute for Bahá'í Studies in Persian, 1995.

Interview with Bibi Khánum, unpublished.

Khoshbin, Parivash Samandarí. "Taráz-i-Iláhí, Mírza Taráz'u'lláh Samandarí." Association for Bahá'í Studies in Persian (2002).

Khusravi, Muḥammad-'Alíy-i-Malik. *Tárikh-i Shuhadá.* Tíhran, Iran: Bahá'í Publishing Trust, 1973.

Ma'ani, Baharieh Rouhani. *Against Incredible Odds.* Oxford, UK: George Ronald, 2006.

MacEoin, D. M. *"From Shaykhism to Bábism: A study in charismatic renewal in Shí'a Islam."* PhD dissertation. Cambridge University, 1979.

Mackey, Sandra. *The Iranians: Persia, Islam and the Soul of a Nation.* New York: Dutton, 1996.

Mahdavi, Shireen. "Qájárs: the Qájár-period household." *Encyclopaedia Iranica*. New York City: Columbia University, July 20, 2009. Accessed December 20, 2010. http://www.iranica.com/articles/Qájárs-period-household.

Mahmúd-i-Zarqání, Mírzá. *Mahmúd's Diary.* Translated by Mohi Sobhani with Shirley Macias. Oxford, UK: George Ronald Publisher, 1998.

Malik-Khusravi, Muḥammad. *Tarikh Shuhadi Amr*. Tihrán, Iran: Bahá'í Publishing Trust, 1974.

Málmirí, Hájí Muḥammad-Táhír. *Khátirát-i-Málamírí*. Langenhain, Germany: Bahá'í Verlag, 1992.

———. *Táríkh Shuhadá Yazd*. Karachi, Pakistan: Bahá'í Publishing Trust of India, 1979.

Martin, Vanessa. *The Qájár Pact: bargaining, protest and the state in nineteenth-century Persia*. New York: I. B. Taurus, 2005.

Mázandarání, Mírzá Asadu'lláh Fádil-i. *Amr Va Khalq*. Germany: Bahá'í Verlag, 1971.

———. *Zuhúr al-Haqq, Volumes 1–4*. Tihrán, Iran: Bahá'í Publishing Trust, 1973.

Mehrabkhani, Ruhu'lláh. *Disciple at Dawn*. Los Angeles, CA: Kalimat Press, 1987.

Mírhádí, Túrán. "Education viii. nursery schools and kindergartens." *Encyclopaedia Iranica*. New York City: Columbia University, December 15, 1997. Accessed December 20, 2010. http://www.iranica.com/articles/education-viii-nursery-schools-and-kindergartens.

Misaghi, Jalal. *Unpublished memoirs*. New York, 1995.

Moghaddam, Siyamak Zabihi. *Váqi'iy-i-Qal'iy-i-Shaykh Tabarsí*. Darmstadt, Germany: 'Asr-i Jadíd Publisher, 2002.

Momen, Moojan, ed. *The Bábí and Bahá'í Religions, 1844–1944: Some contemporary Western accounts*. Oxford, UK: George Ronald Press, 1981.

———. Selections from the Writings of E. G. Browne and the Bábí and Bahá'í Religions. Oxford, UK: George Ronald Press, 1987.

———. An introduction to Shi'i Islam. Oxford, UK: George Ronald Publisher, 1985.

Mottahedeh, Negar. Representing the unrepresentable. Syracuse, NY: Syracuse University Press, 2008.

"Mozaffar ad-Din Sháh Qájár." January 12th, 2011. http://en.wikipedia.org/wiki/Mozaffar ad-Din_Sháh_Qájár

Nabíl-i-A'ẓam. *The Dawn-Breakers*. Translated by Shoghi Effendi. London: Bahá'í Publishing Trust, 1953.

Nasr, Siyyid Hossein. Islam: Religion, History and Civilization. NY: Harper Collins, 2003.

Nayrízí, Siyyid Ibrahim. "The Account of Siyyid Ibrahim concerning Nayriz." Translated by Ahang Rabbani. *Translations of Shaykhi, Bábí and Bahá'í Texts* 4, no. 5 (June, 2000). 1995, http://www.h-net.org/~bahai/trans/vol4/ibrahim/ibrahim2.htm.

Nicolas, A. L. M. *Seyyed Ali Mohammed dit le Bab*. Michigan State University. http://www.h-net.org/~bahai/diglib/books/K-O/N/LeBab/LeBab.htm.

———. *Prophet in Modern Times, Volume I of the Bábí Studies Series*. Translated by Peter Terry. United States of America: Lulu Publications, 2008.

Officer, Lawrence H., and Samuel H. Williamson. *Measuring Worth, 2010*. University of Illinois at Chicago. http://www.measuringworth.com.

Price, Massoume. "Iranian Marriage Ceremony, Its History & Symbolism." New York City: Columbia University, 2001. http://www.iranchamber.com/culture/articles/iranian_marriage_ceremony.php.

Rabbani, Ahang. "Efforts to preserve the remains of the Báb: Four historical accounts." Bahá'í Studies Review 11: (2003).

———. *Nayriz: The First Century*. Ebook Publications: March 2007 edition.

———. *The Bábís of Nayríz: History and Documents, Witnesses to Bábí and Bahá'í History vol. 2*. Ebook Publication, 2007.

———. "Translations of Shaykhi, Bábí and Bahá'í Texts," no. 9 (October, 1997). http://www.h-net.org/~bahai/trans/vol1/khadija/khadija2.htm.

Rouhani, Mírzá Muḥammad Shafi'. *Lam'átul-Anvár vols. 1 and 2*. Tihrán, Iran: Bahá'í Publishing Trust, 1971.

Rouhani, Shidroukh. *Morvareed*. Darmstadt, Germany: ASR-Jadid Publisher, 2002.

Ruhe, Davis S. *Robe of Light: The Persian Years of the Supreme Prophet Baha'u'llah 1817–1853*. Oxford, UK: George Ronald Press, 1994.

Saiedi, Nader. *Logos and Civilization*. Bethesda, MD: University of Maryland Press, 2000.

Sarwal, Anil. *Miracles in Religion: A study of the miraculous in religion in context of the Bahá'í Faith*. Lucknow: Royale Publishers, 1996. http://bahai-library.org/books/miracles/bahai.html.

Sepehr, Arya. "Bábís and Bahá'í role in the Constitutional Revolution." September, 2006. http://www.ohamzodai.com/maghalat.html.

Shafi' Nayrízí, Mullá Muḥammad. *Narrative of Mulla Muhammad Shafi' Nayrízí*. Translated by Hussein Ahdieh and Ahang Rabbani, unpublished. Ahdieh translation available at http://www.nayriz.org.

Sháhbazi, A. Shapur. "Nowruz ii. In the Islamic Period." *Encyclopaedia Iranica*. New York City: Columbia University, November 15, 2009. Accessed December 20, 2010. http://www.iranica.com/articles/nowruz-ii.

Shiva, Manouchehr. "History." 2002–2009. Accessed June 3, 2010. http://www.qashqai.net/history.html.

Siphir, Mohammad Taqi. *Nasikh al-Tavarich*. Tihrán, Iran: Bahá'í Publishing Trust, 1965.

Stockman, Robert. *Origin of the Bahá'í Faith in America, 1892–1900*. Wilmette, IL: Bahá'í Publishing Trust, 1985.

Sulaymání, 'Azizu'lláh. *Masábih Hidáuat*. Nine volumes. Tihrán, Iran: Bahá'í PublishingTrust, 1967–1975.

Taherzadeh, Adib. *Revelation of Bahá'u'lláh, volumes 1–2*. Oxford, UK: George Ronald Press, 1977.

Tavangar, Siamak. "Iran Dried figs." *Estahban Fig Growers Cooperative*. http://www.iranfig.com/Driedfigs.htm.

"The Iranian history 1926 AD." November 3rd, 2010. http://www.fouman.com/history/Iranian_History_1926.html#BKM758.

Whitmore, Bruce. *The Dawning Place.* Wilmette, IL: Bahá'í Publishing Trust, 1984.

———. "The Story of the Cornerstone." October 21, 2011. http://www.bahai.us/bahai-temple/history-and-architecture/cornerstone/.

Yazdani, M. "Iran at the time of the Qájár dynasty, a perspective from the Bahá'í Sacred Writings." *Association for Bahá'í Studies in Persian* (2003).

Index

Names beginning with the titles "Ḥájí," "Mullá," or "Siyyid" are alphabetized according to the second element in the name. Names occurring after 1930 (when last names were introduced in Iran) are alphabetized according to the last name. Page numbers in italics indicate photographs or other illustrations. All locations are in Persia / Iran unless otherwise indicated.

Ábádih, town of, burial of Bábís at, 180–81
  'Abdu'l-Bahá's Tablet for, 182–83
'Abdu'l-'Alí, Ḥájí Shaykh (father-in-law of Vaḥíd), 72, 87, 124, 125, 172
'Abdu'l-Bahá (son of Bahá'u'lláh), 119, 209, 222, 237
  on the Báb's station, 64n, 293–94n21
  and burial of the Báb's remains, 231–32
  as Center of the Covenant, 5, 202, 271
  on Declaration of Bahá'u'lláh, 193
  dreams of, 264–65
  lays cornerstone of U.S. Mashriqu'l-Askár, 261
  Nayrízi Bahá'ís' pilgrimages to, 243–44, 246, 254, 263–64, 317n18, 318n5, 320n13
  passing of, 265–66, 267
  writings of
    The Secret of Divine Civilization, 198–99, 209–10
    Tablet for martyrs, 181, 182–83, 277
    Tablets to Nayrízi Bahá'ís, 169, 202, 204, 223, 226, 235, 279
    Tablets to U.S. Bahá'í Convention, 238–39, 245–46
    Tablet to Nayrízi Bahá'ís, 279
    Will and Testament, 266, 267–68

'Abdu'l-Hamíd Khán, 61n1, 62n2
'Abdu'l-Ḥusayn, Mírzá, 247, 260, 262–63
  on pilgrimage in Haifa, 243, 244, 246
'Abdu'l-Ḥusayn, Mullá (1853 resistance leader), 124, 125, 146
  as prisoner, 162–63, 172n1, 178, 180
'Abdu'l-Ḥusayn, Mullá (grandfather of Mullá Muḥammad Shafí'), 72, 74, 82, 112, 185
'Abdu'l Ḥusayn Lárí, Siyyid
  orders issued by, 213–14, 218, 313n11, 313n16
  takeover of Fárs province, 211, 217, 259
'Abdu'lláh Khán, 89n1
'Abdu'l Majíd, Mullá, 243, 317n17
'Abdu'l Nayrízí, Ḥájí Shaykh (father-in-law of Vaḥíd), 79–80n
'Abdu'l Samí, Mullá, 74n1
'Abid, Ḥájí Siyyid, 96, 98, 147
Abú Bakr, 9, 10
Abú'l-Qasím, Mírzá, 73n2, 84n1
Abú-Talíb (uncle of Muḥammad), 8, 9
Abú-Turáb, Shaykh, 38, 48, 50–51, 131n1, 185, 189, 197, 310n33
Afnáns, 131n1, 199, 211, 251
Agnew, Arthur, 249
agriculture. *See* farming
Ahdieh family, 72n2, 111n, 220n, 273, 310–11n34
Aḥmad (son of the Báb), 40, 43
Aḥmad, Mírzá, 85, 133n
Aḥmad, Tablet to, 194–95, 199
Aḥmad Vaḥídí, Mírzá, 243–44, 270–71
Akbar, Mírzá, 188, 256, 309n8, 316n16, 318–19n8
'Alí (son-in-law of Muḥammad), 1, 10, 11, 37n
'Alí, Ḥájí Mírzá Siyyid (uncle of the Báb), 35, 36, 37, 38–39, 50, 61, 62n2
'Alí, Mullá, 240, 241
'Alí, Siyyid, 154–55, 305n11
'Alí Akbar (nephew of Muḥammad Ismá'íl), 241–42
'Alí Akbar Rafsinjání, Mírzá, 215, 254
'Alí Aṣghar / 'Askar Khán, 85n1, 86n2, 299n23
'Alíe Rafi'i, 252n3
'Alí Heshmatu'lláh Islám, Siyyid, 218–19
'Alí Muḥammad, Mírzá, 317n17
'Alí-Muḥammad, Siyyid. *See* Báb, the
'Alí Murad-i-Sírjáni, 134n2

'Alí-Naqí, Mullá, 72, 146, 160, 185n
'Alí-Riḍá, Mírzá, 73n2
'Alí Sardár, Mírzá, 75, 130, 186
  martyrdom of, 150–55, 270, 305n6, 305n10
  as member of Nayríz resistance, 124, 126, 132
  and mountain battles, 2, 140, 141, 145–46
  nieces of, 197, 220, 310n32
  uncle of, 85, 107
Amru'lláh, Ḥaj, 254, 318n5
Áqá 'Abbás, 255–56
Áqá Abú Talíb, Siyyid, 73n1, 113
Áqá Afnán, Áqá Mírzá, 199
Áqá 'Alí, Siyyid, 152n3, 184n1
Áqá Bábá, Mullá, 186
Áqá Khán (son of 'Alí Aṣghar Khán), 299n23
Áqá Khán-i-Núrí, Mírzá, 116, 128n1
Áqá Muḥammad-Ḥusayn Ardistání, 62n2
Áqásí, Ḥájí Mírzá, 53–54, 59–60
  fate of, 69
  imprisonment of the Báb, 63–67
Asadu'lláh (son-in-law of Muḥammad Ibráhim), 241, 242, 315n9
Asbergun orchards, 156, 161
Ayatu'llah Aqa 'Abdu'l-Ḥusayn, Ḥájí Siyyid, 214
'Azím, Mullá Shaykh 'Alí, 55n2

Báb, the, 5–6, 35–51
  arrests and imprisonments, 50, 61, 63–69
  burial of remains, 231–32
  childhood, 35–36
  Covenant of, 146
  Declaration of, 42, 43–48, 50–51, 293n12, 293n15
  family, 131n, 199, 211, 251
  as Gate, 2, 12, 45–46, 51, 68, 102, 293–94n21
  given name, 1
  laws brought by, 66, 163
  as Manifestation of God, 7, 68–69, 74
  marriage, 38–39
  martyrdom, 15, 102, 128n1
  as merchant, 36–37
  miracles, 61–62, 64n, 67

Báb, the *(cont'd)*
mission, 5, 51, 57
physical description of, 69
pilgrimage, 48–49
as promised Qá'im, 44–45, 49, 51, 68, 95–96
revelation of, 41–42n, 48, 68, 69, 163, 178
Shrine of, 200
son of, 40, 43
transport of remains, 192, 195–96, 203
travels, 293n16
Vaḥíd's interviews with, 55–57, 59
violence forbidden by, 15, 71, 126
writings
Bayán, 93
Tablet to Fáṭimih, *108*
will, 60–61
Bábá, Mírzá (uncle of Mírzá Na'ím), 128, 130, 132, 133
Bábís, Nayríz, 5, 95–96
becoming Bahá'ís, 185–204
education of, 146, 199
growth of community, 49, 74, 80n, 111, 184, 190–91
See also children, Bábí; persecutions, in 1850; persecutions, in 1853; women, Bábí
Bábu'l-Báb. *See* Ḥusayn, Mullá (Letter of the Living)
Badas͟ht, Bábí conference at, 66
Bag͟hdád, Iraq, Bahá'u'lláh in, 192–94
Bag͟hdádi, Najla, 321n25
baghe razi orchard, 240–41n
Bahá'í Faith, 7–8, 198–99, 209, 237
teachings on violence, 15, 88n1, 116, 117, 193, 310n22
Bahá'ís, Nayríz, 255, 271
Bábís' becoming, 185–204
at burial of Báb's remains, 231–32, 244
education of, 199, 215, 268, 310n22
growth of community, 184, 199, 202, 215, 263, 268–69, 277–78
pilgrimages made by
to 'Abdu'l-Bahá, 243–44, 246, 263–64, 317n18, 318n5, 320n13
to Bahá'u'lláh, 194, 198, 254, 306n6
qualities of, 245–46
Spiritual Assembly, 197, 263, 269, 270, 319n9, 319–20n12

See also Muslims, Nayríz, Bahá'ís assisted by; persecutions, in 1909; persecutions, post-1909
Bahá'ís, U.S., first national convention of, 232, 237–39, 245–46, 249
Bahá'í Temple Unity (U.S.), 246, 249
Bahárlú sharpshooters, 151, 152, 153, 154, 157, 304–5n3, 308n18
Bahá'u'lláh
at Conference of Badasht, 66
Covenant of, 186, 194, 199, 202, 271
as culmination of Báb's mission, 5–6, 190, 192–94
Declaration of, 2, 192–94
E. G. Browne's meeting with, 200–201
given name, 1n
growing influence of, 190–91
as Him Who Will Be Made Manifest, 7, 15, 119
imprisonments and exiles, 118–19
Nayrízi Bahá'ís' pilgrimages to, 194, 198, 254, 306n6
passing of, 201–2
proclamation to kings and rulers, 195, 209
prophecies regarding Persia, 203–4
teachings, 7–8, 198–99, 209
on violence, 15, 88n1, 116, 117, 193, 310n22
writings, 190, 197
Book of Laws, 203–4, 310n22
Lawh Ayyúb, 192
Tablet for Vaḥíd, 101
Tablet of Aḥmad, 194–95, 199
Tablet of Job, 86, 192
Tablet of the Holy Mariner, 267
Tablet of Visitation, 202
Tablets to Nayrízi Bábís, 110n, 192, 196, 198, 269
Bahíyyih Khánum (sister of 'Abdu'l-Bahá), 267–68
Bálá-Taram heights, battles at, 115–16n, 145–48, 150, 156, 180, 186
Báqir, Mullá, 74, 99, 297n18, 298n23
Bávanát district (Nayríz), Vaḥíd's teaching in, 71–72
Báyír tribe, 174n2
BibiDokhtaran, Shrine of (Shiraz), *177*
Bibi Khánum, 100–101
Bid-Bikhubih orchards, 302–3n6
Bid Bukhun area (mountains), 150
Bísámán trail, 156, 164n2

Blomfield, Lady, 265–66
British agents, reports by, 89–90, 103, 104, 131n, 136–37, 143–45, 148, 167
Browne, Edward Granville (E. G.), 200–201, 209

Catholic Church, use of violence by, 14
Cháhr-Bulúk, village of, 306n22
Charlemagne, 14
Chase, Thornton, 237
Chihríq, Báb's imprisonment in, 66–67, 69
children, Bábí
  in Asbergun orchards, 156
  at mountain battles, 136, 152
  as prisoners, 5, 104–9, 161–76, 178–81, 184, 240, 295n1, 306–7n7
  return to Nayríz, 185–89
children, Bahá'í
  flight of, 220, 225, 260, 263–64
  in hiding, 225, 227, 231, 233, 239–40, 251
  persecution of, 5, 275, 276, 280
children, in Nayríz, 24–25
Chinár Sháhi district (Nayríz), 22, 255
Chinár-Súkhtih district (Nayríz), 22–23, 74, 75, 80n, 87, 215, 276
  See also Great Friday Mosque of Nayríz; persecutions, in 1850; persecutions, in 1853; persecutions, in 1909; persecutions, post-1909
Christ. *See* Jesus Christ
Christianity, teachings on violence, 13–14
clans, 8, 9, 14
clergy, Muslim
  authority of, 11, 12–13, 28, 32–33
  becoming Bábís, 74, 139, 162–63, 172n1, 178, 189, 196
  corruption of, 1, 15
  persecutions by
    of Bábís, 50–51, 55, 61, 63, 67–69, 76, 89
    of Bahá'ís, 209, 270, 271–74, 278–79, 313n16, 317n18
  political involvement, 211, 214
  takeover of Iranian government, 279–81
  See also Muslims, Nayríz
constitutionalists, 209, 210–11
Cormick [Dr.], description of the Báb by, 69
customs, ancient, 29–33

Darb-i-Shikáft passage, battles at, 137, 139–45, 150, 156–60, 304–5n3
casualties from, 165–66n, 303n1, 304n7
seven defenders of, 146n1
women and children at, 136, 143, 144, 146, 152
Dawhood, Siyyid, 218
death, customs surrounding, 29–30
See also martyrdom
dervishes, 27

Eshraghieh (Bahá'í woman), 275–76

Faḍlu'lláh, Mírzá, 85–86, 309n8
Faizi, Muḥammad 'Alí, 277
Faraju'lláh Khán, 89n1
farming, 23, 27
See also orchards; vineyards
Fars, province of, 34, 270
'Abdu'l Ḥusayn Lárí's takeover of, 211, 217, 259
Fasá, town of, Vaḥíd's teaching in, 72
Fatḥ 'Alí Khán, 189, 196–97
Fathu'lláh-i-Qumí, and attempted assassination of Náṣiri'd-Dín Sháh, 117n
Fatḥu'lláh Maktab-Dár, Mullá, 35n
Fáṭimih (daughter of Muḥammad), 43, 44
Fáṭimih (mother of Karbalá'í Muḥammad-Ṣálih), 188, 254
Fáṭimih Bagum (daughter of Áqá Siyyid Ja'far Yazdí), 196, 200
Fáṭimih Baraghání. *See* Ṭáhirih
Fáṭimih Khánum (niece of 'Alí Sardár), 197, 220
Fazlu'lláh (son of Mullá Muḥammad 'Alí), 228n2, 314n6
Fazlu'lláh, Mírzá, 243, 244, 317n17
Fazlu'lláh Paymani, Mírzá, 263
festivals, 29, 32–33
Fiddih (servant of the Báb), 39, 41, 42
Fírúz Mírzá, Prince, 128n2, 149
Bábí prisoners brought to, 103, 104, 106, 107
and Bábís' occupation of Fort Khájih, 84, 89
Fort Khájih, 22, 83
Bábís' occupation of, 81–90, 197, 200, 297n17
Bahá'ís' purchase of, 269–70
casualties at, 298n5, 299n19, 301n21

Fort Khájih *(cont'd)*
fall of, 91–98, 107, 109, 115–16n, 124, 147, 180, 189, 196
map of, *13*
prisoners from, 103–14
Vaḥíd's family in, 79–80n
Fort Shaykh Tabarsí, siege of, 70
Furútan, 'Alí-Akbar, 277

Gabriel (archangel), 8, 46
Garden of Riḍván (Baghdád), 192–94
Garden of the Martyrs' Heads (Ábádih), 181
Garden of the Merciful, The (Ábádih), 181
Gates. *See* Báb, the, as Gate
Ghámar Sultán, 263–64, 320n13
Ghulám Riḍá-Yazdi, 71, 85, 91–92, 107, 115–16n
God, 7, 9
Goodall, Helen S., 249
government, Bábí and Bahá'í teachings on, 28, 124, 209
Great Friday Mosque of Nayríz, 21, 33, 87, 98, 220
Vaḥíd's proclamation in, 2, 79–80, 215, 281, 296n2, 296n3
Guardian of the Bahá'í Faith. *See* Shoghi Effendi
Gulpáyigání soldiers, 173

hadiths, 1, 12, 32
Hajan (daughter of Karbalá'í Mehdí), murder of, 227
Ḥájí (son of Aṣghar), 146n, 308n17
Hall, Albert H., 249
Ḥasan, Mullá, 227, 232–33, 296n8
martyrdom of, 228, 229, 314n6, 314–15n11, 315n12, 317n20
Ḥasan Lab-Shikarí, Mullá, 73–75, 125, 136, 189, 199, 227
Ḥasan Mírzá, 124
Ḥasan Yazdí, 244, 317n20
Hesamí [Mr.], Bahá'í schools run by, 268
Hidden Imam. *See* Qá'im; Twelfth Imam
Him Who Will Be Made Manifest, Bahá'u'lláh as, 7, 15, 119
Hoar, William H., 249
House of Worship, U.S. *See* Mashriqu'l-Askár, U.S.
Ḥusayn (son of 'Alí-Naqí), and attempted assassination of Náṣiri'd-Dín Sháh, 115–16n

Ḥusayn, Mírzá (son-in-law of Taqí), 73n2
Ḥusayn, Mullá (father of Mehdí), 242
Ḥusayn, Mullá (Letter of the Living), 43–48, 70, 293n15, 316n14
Ḥusayn, Siyyid, 304n7
Ḥusayn 'Ala'í, Mírzá, 318–19n8
Ḥusayn-'Alí, Mírzá. *See* Bahá'u'lláh
Ḥusayn Khán, 62n1
Ḥusayn Quṭbá, Mírzá, 73
Ḥusayn Rawḍih-Khán, Mírzá, 147

Ibráhim, Ḥájí, 186
Ibráhim, Haj Siyyid, 227–28
Ibráhim, Mírzá, 247–48, 249
  Tablet from 'Abdu'l-Bahá to, *226*
Ibráhim Mo'alem, Mírzá, 253
Ímám 'Alí. *See* 'Alí (son-in-law of Muḥammad)
Ímám Ḥusayn (grandson of Muḥammad)
  martyrdom of, 32–33, 37, 84n2, 300n27
    reenacting, 11, 83n1, 178, 317n17
  Shaykhis' devotion to, 1
Ímáms, 11, 12, 37n
Ímámzadeh Ma'sum shrine (Ṭihrán), 192
Ímámzadih Zayd shrine (Ṭihrán), 196
Iran. *See* Persia
Iṣfáhán, city of, the Báb in, 63
Islám, 8–11, 53
  the Báb as fulfillment of prophecies, 7
  renewal of, 33–34
  teachings of, 1, 9–10, 12, 32
    on violence, 13–15, 32–33, 125, 147
  See also clergy, Muslim; Muslims, Nayríz
Ismaí'íl, Ḥájí Siyyid, 88
Ismaí'íl, Mírzá, 146, 188, 256
Ismá'íl, Siyyid (son of Vaḥíd), 60n, 79
Iṣṭahbánát, town of, 34, 76

Jacobsen, Bernard M., 249
Ja'far, Mírzá (aka Mírzá Jalal), 198, 306n6
Ja'far-i-Kashfí Dárábí, Siyyid (father of Vaḥíd), 48–49, 54, 60, 65

Ja'far Iṣṭahbánáti, Siyyid, 87, 218
Ja'far Yazdí, Áqá Siyyid, 110–12, 113, 196, 262
Jahán Bagum (sister of Vaḥíd), 79–80n
Jalálí'd-Dín 'Abdull'áh, Siyyid, shrine of, 100n3
Jesus Christ, 12, 13–14, 47, 238
Jews, beliefs regarding violence, 125–26
jihad, concept of, 15
  See also violence, religious teachings on, Islamic
Jináb Amru'lláh, 242, 316n16
Jináb-i-Bahá. *See* Bahá'u'lláh
Jináb-i-Muḥammad Ḥusayn, Mírzá, 252, 253n2
Jináb Khájih Muḥammad, 257, 263
Jináb Mírzá Báqir Khoshnevis (aka Mírzá Áqá), 197
Jináb Mírzá Fazlu'lláh Paymani, 257, 263, 319n9 (chap. 22)
Jináb Mírzá Muḥammad, 310–11n34
Jináb Mírzá Muḥammad Báqir Paymani, 257, 263
Jináb Mírzá Shuqr'u'lláh, 310–11n34
Jináb Ustád Atau'lláh, 242, 316n16
Job, Bahá'u'lláh's Tablet on, 86, 192

Kaaba (Mecca), 8
Karbalá'í 'Askar Bíraq-Dár, 146n, 150, 151
Karbalá'í Báqir, 187, 257n1
Karbalá'í Ḥusayn, 243–44, 263–64
Karbalá'í Mírzá Muḥammad, 85, 109
Karbalá'í Muḥammad, 85, 125n1, 186
Karbalá'í Muḥammad-Ṣálih, 188–89, 190, 254, 263, 269–70, 318n5
Karbilá, Iraq
  Báb's journey to, 46
  martyrdom of Ímám Ḥusayn at, 11, 37n, 83n1, 84n2, 178
Káẓim, Siyyid, 37, 43, 44, 45
Kazimayn, Iraq, 37n
Káẓim-i-Zanjání, Siyyid, 61n, 62n2
Khadíjih (wife of Muḥammad), 8, 9
Khadíjih Bagum (wife of the Báb), 35, 51
  assistance to Bábí prisoners, 107–8, 179–80, 186
  dreams of, 36–37, 39–40
  marriage to the Báb, 38–39
  memoirs of, 61n, 62n, 293n12

passing of, 199
prayers revealed for, 42–43, 62–63
son of, 40, 43
Khájih 'Alí, 125n1
Khájih 'Alí Izadi, 220
Khájih Ghafar, betrayal by, 134–35
Khájih Ḥasan, 125n1
Khájih Maḥmúd, 125n1
Khájih Muḥammad, 187, 195, 263, 264, 271, 309n6
Khájih Quṭbá
as member of Bábí resistance, 124, 125, 125n1, 126, 129, 132
at mountain battles, 142, 146, 151, 155, 158, 160
wife of, 197–98
Khamseh federation, 308n18
Khán Mírzá, 150n1
Khávar Sultán, 189, 307n9
'Abdu'l-Bahá's Tablets to, *169*
Bahá'u'lláh's Tablets to, 269
marriage to Muḥammad Shafí', 197, 310n33
persecution suffered by, 202, 225
Khobar mill and waterway (Nayríz), *81,* 81–82, 84n2, 134n1
kings of Persia. *See* Muḥammad Sháh (king of Persia); Náṣiri'd-Dín Sháh (king of Persia); Riḍá Sháh (king of Persia)
Kouchak Gostaran, Mírzá, 252n3
Kouhesorkheh area (Nayríz), 91n
Kúchih Bálá district (Nayríz), 214–15, 215–16
Kúhistání tribe, 270

Laqá Khánum (mother of Adib Taherzadeh), 86n1
Letters of the Living, 46–48, 51
Luṭf-'Alí, Mírzá, 59n
Luṭf 'Alí Khán
at mountain battles, 148, 149, 157, 158
treatment of Bábí prisoners, 165–66n, 166, 167
bringing to Shíráz, 174n2, 174n4, 175n1, 306–7n7

Maghtoli family, 317–18n7
magic, belief in, 30–32, 33
Mahdi. *See* Twelfth Imam

Máh-kú, castle of, the Báb’s imprisonment in, 64–66
Majíd, Mullá, 252
Manifestation of God, words and deeds of, 64n
    See also Báb, the; Bahá’u’lláh; Muḥammad
Mansúrí, ‘Alí ‘Askar Khán, 275
Manúchihr Khán, belief in the Báb, 63
marriage(s), 25–26, 141
    Bábí, 93–94, 146
martyrdom
    Bábís’ desire for, 84n1, 87, 133, 135, 141, 145, 150–51, 155–56, 158, 160, 178
    Bahá’ís’ readiness for, 193, 227, 241–43, 248, 256, 278
    Islamic ideal of, 11, 32–33
Maryam Jan (wife of Mírzá Muḥammad-Ḥusayn), 317n17
Mashadí Ḥasan, 231, 233
Mashhadí Báqir Sabbágh, 161n
Mashhadí Djafir, 140n1
Mashhadí Ḥasan Shu’á’’i, 218
Mashhadí Ḥusayn, 315n12
Mashhadí Shamsa, 256n
Mashhadí-Taqí, 86
Mashriqu’l-Askár, U.S.
    ‘Abdu’l-Bahá lays cornerstone, 261
    decision to build, 232, 237–39, 246
Mecca, Saudi Arabia, 8
    Báb’s pilgrimage to, 48–49
Medina, Saudi Arabia, 9
    Báb’s pilgrimage to, 48–49
Mehdí (son of Mullá Ḥusayn), 241, 242, 315n9
Memar, Ustád Habíbu’lláh, murder of, 274–75
men, in Nayríz, 27–28
Messiah, 125–26
Mihdí, Mírzá, 107
Mihr / Mir ‘Alí Khán, 89, 90, 129–30, 200
mills. *See* Khobar mill and waterway (Nayríz)
Mills, Mountfort, 249
miracles, by the Báb, 61–62, 64n, 67
Mír Muḥammad-Ḥasan, 251–52
Míssáqí, Nurat, 263, 268
Mohammad Rahim, Ḥájí, 86n1

monarchists, 209, 214
Mosleh [Mr.], Bahá'í boys school run by, 268
mosques. *See* Great Friday Mosque of Nayríz; Vakíl mosque (Shíráz), Báb's declaration in
Mostaghim, Bahíyyih Khánum, Bahá'í girls' school run by, 268
mountains, battles in, 23, 136, 180, 185
  casualties in, 152n3, 306n25
  commanders of, 150
  See also Bálá-Taram heights, battles at; Bid Bukhun area (mountains); Darb-i-Shikáft passage, battles at
Mubárak (servant of the Báb), 39, 44, 48–49
Muḥammad, 8–11
  first community founded by, 49
  proclamation as Manifestation of God, 9
  revelation of, 60
  successors to, 10–12
  teachings of, 9–10
    on violence, 13–15
  Vaḥíd as descendant of, 95, 96, 101
  See also Islám
Muḥammad (son of Mírzá Aḥmad), 133n, 134n2
Muḥammad, Ḥájí, 188, 197, 310n32
Muḥammad, Mullá (calligrapher), 86
Muḥammad, Siyyid, Tablets from Bahá'u'lláh to, 196
Muḥammad 'Ábid, Mírzá, 174
Muḥammad 'Abid, Siyyid Mírzá, 188, 288
Muḥammad 'Alí, Mullá, martyrdom of, 227, 228–29, 244, 247, 248, 314n6, 314–15n11, 315n12
Muḥammad 'Alí-i-Bárfurúshi, Mullá. *See* Quddús (Letter of the Living)
Muḥammad-'Alí Khán, 106
Muḥammad-'Alí Qábid, Mullá, 174
Muḥammad Báqir, 187
  murder of, 93
Muḥammad-Báqir, Áqá Siyyid, 188, 197
Muḥammad Ḥasan, 219
Muḥammad Ḥasan Khán (governor of Nayríz), 217, 313n11
Muḥammad Ḥusayn, Mírzá, 317n17
Muḥammad Ḥusayn Mubraem Ain, 247
Muḥammad Ibráhim, 188, 241, 316n11, 316n14

Muḥammad-Ibráhím-i-Amír, 85n2
Muḥammad Ismá'íl, 188, 196, 240–41, 315n8, 315n9
Muḥammad-Ja'far, Mírzá, 85
Muḥammad Kázim, 187
Muḥammad Nayrízí, Ḥájí, 155
Muḥammad Nayrízí, Mullá Mírzá, and attempted assassination of Náṣiri'd-Dín Sháh, 114, 115, 117
Muḥammad-Sádiq Mu'allim, Hájí Mírzá, 293–94n21
Muḥammad Shafí' (youth), 239–40
Muḥammad Shafí', Mullá, 72, 202, 257
'Abdu'l-Bahá's Tablet to, *204*
Abú-Turáb's rescue of, 185, 189
chronicling persecutions, 3, 164n5, 310n22
educating Bábís and Bahá'ís, 196, 199, 310n22
marriage to Khávar Sultán, 197
pilgrimage to Bahá'u'lláh, 190
rebuilding Chinár-Súkhtih district, 194, 196
son of, 220, *222*
Muḥammad Sháh (king of Persia), 53–54, 59, 69
Muḥammad Sho'a, Mírzá, 218, 240
Muḥammad Taqí, Ḥájí, 73, 86
Muḥammad Taqí, Mullá, 136n2
Muḥammad-Taqí Nayrízi, Ḥájí, 110, 112–13, 192
Muḥarram, month of, 32–33
mullás. *See* clergy, Muslim
Munir Nabílzádih, Mírzá, 268–69
Musá Namad-Mál, Mullá, 161n
Muslims, Nayríz
Bábís assisted by, 196–97, 215
Bahá'ís assisted by, 227–28, 240, 242, 246–47, 251–52, 314–15n11
Shaykh Dhakaríyyá's betrayal of, 217–18, 231
See also clergy, Muslim; Nayríz, town of, Bahá'í-Muslim accord in
Musṭafá-Qulí Khán, 89, 90

Nabíl-í-A'ẓam
compilation of Tablet of Visitation for Bahá'u'lláh, 202
The Dawn-Breakers, 3, 64n, 297n18
death of, 202
on Declaration of Bahá'u'lláh, 192–93

Na'ím, Mírzá
and 1850 persecutions, 106, 107
and 1853 persecutions, 128, 129–32
bringing prisoners to Shíráz, 172, 174–75, 176, 178–80, 306–7n7
and mountain battles, 137, 140–43, 143–45, 148–49, 150–51, 154, 304n1
treatment of prisoners, 162–64, 165–66n, 167, 184n1
fate of, 198
Najaf, Iraq, 37n
Nakhjavání, 'Alí, 85n2
Náṣiri'd-Dín Sháh (king of Persia)
assassination of, 203, 208
attempt on life of, 114, 115–19
petition to, 109, 300n9
names of petitioners, 109n
son of, 208, 209
Nasru'lláh, Siyyid, 228
Nayríz, town of, 15, 19, 21–34, 269, 271
the Báb's Revelation brought to, 49
Bahá'í-Muslim accord in, 218–19, 220, 225, 232–33, 260, 262, 263, 313n17
maps of, *12, 13*
Shaykh Dhakaríyyá's invasion of, 211, 213–20, 259, 312n1, 312n2, 312n3, 312n4, 313n13, 319n2
Vaḥíd's teaching in, 70, 74, 75–76n1, 124, 198, 296n1
See also Bábís, Nayríz; Bahá'ís, Nayríz; Fort Khájih; Great Friday Mosque of Nayríz; persecutions, in 1850; persecutions, in 1853; persecutions, in 1909; post-1909 persecutions
Núríján (wife of Mírzá 'Abdu'l Ḥusayn), 240, 246–47, 260, 263, 279
nusrat, concept of, 15
Nuṣratu'd-Dawlih, 319n1

orchards, 23, 302–3n6
Bahá'ís hiding in, 156, 161, 240–41n, 247
destruction of, 260, 272

Pahlavi dynasty, 270
Páriján (grand-daughter of Ḥasan Lab-Shikarí), 199, 216, 270
Páríján Shahídpúr (daughter of Mullá Muḥammad 'Alí), 74n1, 228, 229, *230*, 314n6
Parmerton, Anna L., 249
peace, Bábí and Bahá'í teachings on, 7–8, 14

persecutions, in 1850, 79–119
attempt on life of Náṣiri'd-Dín Sháh, 115–19
in Chinár-Súkhtih district, 81, 104, 109–14
martyrs, 84n1, 100n1, 103–8, 306–7n7
memorial to, 269–70
Mírzá Na'ím's role in, 106, 107
in Nayríz, 2, 5
occupation of Fort Khájih, 81–102
prisoners, 103–9, 115–16n
survivors of, 196, 215
See also children, Bábí; women, Bábí
persecutions, in 1853, 114, 123–90
in Chinár-Súkhtih district, 123, 147, 173
martyrs, 154–55, 163–64, 167, 172–74, 176, 181, *182–83,* 184n1, 306–7n7, 307n14, 307n25
Mírzá Na'ím's role in, 128, 129–32
mountain battles, 139–60, 165–66n
Muḥammad Shafí''s chronicling of, 3, 310n22
in Nayríz, 2, 5, 123–37, 181
prisoners, 34n2, 160–68, 171–76, 178–81, 184, 256, 308n17, 308n23, 308–9n27, 309n28
resistance to, 123–32
revenge for, 147–48
survivors, 185–90, 194, 215, 240–41, 247, 256–57, 264, 269–70
vineyard battles, 133–37
See also children, Bábí; women, Bábí
persecutions, in 1909, 5, 32n, 207–60, 262
breakdown of Persian government, 207–11
in Chinár-Súkhtih district, 219–20, 227
flight to Sarvistán, 219–20, 251–57, 309n6, 317n17, 318n6, 319n2
invasion of Nayríz, 213–20
martyrs, 2–3, 227–29, 232–33, 239–44, 270, 277, 316n16, 317n17
material losses, 231, 240, 247, 259–60, 263–64
resistance to, 269
rewards given for capture of Bahá'ís, 218–19, 220, 225, 227–29, 233, 240–43, 247–49, 313n11, 313n17
survivors of, 259–60, 268–70, 279
See also children, Bahá'í; women, Bahá'í
persecutions, post-1909, 2–3, 262, 270, 271–81, 321n25

Persia
    'Abdu'l-Bahá's recommendations for modernizing, 198–99, 209–10
    ancient customs, 29–33
    Bahá'u'lláh's prophecies regarding, 203–4
    corruption in, 1, 207–8, 210
    government crises, 207–11, 262, 270
    last names introduced in, 271
    religion, 13, 15
    See also Muḥammad Sháh (king of Persia); Náṣiri'd-Dín Sháh (king of Persia); Riḍá Sháh (king of Persia)
Peymani family, 255
prayer, Muslim call to, 9, 21, 30
Promised One. *See* Qá'im

Qabr Bábí (Bábí's burial spot), 104
Qahru'lláh (darvish), 67n
Qá'im, 12
    the Báb as, 44–45, 49, 51, 68, 79–80, 95–96
    search for, 1, 33–34, 43–44
Qájár dynasty
    collapse of, 207–11, 262, 270
    histories of, 54, 74n2, 75–76n, 84n2
Qashqá'í tribe, 165–66, 180, 308n18
Qasím, Ḥájí, and occupation of Fort Khájih, 146, 151, 197
Qasím, Haj Siyyid, 227–28
Qasím-i-Nayrízí, Ḥájí, and attempt on life of Náṣiri'd-Dín Sháh, 115–16n, 117n
Qaṭrúyih, town of, tax revolt in, 130
Qavámu'l-Mulk, the, 211, 268, 308n18, 319n1
quanats (canals), 22, 23n
    See also Khobar mill and waterway (Nayríz)
Quddús (Letter of the Living), 47
    at Conference of Badasht, 66
    martyrdom of, 70
    mission to Shíráz, 49–50
    on pilgrimage with the Báb, 48–49
Qur'án, 1, 10, 11, 12, 28, 30, 31, 32

Rahmán (son of Muḥammad Ismá'íl), 241, 242
recantation, Bábís' and Bahá'ís' refusing, 178, 184, 228, 241–43, 248, 275

religion. *See* Bahá'í Faith; Islám; Sufism; violence, religious teachings on; Zoroastrianism
Remey, Charles Mason, 249
Revelation, Divine, advent of new, 1, 5, 60
See also Báb, the, Declaration of; Báb, the, revelation of; Bahá'u'lláh, Declaration of
Riḍá Sháh (king of Persia), 270
Rouhani, 'Alí Akbar, 272
Rouhani [Mr.], Bahá'í schools run by, 268
Runíz, village of, 251–52
Vaḥíd teaching Bábí Faith in, 72–76

Sádát district (Nayríz), 22, 73n2, 100, 147, 215
Sádiq-i-Tabrízí, and attempted assassination of Náṣiri'd-Dín Sháh, 117n
Saheb Jan Khánum, 220, *221,* 310–11n34
Samandarí, Tarázu'lláh, 215, 254, 273, 277
Samara, Iraq, 37n
Sardári family, 276
Sarvistán, town of, 34
Bahá'ís' flight to, 219–20, 251–57, 309n6, 317n17, 318n6, 319n2
Sayf-Ábád, village of, 215, 216, 313n11
Sháh Abdul Azim, 203n
Sháh 'Alí, Mullá, 146
Shahídpúr, 'Abdu'l-Samí, 272–73, 278–79
Shah Mirhamzeh, Shrine of (Shiraz), *177*
Shaybání, Shokuh, 280, 321n25
Shaykha (executioner from Fort Khájih), 85, 107
Shaykh 'Abdu'l 'Alí, 146
Shaykh 'Abid, 35n, 36
Shaykh Aḥmad, 49
Shaykh Bahá'í, 273
Shaykh Dhakaríyyá
brothers of, 260, 262
invasion of Nayríz by, 211, 213–20, 259, 312n1, 312n2, 312n3, 312n4, 313n14, 319n2
persecution of Bahá'ís by, 227–29, 231, 240–43, 248, 252, 256, 314–15n11, 315n6
Shaykhís and Shaykhísm, 1, 33–34, 37, 43, 49, 68
Shaykh Muḥammad-Ḥusayn, 260, 270

flight of family of, 220, 225, 229, 231, 233, 251, 310–11n34
as member of Nayríz Spiritual Assembly, 197, 263
Tablets from 'Abdu'l-Bahá to, *223, 235*
Shaykhu'l-Islám, 28, 213–14, 217–18
Shi'ite Islám, 1, 10, 11–13
use of violence in, 125, 147
Shimr. *See* Zaynu'l-'Ábidín Khán
Shíráz, city of, 28, 34, 43, 89, 131, 278
bringing Bábí prisoners to, 103–8, 172–76, 178–80, 256–57, 306n5, 306–7n7, 307n13, 308n23
Quddús' mission to, 49–50
Vaḥíd in, 72n1
Shoghi Effendi
God Passes By, 3
as Guardian of the Bahá'í Faith, 268, 269, 271, 277, 278, 317n18
on passing of 'Abdu'l-Bahá, 265–66
Shrine of the Báb (Haifa, Israel), 200
Shu'á'y, 'Abdu'l Ḥusayn, 273
Shukru'lláh, Mírzá, 252–53
siyyid, use of term, 39n
spirits, belief in, 30–32
Spiritual Assembly, Bahá'í, 237
See also Bahá'ís, Nayríz, Spiritual Assembly of
Sufism, 53
Ṣughrá (wife of Vaḥíd), 60n, 79
Sultanu'l-Muslimin, 214
Sunni Islám, 10, 11, 13
Súrih of Abundance, Báb's commentary on, 56–57

Tabríz, city of, trial of Báb in, 67–70
Taherzadeh, Adib, 86n1
Ṭáhirih (Letter of the Living), 47
at Conference of Badasht, 66
Ṭahmásb (son of Muḥammad 'Alí), 247, 248
Ṭahmásb Mírzá, 128n2
Taliati'e Khánum, 249, 317–18n7
Tang-i Láy-i Ḥiná, caves of, 220, 225, 246–47, 251
Taqí Khán, Mírzá (prime minister), 128n1
Third Ímám. *See* Ímám Ḥusayn (grandson of Muḥammad)

Ṭihrán, city of
persecution of Bahá'ís in 1956, 278
sending Bábí prisoners to, 130, 132, 180–81, 184
Tobin, Nettie, 261
tribes, 8, 9, 14
True, Corinne, 238, 249, 260–61
Ṭubá Khánum (daughter of Vaḥíd), 93–94, 102
Twelfth Ímám, 11–13, 217
See also Qá'im
Twin Manifestations of God, 1, 7
See also Báb, the; Bahá'u'lláh

'Umar, as successor to Muḥammad, 10–11
United States (U.S.), first national Bahá'í convention in, 232, 237–39, 245–46, 249
unity, Bábí and Bahá'í teachings on, 7–8, 47n, 209
Ustád 'Alí, 309n28
Ustád 'Alí Sabbágh, 247, 248, 249
Ustád Qásim, 125n1
'Uthman, as successor to Muḥammad, 11

Vafa (son of Mullá Báqir), 189, 194
Vaḥíd, 53–57
as descendant of Muḥammad, 95, 96, 101
family, 49, 55n1, 60n, 71, 75–76n, 79
interviews of the Báb by, 55–57, 58
leadership by, 87–88, 91, 92n, 135, 147
martyrdom, 99–100, 101, 103, 147, 153, 299n23
Nayrízis going out to meet, 72–75
and occupation of Fort Khájih, 81–96
as prisoner of Zaynu'l-'Ábidín Khán, 96–98
proclamation in Great Friday Mosque of Nayríz, 2, 79–80, 215, 281, 296n2, 296n3
supporters of, 110, 189, 196, 262
teaching Bábí Faith, 65, 70, 71–72, 74, 75–76n, 124, 198, 296n1
Vaḥíd, numerical value of, 46–47n, 124–25, 145n
Vaḥídí, 'Abdu'l-Ḥusayn, 275
Vaḥídí, Mírzá Aḥmad, 277, 278
Vakíl mosque (Shíráz), Báb's declaration in, 50–51
Victoria, queen of England, Bahá'u'lláh's Tablet to, 209

vineyards, battles in, 132, 133–37
violence, religious teachings on
Bábí, 15, 71, 126
Bahá'í, 15, 88n1, 116, 117, 193, 310n22
Christian, 13–14
Islamic, 13–15, 32–33, 125, 147
Jewish, 125–26
See also martyrdom

water, distribution of, 22, 23n
See also Khobar mill and waterway (Nayríz)
women, Bábí
in Asbergun orchards, 156–57
at mountain battles, 136, 143, 144, 146, 152
and the occupation of Fort Khájih, 79–80n, 92
as prisoners, 5, 104–9, 161–68, 171, 173–76, 178–81, 306n5, 306–7n7, 307n14, 308n21
relinquishing marriages to non-Bábís, 141
returning to Nayríz, 185–89
women, Bahá'í
flight of, 220, 225, 246–47, 260, 263–64
in hiding, 227, 229, 231, 233, 251
persecution of, 275–77, 279, 280
women, in Nayríz, 23–24, 26, 28–29

Yaḥyáy-i-Dárábí, Siyyid. *See* Vaḥíd
Yaqútí spring, battles at, 150–51, 157, 304–5n3
Yathrib. *See* Medina, Saudi Arabia
Yazd, city of, persecution of Bábís in, 71
Yúsuf, Shaykh, 85, 109

Zardosht mill and waterway (Nayríz), 134n1
Zarghan family, 277–78
Zaykr'u'lláh Loghmanee, 316n15, 316n16
Zaynu'l-'Ábidín, Mírzá, 151
Zaynu'l-'Ábidín Khán, 74–76
assassination of, 125, 126–27, 128, 189, 196
and attempt on life of Muḥammad Sháh, 115–16n
brother of, 296n8, 299n23

Zaynu'l-'Ábidín <u>Kh</u>án *(cont'd)*
opposition to Vaḥíd, 79, 80–81
persecution of Nayríz Bábís by, 109–14
resistance against, 123–27
and siege of Fort Khájih, 82–90, 94–99
sons of, 84–85
wife of, 113, 129
Zoroastrianism, 29, 281

Bahá'í
PUBLISHING

Bahá'í Publishing and the Bahá'í Faith

Bahá'í Publishing produces books based on the teachings of the Bahá'í Faith. Founded over 160 years ago, the Bahá'í Faith has spread to some 235 nations and territories and is now accepted by more than five million people. The word "Bahá'í" means "follower of Bahá'u'lláh." Bahá'u'lláh, the founder of the Bahá'í Faith, asserted that He is the Messenger of God for all of humanity in this day. The cornerstone of His teachings is the establishment of the spiritual unity of humankind, which will be achieved by personal transformation and the application of clearly identified spiritual principles. Bahá'ís also believe that there is but one religion and that all the Messengers of God—among them Abraham, Zoroaster, Moses, Krishna, Buddha, Jesus, and Muḥammad—have progressively revealed its nature. Together, the world's great religions are expressions of a single, unfolding divine plan. Human beings, not God's Messengers, are the source of religious divisions, prejudices, and hatreds.

The Bahá'í Faith is not a sect or denomination of another religion, nor is it a cult or a social movement. Rather, it is a globally recognized independent world religion founded on new books of scripture revealed by Bahá'u'lláh.

Bahá'í Publishing is an imprint of the National Spiritual Assembly of the Bahá'ís of the United States.

For more information about the Bahá'í Faith,
or to contact Bahá'ís near you,
visit http://www.bahai.us/
or call
1-800-22-UNITE

Other Books Available from Bahá'í Publishing

CALL TO REMEMBRANCE
THE LIFE OF BAHÁ'U'LLÁH IN HIS OWN WORDS
Geoffrey Marks
$17.00 US / $19.00 CAN
Trade Paper
ISBN 978-1-61851-030-3

An excellent introduction to the distinction and purity of the life of Bahá'u'lláh, the Prophet-Founder of the Bahá'í Faith.

Call to Remembrance is the first book to tell the story of Bahá'u'lláh, the Prophet-Founder of the Bahá'í Faith, largely through His own words. Combining extracts from Bahá'u'lláh's writing and supplementing with additional background information, many major events in His life and ministry are presented. This unique compilation chronicles all periods of Bahá'u'lláh's life, and is organized into five sections.

PRAYERS FOR CHILDREN
Constanze von Kitzing
$12.00 US / $14.00 CAN
Paper Over Board
ISBN 978-1-61851-032-7

A beautifully illustrated collection of Bahá'í prayers for children; a perfect book for the whole family to treasure.

Prayers for Children is a collection of Bahá'í prayers compiled specifically for young children. Beautifully illustrated, this book will help parents cultivate a lifelong habit of daily prayer in their child. The beautiful color illustrations will appeal to children of all ages and will make it an appealing book for daily use for parents and children alike.

SPIRIT OF FAITH
SACRIFICE AND SERVICE
Bahá'í Publishing
$12.00 US / $14.00 CAN
Hardcover
ISBN 978-1-61851-031-0

The sixth book in the Spirit of Faith series focuses on the vital spiritual topics of sacrifice and service.

Spirit of Faith: Sacrifice and Service is a compilation of writings and prayers that focus on sacrifice and service—subjects that are given great importance in the Bahá'í writings. The passages compiled here implore all people to make sacrifices and expend their energies in service to mankind as a means to improve the world of humanity and bring about its oneness. The *Spirit of Faith* series continues to explore spiritual topics—such as the unity of humanity, the eternal covenant of God, the promise of world peace, and more—by presenting what the central figures of the Bahá'í Faith have written regarding these important topics.